THE
EVERYTHING®
GHOST HUNTING
BOOK

Dear Reader,

It is an exciting time to be a paranormal investigator, or even just someone interested in the supernatural. Have you noticed that there has been a whole lot going on in the field lately?

The field of paranormal research is very hot right now, but its history stretches far back into the past and raises as many questions now as it did 5,000 years ago. The only difference is that we may now be standing at the threshold of some very new approaches and discoveries that will at last give us the answers we've been seeking for millennia.

This book is full of helpful, interesting, and thought-provoking information, and whether you skip around or read it straight through, I hope you enjoy reading it as much as I did writing it.

Best,

Melissa Martin Ellis

Welcome to the EVERYTHING® Series!

These handy, accessible books give you all you need to tackle a difficult project, gain a new hobby, comprehend a fascinating topic, prepare for an exam, or even brush up on something you learned back in school but have since forgotten.

You can choose to read an *Everything*® book from cover to cover or just pick out the information you want from our four useful boxes: e-questions, e-facts, e-alerts, and e-ssentials.

We give you everything you need to know on the subject, but throw in a lot of fun stuff along the way, too.

We now have more than 400 *Everything*® books in print, spanning such wide-ranging categories as weddings, pregnancy, cooking, music instruction, foreign language, crafts, pets, New Age, and so much more. When you're done reading them all, you can finally say you know *Everything*®!

E-QUESTION

Answers to
common questions

FACTS

Important snippets
of information

ALERTS!

Urgent
warnings

ESSENTIALS

Quick
handy tips

PUBLISHER Karen Cooper

DIRECTOR OF ACQUISITIONS AND INNOVATION Paula Munier

MANAGING EDITOR, EVERYTHING SERIES Lisa Laing

COPY CHIEF Casey Ebert

ACQUISITIONS EDITOR Lisa Laing

DEVELOPMENT EDITOR Elizabeth Kassab

EDITORIAL ASSISTANT Hillary Thompson

Visit the entire Everything® series at *www.everything.com*

THE
EVERYTHING®
GHOST HUNTING BOOK

Tips, tools, and techniques
for exploring the supernatural world

Melissa Martin Ellis

Adamsmedia
Avon, Massachusetts

This book is dedicated to the seekers and searchers of the world. It is also dedicated with great respect and appreciation to Lisa Laing, Mark Ellis, Deirdre DeLay, and the always incredible and inspirational Colin Wilson.

An Everything® Series Book.
Everything® and everything.com® are registered trademarks of F+W Media, Inc.

Published by Adams Media, a division of F+W Media, Inc.
57 Littlefield Street, Avon, MA 02322 U.S.A.
www.adamsmedia.com

ISBN 10: 1-59869-920-2
ISBN 13: 978-1-59869-920-3

Printed in the United States of America.

J   I   H   G   F   E

Library of Congress Cataloging-in-Publication Data
is available from the publisher.

This publication is designed to provide accurate and authoritative information with regard to the subject matter covered. It is sold with the understanding that the publisher is not engaged in rendering legal, accounting, or other professional advice. If legal advice or other expert assistance is required, the services of a competent professional person should be sought.

—From a *Declaration of Principles* jointly adopted by a Committee of the American Bar Association and a Committee of Publishers and Associations

Many of the designations used by manufacturers and sellers to distinguish their products are claimed as trademarks. Where those designations appear in this book and Adams Media was aware of a trademark claim, the designations have been printed with initial capital letters.

This book is available at quantity discounts for bulk purchases.
For information, please call 1-800-289-0963.

Contents

ACKNOWLEDGMENTS

This is where I get to thank the many people who so generously shared their time, talents, and expertise with me. I'd like to thank my husband Mark, who helped so much in the research and proofreading, my daughter Deirdre DeLay for her support and research links, and my friends Douglas Clegg and Raul Silva for their interest and support.

Thanks to Gina Panettieiri, who likes to stroll around cemeteries, too. You started the wheels rolling.

Especially helpful and informative were all the people at the Rhode Island Paranormal Research Group (T.R.I.P.R.G.) and its founder and director, Andrew Laird, who gave invaluable help and support when it was most needed. My thanks also to T.R.I.P.R.G. sensitives and investigators Maggie Florio and Kym Black, whose e-mails, interviews, and phone conversations were so amazingly detailed and helpful.

A big thanks also to the Demon Hunter, AKA Nathan Schoonover, and his talented mate, Kristy Petersen Schoonover.

Nelia and John Petit were quite helpful in sharing their knowledge for the section on malevolent hauntings; thanks very much for filling me in on entities that made my blood run cold!

Many thanks also to Kathy Conder at Michigan Paranormal, Will Murray, and Elizabeth Bissette. Liz is the world's fastest typist and had some great anecdotes to relate and photos to share.

Top Ten Things about
Approaching the Paranormal World

1. Read all you can about ghosts, psychics, and hauntings.

2. Write down any paranormal experiences that you or your family members have had.

3. Maintain a skeptical but open mind and attitude.

4. Be prepared to enter uncharted waters.

5. Keep a journal of your experiences with any sort of psychic experiments involving pendulums, scrying, séances, or any other means of divination.

6. Sign up for a class to learn from experienced teachers.

7. Ask questions and follow your instincts.

8. Respect the research and work that has gone before.

9. Be prepared to be disappointed sometimes.

10. Be prepared to be totally amazed!

Introduction

▶ DO GHOSTS LURK in the twilight, waiting to remind us that they have unfinished business to conduct, scores to settle, or wrongs to right? Or are spirits merely the work of our wild imaginings and superstitions?

Perhaps what we call ghosts have messages to impart before they are able to leave this material plane of existence . . . and perhaps they only need for someone to hear those messages before they find peace at last.

No matter who you are or where you live, chances are that at one time or another you will be brushed by the wings of the unearthly. You may feel the sudden chill of goose bumps or the hairs rising on your neck as you hurry from a dark room toward the light.

Even hardened investigators have been quite literally spooked. A physical response to fear cannot be controlled once the adrenaline courses through the blood and the heart starts to race. One can either stand or run, and the urge to run is hardwired into our bodies.

The mere thought of an apparition, ghost, or spirit is disturbing, because by definition such an entity is a remnant, a fragment of a soul desperately trying to move forward but trapped in a prison woven from its own dark dreams of violence, pain, and betrayal.

Perhaps some stay on the earthly plane for love, but if paranormal literature tells us anything, we know that haunted sites are places in which some human drama or tragedy has occurred, and the revenants that remain have their own agenda.

Ghosts are part of all human cultures, and the questions surrounding them are the same whether they were asked 5,000 years ago or just yesterday: Are ghosts real? Can they hurt us? Why do they seem to linger in some places?

The Everything® Ghost Hunting Book addresses many of these questions and attempts to answer some of them. Whether any aspect of human consciousness survives beyond the death of the body is one of the most fundamental and universal mysteries. It has been a source of curiosity since the dawn of time.

Do you have questions about the reality of ghosts and hauntings? Have you had experiences too strange and unbelievable to share— even with your closest friends? If so, this book has been written with you in mind.

Do you have a more skeptical nature? Are you only able to accept what you hear with your own ears or see with your own eyes? This book is written for you as well.

Armed with a need for answers, today's ghost hunters are committed to stripping away any ambiguity from the equation of the supernatural. They are men and women on a mission to discover the hard evidence necessary to prove—or, ironically, disprove—the existence of spirits. A minority of these individuals are on a very different mission—their goal is to prove that all this talk of ghosts is hokum, and that all things that go bump in the night can be naturally explained. *The Everything® Ghost Hunting Book* presents both sides of the mystery.

CHAPTER 1

So You Want to Be a Ghost Hunter

Whether you are a believer or a skeptic, ghost hunting can be a totally fascinating experience that blends spirituality and science. Have you ever caught a glimpse of the world beyond? If you are interested in the world of spirits and have asked the age-old question, "Does the soul continue after death?" you may have what it takes to be a ghost hunter . . . and you are in good company.

Not for the Faint-Hearted

To become a paranormal investigator or ghost hunter, you must have some great qualities: objectivity, patience, courage, strength of character, and total honesty. However, both believers and nonbelievers must also have the ability to suspend their judgment long enough to gauge all of the facts objectively. Be sure you're emotionally ready to obtain tangible knowledge about the other side should you find evidence to support it. The reverse is also true.

Today's ghost hunters know all the technological tricks of the trade, including how to stay safe and what to do. Just as important, they know what not to do to ensure a professional investigation. Investigation of paranormal phenomena should be approached seriously, with respect and an abundance of caution. This is not a parlor game or a fun party activity. If you have an open mind and really want to explore the supernatural objectively, you'll find the tools you need to do so here.

The New School

The paranormal investigators of the twenty-first century are a few steps ahead of those who pursued answers in the past. In the upcoming chapters, you'll learn a little about ghost hunting through history and how the universal belief in spirits exists in numerous cultures.

Ghost Hunting Fever

The differences between types of hauntings—ghosts, apparitions, and poltergeists—will be explained. Various ways of protecting yourself during your investigations will also be discussed.

Over the last decade, ghost hunting fever has gripped the imagination of the world. With the rise of digital technology, there has been an incredible worldwide upsurge of interest in the topic.

Many organized groups attempt to pierce the barriers and contact the other side, but unlike their forebears, they do not use mediums or spiritualists as intermediaries. Today's ghost hunters have scientific tools in their arsenal, such as electromagnetic field (EMF) meters, infrared cameras, digital thermometers, tape recorders, and motion detectors.

Hobbyist or Professional?

Although it is true that many people who start out in this field as a hobby eventually find themselves working at it full-time, the transition from amateur to professional isn't always easy.

Making It Work

There is no one-size-fits-all solution to making a living as a paranormal investigator. However, unless you are independently wealthy and have the free time to conduct your investigations, you must derive income from some aspect of your work. Every individual must strive to find the correct balance to make it work; no two people will make the same choices.

E-QUESTION

Is possession always by evil spirits or demons?
In many traditions, possession is not thought to be demonic. Reports of spontaneous and deliberate possession are found throughout history and throughout the world. In more primitive societies, it is considered a form of shamanism and is likely the world's oldest spiritual tradition.

The best advice is to follow your own instincts and to walk the career path that offers you the most satisfaction. After pursuing the paranormal for a year or so, you will know whether you are ready to make the commitment necessary to do the job full-time. Most paranormal investigators truly love their work because it is interesting, challenging, and exciting. Additionally, they derive great satisfaction from rescuing others who are in crisis. Remember, it is possible to help people, whether you are doing it full- or part-time and whether you're an amateur or a pro.

Amateur Ghost Hunters

Being an amateur ghost hunter can be a very absorbing pastime. As you explore allegedly haunted sites and learn more and more about the supernatural world, you may find many overlapping areas of interest in related paranormal fields as well.

People who find the study of ghosts fascinating often find themselves drawn to the study of crop circles, extrasensory perception (ESP), psychokinesis (the ability to move objects without touching them), psychometry (the ability to pick up information from objects by merely touching them), and precognition (the ability to predict future events).

In short, you may feel drawn to any of the many types of unexplained phenomena. Lately, there has been an explosion of interest in all of these topics, and you have a wealth of resource material to explore. The Internet is a good place to start your search for information, but keep in mind that much of the data on the web is from unverifiable sources. Used wisely,

Michael the Archangel is an iconic figure for those battling the forces of darkness.

Photo copyright Melissa Martin Ellis, 2006.

however, the Internet can provide you with a good general overview of many topics, and you can use bibliographies to steer you toward further research. The ideal situation for a beginner is to find a group or individual mentor to help you gain the proper experience in the paranormal realm.

Professional Ghost Hunters

Many people ask whether you can actually earn a living as a ghost hunter. Unfortunately, the answer is no—certainly not at first. Although paranormal investigating can be rewarding on a personal level, it is not a particularly lucrative field. The people who go into it do so primarily for unselfish reasons—to help others. You may also find yourself in competition with other ghost hunting organizations that do not charge for their services.

Realistically, though, not many professional ghost investigators could support themselves without deriving income from some peripheral aspect of their work. Therefore, some may charge an hourly fee or a flat fee for a minimum number of hours. In addition, they supply their client with a written report, photos, and digital videos of the site investigation if any evidence is found. Most, however, find this approach unthinkable and charge no fee whatsoever for their services.

FACT

The Myrtles Plantation in St. Francisville, Louisiana, is supposedly the most haunted location in the United States. Reportedly, ten murders took place in the house. Now a bed and breakfast, the plantation is listed on the National Register of Historic Places and offers daily ghost tours.

Although it is true that there are few careers that provide the kind of satisfaction that comes from freeing frantic clients from disturbances, you may have to find other ways of supplementing your income. Here are ideas:

- **Teach paranormal classes.** If you are comfortable speaking to groups, you might consider the option of teaching classes on ghosts and paranormal-related subjects. These sessions could be held privately, through a community group, or at a college.

- **Cleanse spaces.** People increasingly want to clear their homes of any possible negative energy. Interestingly enough, the real estate laws of many states require full disclosure of paranormal activity when a house is sold, so real estate agents can be a source of referrals for your services.
- **Write an article, book, or script.** People with an interest in the paranormal can often build a network once they have established their credentials by writing about the subject. These credentials often lead to other writing assignments.
- **Work as a media consultant.** Consultation jobs can pay well, and with the growing interest in the paranormal there are more movies and television shows that will need advice and insight.
- **Debunk.** Most reports of hauntings turn out to have totally normal explanations. If you as an investigator can alleviate clients' fears and debunk the notion that ghosts are haunting their premises, you'll provide a very valuable service.
- **Maintain a members-only website.** These days, professionals should maintain a site. These sites may have content that is available to the public and a paid membership section as well.

Financial Resources and Considerations

You are probably wondering what entering this field will cost you financially. Credible investigators usually operate as nonprofits and do not charge clients for their investigations. Some investigate cases with their own finances or with money collected from donations and sponsors. You might consider making local investigations free of charge, but ask to be reimbursed by your clients for your hotel costs and travel expenses if you have to travel long distances.

Opinions differ widely and there is a heated debate among paranormal investigators as to the ethics of allowing clients to reimburse traveling expenses and other costs. Some will not charge a client under any circumstances, while others will only accept payment from an organization and never from an individual.

Purchasing Equipment Inexpensively

If you want to build your ghost hunting toolbox, try to acquire equipment as your budget allows and keep an eye on it when you're in the field. You should keep your investment in equipment to a minimum until you are totally sure that your interest in the paranormal will continue. Investigators have shown significant results with less expensive equipment, so don't let the cost of the more expensive items discourage you.

Build your ghost hunting toolkit over time if you are on a budget. Start with relatively low-tech items that are most essential to the hunt until you can afford to buy the more expensive ones. Make a wish list and prioritize the items on it.

ESSENTIAL EQUIPMENT LIST

- **A flashlight and extra batteries.** It is not at all unusual for a flashlight to go out during an investigation. Some believe paranormal entities cause modern devices to stop working. The theory posits that entities try to manifest by drawing energy from their immediate environment and will often drain even brand new batteries within minutes. $10.
- **A first aid kit.** As you're walking around in old buildings in pitch darkness, be prepared to deal with a few scratches, bumps, and scrapes. $15.
- **A notebook and pencil or pen.** Old-fashioned writing devices are vital for keeping track of observations and sequences of events. $8.
- **A watch.** Invest in an old-fashioned wind-up watch that doesn't run on batteries. If possible, get one with a second hand. $35.
- **A tape recorder.** It can be either analog or digital, but it must have an external microphone that can be placed away from the recorder to minimize static and noise. $30.
- **A camera.** It can be a digital or film camera. Bring extra camera batteries. Used film cameras are available on eBay and Amazon.com for around $50. Digital cameras start around $80.

- ❏ **An EMF meter.** This new ghost hunting tool measures the electromagnetic field in the area. Around $80.
- ❏ **A cell phone.** They often don't function well in paranormal hot spots, but bring one anyway. The pay-as-you-go kind are around $30.

These items can all be purchased for less than $300 total. You probably already have several of the items on the list, and you might be able to buy some of the others used. Other inexpensive low-tech items to include in your ghost hunting kit include the following:

- ❏ **Candles and matches or a kerosene lantern.** These are a good backup in case the flashlight goes dead.
- ❏ **A pendulum.** This is an ancient way of communicating with spirits.
- ❏ **Dowsing rods.** These are used by some in the same way as an EMF meter.
- ❏ **Rubber cement and black string.** These can be tacked across access points to detect whether someone is entering or leaving the site without your knowledge.
- ❏ **A military-type compass** to gauge the presence of magnetic field anomalies.
- ❏ **A tape-measure or yard-stick** to measure any object that may appear to have moved from its former position.
- ❏ **A map of the area** to acquaint yourself and the team with the site's layout.

The most important things to bring to an investigation are your common sense, your sensitivity and investigative skills, and a buddy to go onsite with you. Never go into the field alone.

Observational Skills and Information Gathering

As a paranormal investigator, you must learn to hone your observational skills to almost superhuman levels. When you have learned to use the equipment and mastered all the many dos and don'ts for effective field work, you still have to develop the skills you need to observe your surroundings with a truly critical eye.

To do this, you must assess and observe the location objectively. Learn to release your emotions and let go of the preconceived ideas you have about a site or situation. First consider the facts. You will take a statement of unusual events from the client. Then you will make your own observations and judgments of those events.

Over the centuries, there have been many ways to foretell the future by supernatural means, including scrying, crystal balls, the Tarot, pendulums, and mirror magic. In ancient times, the future was also foretold and omens were read by examining the entrails of sacrificial animals.

Keeping Accurate Records

You must take good notes to keep track of unusual phenomena, even if someone is simultaneously videotaping the investigation. Notes can be a valuable way of recording important data; the camera can't catch every angle at once, nor can it know what you have just experienced on a personal level—an impression, a cold spot, or a ghostly touch. Keeping a record of your reactions to the things that happen can help you better reconstruct the investigation later.

- Make a note of anything you think is significant. Record any possible ordinary explanations.
- Later, eliminate all events or discrepancies that seem to be suspect and those for which there may be perfectly ordinary explanations.
- List the remaining items separately, in order of significance, to ensure clarity of thought and to help you arrange your list logically.
- Don't discard less significant facts. Instead, move them to the bottom and be aware that their status can change as the investigation proceeds.
- Never ignore the influence of random coincidence. Most investigations involve some elements of coincidence or randomness.

Analyzing Data

Seek meaningful probabilities and correlations from the facts in order to limit the amount of guesswork in your analyses and conclusions. Dispassionately reviewing the evidence, both from your own personal experiences and from the electronic voice phenomena recordings, digital video recordings (DVRs), and even digital thermometer readings will help you make a balanced assessment that can withstand the scrutiny of critics and debunkers.

Sensitivity to the Supernatural

Some people are born with a unique sensitivity to the supernatural and some develop it through hard work and rigorous training. Most people are aware of and use the five ordinary senses they are born with, but now it is generally accepted that a sixth sense exists as well; it just lies latent in most people and is seldom accessed. We have all experienced it at one point or another. For instance, we know who is calling when the phone rings, or a commercial we are thinking about suddenly appears on the television. These sorts of things happen often in our daily lives, and we chalk them up to coincidence. Sometimes that's just what it is. But what if coincidence isn't a convincing explanation? Is there really an intuitive sense? Perhaps this sense is part of every human being, and it can be used as a practical tool.

Intuition or Coincidence?

If this sixth sense does exist and isn't just coincidence, how can you plug it into your intellect to help you interpret the data correctly? Can you actually learn to develop your intuition and sensitivity? Here are the first steps:

1. **Acknowledge that the ability exists.** Without this vital first step, you cannot move forward and trust the information you're receiving.
2. **Listen to your gut feeling.** Intuition comes in flashes. When it sweeps over you, note it. Analyze it. Respect it.
3. **Engage your intellect.** It must be brought in to analyze the information correctly. Trust that something significant has occurred and attempt to figure out exactly what it means.

Remember that in order for your mind to listen to your intuitive feelings, it must value those feelings. Your mind needs a logical reason to value the information. The best way to convince your mind to pay attention to intuitions is to introduce it to the origins of these feelings.

Tapping the Source

Where does the psychic or intuitive information come from? There are different theories, but we can perhaps condense it into three sources.

The Subconscious Mind

Our minds are like organic computers that store the details of every experience we've ever had. Our conscious minds allow us to quietly store all this extra data in our huge biological hard drive. If the subconscious is prompted, it will allow the conscious mind the necessary access to all kinds of helpful information.

Telepathy or ESP

One theory posits that thoughts are energy. They have a bandwidth or frequency that is similar to a broadcast signal. Perhaps, when others are operating at the same bandwidth, we may experience a bleed-through effect, similar to what happens when a radio signal allows us to hear two stations at once. Some have speculated that this is what creates mass consciousness, also known as groupthink. This is the phenomenon of a large number of people thinking in similar ways. These mental energy signals may influence many aspects of our lives: social and moral values, politics, and religious beliefs. It is just a theory, but it might be one explanation for some very disturbing periods in human history, such as the rise of Nazi Germany.

FACT

Franz Anton Mesmer discovered what he called *magnétisme animal* (animal magnetism), which came to be called mesmerism. The evolution of his ideas and practices led to the development of hypnotism in 1842. Under hypnosis, patients in trance states have been known to communicate with spirits through speech and automatic writing.

If we can consciously tune in or block the signal, we are in much better control of our thoughts and intuitions.

The Superconscious Mind

The third source of psychic intuition may come from the superconscious. It is theorized that everyone has access to a higher source of knowledge.

Information from the superconscious level of psychic guidance is said to influence your consciousness for your own higher good and helps you make observations and choices from a fresh perspective. This influence can be perceived as an inspiration, warning, or sudden flash of insight.

Supernatural Studies

Princeton University maintains one of the most well established research centers, known as Princeton Engineering Anomalies Research (PEAR). After twenty-five years of researching unexplained phenomena and anomalies, PEAR's laboratory manager, Brenda Dunne, explains that PEAR is trying to acquire reliable information that shows human consciousness is: 1) capable of somehow changing or affecting things in the physical world, or 2) is capable of getting information about remote locations without actually being there physically.

E-QUESTION

What is ectoplasm made of?
No one knows for certain. The physical existence of ectoplasm is not accepted by mainstream science. Psychics say it is a substance that holds energy derived from the medium.

The research at prestigious institutions of higher learning such as Princeton lends credibility to the pursuit of information about all paranormal phenomena using scientific methods and protocols.

Patience and Reliability Pay Off

As the old adage goes, slow and steady wins the race. The best investigators in the psychic world are those who have actively cultivated patience and reliability. The individual who is calm, mature, and patient brings stability and credibility to the investigation. Both qualities are vital when dealing with panicky clients in a state of high anxiety.

You should cultivate patience and reliability not only for your own good, but also for the sake of your colleagues and clients. By its very nature, the paranormal field is full of chaotic activity and confusion. You, as the person brought into the situation to resolve the scary issues and answer the difficult questions, must be an absolute rock of stability and confidence.

Maintaining Objectivity

Critics and skeptics don't believe that most ghost hunters are credible. Ghost hunters are often labeled fantasy-prone personalities, a designation used to describe an otherwise normal person's heightened propensity to make things up.

Although we may find the skeptics' analysis of the facts about ghost hunters a bit skewed, it does underscore how important it is that paranormal investigators be totally professional and reliable in the course of their work. Keeping scrupulous records and honoring client commitments and confidentiality while looking for normal everyday explanations should be standard operating procedure for today's investigators.

FACT

Ed and Lorraine Warren, two well-respected early ghost hunters, became involved in a case known as the Smurl Haunting. The Warrens' investigation revealed four spirits in residence, which wreaked havoc on one family, including two teenagers. The Catholic Church sent in an exorcist in 1989, after which the activity ended.

Skepticism, Not Dogmatism

Keep a skeptical but open mind as you explore the supernatural realm. As scientist Rupert Sheldrake says, "Healthy skepticism plays an important part in science, and stimulates research and critical thinking. Healthy skeptics are open-minded and interested in evidence. By contrast, dogmatic skeptics are committed to the belief that 'paranormal' phenomena are impossible, or at least so improbable as to merit no serious attention. Hence any evidence for such phenomena must be illusory."

CHAPTER 2

Manifesting Through Time

Our history is fraught with ghostly interactions. One of the earliest ghost stories appears in "The Epic of Gilgamesh," a poem from ancient Mesopotamia. Ghost stories are found in all cultures and all times, and the accounts of how ghosts look and behave is remarkably consistent. In the ancient world, ghosts were often seen as fog-like figures, made of subtle material like the white mist exhaled in cold climates. Perhaps this is why the Latin word for breath is *spiritus*.

An Ancient Belief in the Afterlife

There have been many reports of ghosts appearing to be so substantial that they are indistinguishable from living people until they disappear into thin air or walk right though a wall.

What are we to make of the frightening apparitions that appear as dark, darting shadows, which bring a sense of dread and despair with them? Are these ghosts or ghouls? According to eminent paranormal researcher Colin Wilson, there are differences between nature spirits or elementals and true hauntings. Wilson refers to nature spirits as ghouls and human apparitions as ghosts.

In most ancient cultures, ghosts were believed to be the restless spirits of the dead, seeking vengeance or attempting to complete unfinished business. Although they no longer had physical bodies, they could still manifest themselves, not only visually, but also through other sensory phenomena. They were able to move furniture, throw projectiles through walls, and create loud noises and other disruptions.

Deliver us from evil! Amulets and talismans have been used for millennia to protect the wearer from evil spirits, sorcery, and other harmful paranormal phenomena. Depending on the culture, these wards can take many forms. Horns, evil eyes, and scarabs are still in use today.

Eastern and Western Ghosts

In the traditions of India, where it is widely believed that souls will reincarnate after death, bereaved relatives sometimes followed an ancient ritual. At night, in a corner of the room where the deceased had slept, a saucer of water, rice, and ashes were placed on a sheet of white paper on the floor. No one was allowed to sleep in the room, and any kind of noise was forbidden.

It was believed that an imprint would appear on the ashes to foretell what would become of the deceased. If the imprint was of a human baby's foot, the person would be reborn as a human. An Om imprint meant the

Painting from a photo, both copyright Melissa Martin Ellis, 2002.

The ancients believed that elementals called dryads were the spirits of trees.

person had gone to heaven and would not be reborn. An animal imprint meant the person would be reborn as an animal. If there was no imprint, it meant the person's spirit had not moved on. As the *Garuda Purana*, an ancient Hindu scripture states, "All these are sure to be born as ghosts— a man misappropriating a trust property, a man treacherous to his friend, a man fond of another man's wife, a faithless man and a deceptive wretch."

Ghosts in Ancient Egypt, Greece, and Rome

The ancient Egyptian belief in the afterlife is described in "The Book of Going Forth by Day," which is more commonly known as "The Book of the Dead." It contained all the instructions that Egyptian royalty would need to make a comfortable transition to the afterlife. Those Egyptians who could afford the rites of beatification were assured an extenuation of their normal life on earth, full of banqueting and socializing. The dead could receive letters from the living and could visit them in dreams or visions to impart their own wisdom.

E-QUESTION

What is a spirit guide?
A spirit guide carries communications between a medium and the spirits of the dead. Many mediums claim to have specific guides who regularly work with them and contact the departed entities. The spirit guide acts as a moderator and keeps low-level spirits at bay.

Part of what we know about ancient Egypt's beliefs in ghosts is derived from a historical text that describes a conversation between the first king of the twelfth dynasty, Amenemhet I, and his son and successor, Senusret I. The *Instruction of Amenemhet* primarily takes the form of a testament. The author is the ghost of King Amenemhet I, returning to tell his son how to govern well and to urgently warn him to trust no one in the court. This admonition might have arisen because a palace coup probably caused the death of the king.

Ghosts of Ancient Greece

Ghosts appear in many stories that have come down to us from ancient Greece, through such renowned storytellers as Pliny, Homer, and Virgil. Interwoven with tales of mythical gods and heroes, the ghosts of ancient Greece were very much a part of its culture.

"The Odyssey" contains a long passage that describes the hero, Odysseus, going to the Underworld to talk to the shades of the dead, to figure out the next actions he should take to return home. Circe tells him that he should travel past the groves of Persephone, where he will find the house of Hades, which is described as a place where the light of Helios (the sun) never shone. Circe instructs him in the rituals he must perform to fend off the shades of the dead until he is able to get the answers he seeks.

From Virgil's "Aeneid Book VI," a Sybil (a sort of seeress or medium) tells of ghosts who wander because they did not have a proper burial:

The ghosts rejected are the unhappy crew
Deprived of sepulchers and funeral due:
The boatman, Charon; those, the buried host,
He ferries over to the farther coast,
Nor dares his transport vessel cross the waves
With such whose bones are not composed in graves.
A hundred years they wander on the shore;
At length, their penance done, are wafted o'er.

Even today, we hear of ghosts who wander eternally because their mortal remains aren't properly interred. It is a recurrent theme associated with hauntings.

Malevolent Spirits

The ancient Romans celebrated Lemuria, a nine-day festival in May that was designed to soothe the harmful spirits, or *lemures*. According to a passage in Ovid's poem "Fasti," the festival was instituted to appease Remus, whose spirit haunted early Rome. The Romans apparently had three classifications for spirits. They were called *lares* if they were good, *lemures* if they were evil, and *manes* if their disposition was yet to be determined.

Often referred to as "the night-wandering shades of the prematurely dead," the lemures may have been souls who could find no peace, either because they had met with a violent death or had unfinished business. They wandered among the living, tormenting people and sometimes driving them to early deaths or madness. That rather sounds like the entities we call poltergeists.

Parentalia and Feralia

During the festival of Parentalia and the feast of Feralia, held on the eighteenth and twenty-first of February, the living descendants of benevolent and beloved spirits shared a meal with their honored ancestors, often called *manes* or *di parentes*. At first, manes was used as a generic term for the dead, but when they were subsequently identified with the ancestors of the family, it was believed that they watched over the welfare of the family along with the other household deities.

Hauntings in Great Britain

Great Britain, with its long history of political intrigue and murder, has scores of ancient structures that are said to be haunted. Some reports go back hundreds of years.

The Princes in the Tower

The Tower of London was a royal residence that evolved into a prison where many famous royals were detained while their relatives in power decided their fate. According to the legend of the princes in the tower, two young royals, Edward V, age twelve, and Richard, Duke of York, age ten, were murdered in the Tower of London in 1483. Their uncle, the Duke of Gloucester, had placed them in the tower, ostensibly for their own protection. But Gloucester had the princes removed from the line of succession and seized the throne for himself as Richard III. The boys disappeared under mysterious circumstances. No one knows what happened to them or how and when they died, but it was widely believed that they were murdered under Richard's orders. Their ghosts were seen in the Tower on many occasions throughout the centuries. Guards in the late fifteenth century reported seeing the shadows of two small figures walking down the stairs in the Tower.

FACT

Unusual cold spots can be detected and measured by thermometers and thermal imagers. When a cold spot is detected, unusual or anomalous phenomena usually follow, such as electronic voice phenomena (EVPs), unexplained sounds, unexplained movements of objects, or a sudden feeling of apprehension in witnesses, who may also experience a ghostly touch.

In 1674, workers found a chest that contained the skeletons of two young children, which were believed to be the bones of the princes. They were given a royal burial not long afterward and the sightings of the spirits ceased.

The Ghosts of Stirling Castle

Most of present-day Stirling Castle in Scotland dates from the fifteenth and sixteenth centuries, but there were defensive structures on the site as early as the twelfth century. William Wallace fought successfully to wrest it from English control in 1297, and it was the site of the coronation of Mary, Queen of Scots, in 1543—but not all of its history is happy.

Three ghosts continue to haunt the castle, and other strange occurrences point to other supernatural inhabitants.

The Highland Ghost

This ghost allegedly wanders about in period costume, and tourists sometimes mistake him for a tour guide. When asked for directions, he usually turns and walks away, much to their annoyance. Only when he has walked through a wall or into a closed door do they realize what they have seen.

In 1935 the spirit was captured on film by an architect who went to the castle in the wee hours of the morning to take photos of the castle. He deliberately arrived early to avoid crowds. But to his dismay, the developed photos showed one person standing under an archway. Since he had been very careful while taking the photos, he was surprised to see the person there—until he realized the figure must be that of the Highland Ghost.

The Green Lady

The Green Lady was allegedly a maidservant to Mary, Queen of Scots. One night, when she had retired for the evening, she had a premonition that the queen was in danger—specifically, that her bed curtains were on fire. When she rushed into the queen's bedchamber, they were indeed ablaze. Although she managed to save the queen, she died of injuries she sustained.

Now her appearance always foreshadows the coming of bad events at the castle. When she appears, the staff knows to be on the lookout for a fire or some other crisis.

The Pink Lady

The Pink Lady, always bathed in an unearthly pink light, has been seen walking from the castle toward an adjacent church. She is believed to be the ghost of a woman looking for her lost husband, who was killed when the English took the castle in 1304. Others say the beautiful apparition is none other than Mary, Queen of Scots.

Elphinstone Tower

The staff of Stirling Castle avoids Elphinstone Tower, located on the east side of the castle. Many unexplained incidents, perhaps attributable to the castle's bloody history, have taken place there. Much of the tower is gone; only crumbling ruins remain. It is believed that the tower was used as a torture chamber, where people were locked up with no hope of release. Local legend has it that James V kept a pair of conjoined twins locked up within it, using them as an oracle. It is rumored that when one twin died, the other was forced to live on there for ten months, still attached to his brother's dead body. Although this may seem highly unlikely, the legend lives on.

Wotton-under-Edge

The Ancient Ram Inn in the town of Wotton-under-Edge is host to a great deal of unexplained phenomena. Stories of devil worship and grisly deaths fill its long history. Some allege it is one of England's most haunted houses.

FACT

Ghost lights and spectral lights have been reported frequently in the literature of the supernatural. In Britain, these ghostly lights are called will-o-wisps and are thought to be an omen of impending misfortune or death. Sometimes called *ignis fatuus*, or fool's fire, they are thought to be the souls of the dead in some cultures.

The Ram was a pub built on an old pagan burial site. Parts of the ramshackle structure date back to the twelfth century. It has become a popular spot with ghost hunters and is reportedly susceptible to sudden inexplicable temperature drops, orbs, dancing lights, and spectral shadows. Most visitors and investigators feel that whatever is lurking at the Ancient Ram is decidedly unfriendly; many describe the atmosphere as oppressive or evil. The owner states that eight people who stayed there had to undergo exorcisms.

Chillingham Castle

Chillingham Castle, near the Scottish border, bills itself as one of the world's most haunted castles. For almost eight centuries, the castle has been continuously occupied.

The Blue Boy

The Blue Boy's hauntings always began on the stroke of midnight, when wailing and shrieking echoed off the ten foot thick castle walls. After the cries died away, witnesses reported that a bright halo of light began to form near an old four-poster bed in the room. A childish figure in blue appeared, surrounded by an eerie light. In the 1920s, renovations near this room uncovered the bones of a young boy and some fragments of blue material. The remains were removed and properly buried in consecrated ground. The boy's apparition has not been seen since.

Lady Mary Berkeley

Lady Mary Berkeley, wife of the Earl of Tankerville, occasionally strolls the stone corridors looking for her bounder of a husband. He ran away with her sister, Lady Henrietta, leaving Lady Mary and her child to cope with life alone in the castle. Legend has it that the nursery where her portrait hangs has been repeatedly disturbed by her apparition, which steps out of the frame to frighten children by following them.

Other Chillingham Ghosts

Two invisible men have been overheard talking in the library. Exactly what they're discussing isn't clear, and their conversation stops abruptly when they detect eavesdroppers.

In the pantry where the silver is stored, a frail woman in white has been seen repeatedly. One footman whose job it was to care for the silver simply presumed she was a guest—until he remembered he was behind the locked pantry door. When he turned back to confront her, she had vanished.

Victorian Ghost Hunters

Table tilting, spirit writing, Ouija boards, séances, mediums, and apparitions were all the rage in the nineteenth century. The investigation into the world of ghosts gained momentum in the Victorian era and the age of spiritualism. Fueled by a belief that science would soon unravel all the mysteries of the spirit world, the Victorians were very avid ghost hunters. They lived in a society that, for the first time in centuries, did not blindly accept religious dogma as the absolute truth.

The Spiritualist Movement

The Spiritualist movement began in 1848, when many reputable eyewitnesses observed poltergeist activity in a house in Hydesville, New York. The activity began with loud rapping, which occurred first in the presence of two teenaged girls, Margaret and Kate Fox.

The Victorians had an incredible interest in all things bizarre and paranormal and enjoyed grotesque images such as this sphinx with the head of a Victorian lady.

Photo copyright Melissa Martin Ellis, 2008.

The Fox sisters believed the noises were made by some intelligent entity or entities. A spirit they called Mr. Splitfoot could answer questions and told the girls things they could not have known on their own. The Fox sisters became a sensation and were soon traveling throughout the eastern United States, demonstrating their powers and bringing messages from the spirit world. They rented large halls and held demonstrations of their abilities. The public was riveted and their appearances stirred up huge controversies. Soon other mediums sprang up in their wake, including the Eddy brothers, Madame Blavatsky, and Daniel Dunglas Home, to name a few.

FACT

In séances held in the nineteenth century, a phenomenon often reported was table knocking or tapping, often called spirit rapping. This sort of phenomena has actually been associated with spirits for centuries, but the Fox sisters revived it in the 1850s.

Spiritualism in England

It was not in the least unusual to find middle- and upper-class people with an interest in spiritualism. Some scientists of great standing and reputation took psychic research very seriously. Men of letters who were open to the claims of mediums included poet Alfred, Lord Tennyson; philosopher Henry Sidgwick; and Nobel Prize winners Charles Richet and Lord Rayleigh. Two of the paranormal world's most respected supporters were William James, a writer who authored one of the earliest books on psychology in nineteenth-century America, and Sir Arthur Conan Doyle, creator of Sherlock Holmes.

In 1882, some of the intellectuals in London decided to form an organization to study the world of psychic powers and paranormal abilities. The Society for Psychical Research (SPR) was formed. The founders were Edmund Gurney, an English psychologist, poet and essayist; Frederic William Henry Myers, professor of physics at the Royal College of Science; philosopher William Barrett; philosopher Henry Sidgwick; and journalist Edmund Dawson Rogers. The SPR exists to this day and has a branch in America as well.

Ghost Hunting in the Twenty-First Century

Since the SPR was founded, many new elements have been added to the study of ghosts and apparitions. Surprisingly, some of the tools at the modern ghost hunter's disposal are similar to those used in the 1880s. Good observational skills, accurate recording of information, and an inquiring and skeptical mind are prerequisites that will probably never change.

Electronic Spook Sleuths

The invention of radio and television ushered in a new age in ghost hunting. It was widely reported that people were picking up transmissions from the other side through these mediums. Televisions that were turned off displayed the ghostly faces of deceased relatives, or more frequently, total strangers.

Recordings of garbled voices surfaced as well. These voices came to be known as electronic voice phenomena (EVPs). One of the characteristics of EVPs is the reaction they produce in the listener. Sometimes they will literally send chills up the spine or cause the hair on the back of the neck to stand up. Critics allege that the sounds are random signals that the human mind interprets as meaningful.

Digital Necromancy

Only in the twenty-first century has digital photography been readily accessible to paranormal investigators. The new generation of audio software can be loaded onto home computer systems and can filter out background noises and boost weak audio signals, allowing paranormal investigators to more easily analyze audio data captured on both analog and digital recorders.

Digital thermometers, too, have increased in sophistication. They are more sensitive than ever to slight temperature fluctuations and the movement of cold spots. Electromagnetic field (EMF) meters have increased in ease of use and sensitivity, with red lights that signal users of readings beyond normal ranges.

Is Something Out There?

Perhaps the question is not *whether* something is out there but *what* is out there. When people see ghosts, are they actually experiencing a form of mental telepathy? Are they seeing remnants of an event from the past that has been imprinted somehow on the surroundings? Or are they seeing the projection of a person who has died?

Credible witnesses over decades, even centuries, have reported seeing things that have no rational explanation according to the laws that govern the natural world. About 33 percent of Americans believe in ghosts and UFOs, and almost half—48 percent—believe in extrasensory perception, or ESP.

Most people who are interested in the paranormal are just average folks who have had an experience they cannot explain. An inexplicable experience changes a person's perception of the world. It leads people to search for answers. In essence, they become ghost hunters.

CHAPTER 3

The Psychic Skill Set

If you have experienced paranormal phenomena, you may be confused, frightened, and perhaps even a little fearful of being ridiculed. Or, you may have just discovered that you are a little bit psychic. The best defense against fear of the unknown is to educate oneself. There are hundreds of books and websites about the paranormal world. Consult the recommended reading list at the end of this book to help you find the materials that are the most informative and credible.

Cultivating Your Talents

It is possible to hone your natural observational skills and objectivity and train yourself to develop whatever latent psychic skills you may already have. In *The Everything Psychic Book: Tap into Your Inner Power and Discover Your Inherent Abilities* by Michael R. Hathaway, you'll find a great deal of helpful information.

The primary question you must ask yourself if you are eager to develop your natural psychic talents is why. If you wish to explore the boundaries of human consciousness and connect with higher realms—in short, if your intentions are honest and not selfish—you can proceed with confidence. It's hypothesized that everyone has some amount of psychic ability, but the extent of the development of these talents can vary widely.

Types of Abilities

There seem to be roughly four kinds of psychic ability, and people can develop one or more of them. The four psychic senses are psychic intuition, psychic feeling, psychic vision, and psychic hearing.

- **Clairsentience, or psychic feeling:** The sense of psychic feeling is what people mean when they say they have a gut feeling or a hunch. When people have a feeling something is about to go wrong, they often experience a sinking feeling in the pit of their stomach.
- **Claircognizance, or psychic knowing:** Psychic intuition is similar to psychic feeling, but there is no physical sensation involved; the person simply knows an event is about to take place.
- **Clairvoyance, or psychic seeing:** This is perhaps the best known psychic skill. When you have a psychic vision, it is as if you're viewing the scene through your mystical eye, or third eye. This is located between your eyebrows and is said to be a powerful psychic tool. Often, you will experience a very brief flash of an object or person. The image slips away if you try too hard to grasp it. People who are clairvoyant often see auras—a glowing energy field—around people and even plants and animals.
- **Clairaudience, or psychic hearing:** People who have the gift of psychic hearing are called clairaudient. They say it is as if they are

hearing a voice inside their head, perhaps just above their ears. A very common clairaudient experience is hearing your name called even though no one is there. This can happen as you're falling asleep, and it is very startling. Another frequent occurrence is parents who believe they hear their children crying or calling to them when they are totally out of earshot.

Psychics and Seers

Since the dawn of time, there have been people whose senses were tuned to events that were inaccessible to the average person. These people have often been consulted and exploited for their talents, but they have also been regarded with suspicion, fear, and sometimes contempt. It is small wonder that many psychics simply chose to keep their knowledge to themselves. At many times, during the medieval era and even as recently as seventeenth-century America, people with these paranormal abilities were burned at the stake or suffered other dreadful fates for the audacity of showing their abilities.

Today we are somewhat more civilized and more tolerant of those who are a little different. Sure, skeptics may scoff, but that has never killed anyone.

Divining the Differences

Psychics and seers generally fall into three categories:

1. The real deal
2. Total charlatans
3. People with actual abilities who cheat for unknown reasons

How do you tell the real psychics from the frauds? Use your own powers of perception. Ask yourself if you have a gut feeling about a person. Does she make you feel uneasy or try to frighten or intimidate you? Does she ask you for money or request that you do something that is against your better nature? You should leave the presence of this person as quickly and politely as you can. Even if she truly does have psychic powers, the effect she can have on your energy and senses is not good. It is reasonable to assume that the outcome of being near her will not be good either.

FACT

Automatic writing is a term for the delivery of messages from the other side by the means of writing. It is done without any conscious cooperation of the person doing the writing. Sometimes the information conveyed proves to be far beyond the knowledge and capabilities of the medium.

You will sense that a genuine psychic or seer is surrounded by a special energy. Although you may be nervous, you should not feel threatened or afraid. A good psychic is usually a good person who has taken all the steps required to build his psychic talents. He meditates to learn to place himself in a receptive state of mind, and he has also learned the skill of creative visualization. He studies, practices, and eventually grows in skill and accuracy over time.

Old stone houses and older structures are featured often in stories of hauntings.

Photo copyright Melissa Martin Ellis, 2006.

Both the real psychics and frauds sometimes use special tools, such as pendulums, crystal balls, or cards in their work. These tools can help focus concentration and assist in visualization, which is helpful for clairvoyants.

Sadly, there have been psychics with genuine abilities who chose to exploit them. When their powers failed them, they were so invested in their situations that they tried to cover up their loss with chicanery. These people have done a lot of harm to themselves and others and should be avoided.

Your Paranormal Self-Education

If you decide you want to pursue a career as a paranormal investigator, either as a hobby or as a profession, it is very important to gather a library of reference materials and educate yourself about the many sorts of unexplained phenomena and hauntings. Today there are some truly wonderful books and reference materials available. Bookstores and online sources such as Amazon.com make these reference materials, magazines, books, and websites available to everyone. It is a totally fascinating field, and we are fortunate to have more material available to us today than at any time in history.

Beginning the Journey

If you have an inquiring and open mind, you have a very fascinating experience ahead of you. There is much to learn and much to explore. In addition, what you learn will change how you view the world, yourself, and the people around you.

So where should you begin? You'll find a reading list of reference material at the back of the book, but a few authors stand out. They have written extensively about the paranormal and are consistently informative, intelligent, and honest.

The occult books by British author Colin Wilson are very thorough and insightful. *Mysteries*, *The Occult*, and *Poltergeist* are particularly recommended. D. Scott Rogo's *The Welcoming Silence: A Study of Psychical Phenomena and Survival of Death* and *The Haunted House Handbook* and Loyd Auerbach's *ESP, Hauntings and Poltergeists* are excellent works for people seeking to get an overview. As you read books on the paranormal, keep paper and pen handy to take notes on ideas and concepts that you find of particular interest or would like to follow up on.

E-QUESTION

Are ghosts and poltergeists the same thing?
Some investigators say they are different. Poltergeists are classified as nonhuman entities that produce destructive phenomena. They are capable of starting fires, rearranging furniture, throwing objects, and producing human-sounding voices. Poltergeists are usually heard but not seen.

Internet Research

Make sure the sites you look at have credibility and are run by people with a background in, respect for, and history within the paranormal community. Research which websites have long histories of credibility and which organizations have been around for years and have proven themselves. The Atlantic Paranormal Society (TAPS) website (*www.the-atlantic-paranor mal-society.com*) has a great deal of information, as do the sites run by Troy Taylor (*www.prairieghosts.com/abtauthor.html*) and the Rhode Island Paranormal Research Group (T.R.I.P.R.G.; *www.triprg.com*).

Taking Specialized Classes

Although reading and research can prepare paranormal investigators for the possibilities of ghost hunting, actual classes can better help you grasp subtleties and procedures. They are also useful for learning the technical aspects of the business, such as how to properly operate an EMF meter and how to handle an EVP investigation.

Connecting the Dots

Any class you take should cover the following information:

- How to locate haunted sites
- How to research the site's history

- How to interview eyewitnesses
- How to build a ghost hunting kit
- How to record EVPs
- How to use EMF meters and digital thermometers
- How to properly use a digital camera in the investigation
- How to form a team or paranormal group

This information should be covered whether you take an online class, a home-study class, or a class at a continuing education institution. Sign up for classes only after you have checked out the credentials of the instructors and institutions.

Double-check all classes, particularly Internet classes. If the quality of the classes or the institution has slipped, you can easily get feedback from other students who may have had unsatisfactory experiences there.

If you live in Connecticut, Rhode Island, or Massachusetts, you may be within easy driving distance of TAPS's one-day seminars and lectures. TAPS is the organization featured on the Sci Fi Channel's *Ghost Hunters* TV show. Although the cost of their workshops is generally very reasonable ($40 for a one-day seminar), they sell out very quickly.

Online classes vary widely in cost. Classes priced at $100 are at the high end of the scale. Flamel College (*www.flamelcollege.org*) offers a paranormal investigator certification for $99. This fee includes an EMF meter. Universal Class (*http://universalclass.com*) has a very reasonably priced ($20) online class for beginning investigators, and with certification, it is $45.

The case of the Epworth Rectory Poltergeist is one of the best-known examples of poltergeist activity ever recorded. Because it happened in the home of famous British clergyman John Wesley and was particularly noisy, it became something of a legend. As in the case of most poltergeist activity, there was a teenager in residence.

Fiona Broome is the founder of Hollow Hill (*www.hollowhill.com*), a ghost hunters' website. Hollow Hill offers classes in different levels so students can take classes appropriate to their situation. Her courses are offered on CDs.

Chilling Conferences

In the Pacific Northwest, the Ghost Hunters Getaway Conference might be an option if you have some experience already. It is an annual conference hosted by the paranormal research group Advanced Ghost Hunters of Seattle-Tacoma (AGHOST). This conference is held over a two-day period, with workshops, ghost tours, paranormal investigations, and media presentations. See the website *www.aghost.us/101.html* for more information.

Instinct Versus Intellect

Many skeptics dismiss the topic of investigating the paranormal as a black-and-white issue of intellect versus instinct. The two should never be viewed in conflict with each other, because as you pursue your paranormal studies and investigations you will definitely need to rely heavily on both qualities.

Your intellect and observational skills play a key role in your investigations. You should always look for a natural explanation for any observed or reported phenomenon before concluding that an event is paranormal in origin. Frankly, in most cases you will be able to find a mundane explanation when you examine the evidence thoroughly.

But listening to your instinct is important, too. Instinct can tell you when a situation is potentially dangerous or lead you to a certain room or area where your investigation will bear fruit. The important thing is to keep a good balance between intellect and intuition.

Stumped by the Spirits

If you investigate long enough, you will inevitably encounter a circumstance that cannot be explained by any natural law or debunked by an everyday explanation. When this happens, it is important to maintain an open and alert state of mind. This is easily said but hard to do. When the human mind is confronted by phenomena it cannot quickly categorize or readily understand, it tends to either freeze or race out of control. Your heart may pound and your thoughts may grow chaotic or confused. So how do you cope with these reactions? The answer isn't a simple one; each individual has a different threshold for dealing with anxiety and fear.

If you are a total skeptic, you may find that you completely shut down and simply refuse to process or believe what you are seeing. On the other hand, if you have a tendency to be open-minded, you may be better prepared to handle the situation. In either case, you should work with a partner and use technology to help you keep an objective record of the event. Try to maintain as professional a demeanor as you can, given the circumstances.

Digital's Got Your Back

Additionally, a DVR, digital camera, or tape recorder should be in use at all times as you work. It's best to use at least two of the three at all times. They will provide you with valuable data to be analyzed and verified. If you capture something unexplained, evidence from these devices will force you to realign your thinking. If you're a believer, it will reinforce your existing belief system. Of course, some skeptics have their beliefs validated if nothing turns up on tape or film. That is why it is so important to have credible eyewitness accounts and independently verifiable evidence.

Divination, Necromancy, and Dowsing

Divination is a way of gathering information by paranormal means, using tools and symbols to acquire knowledge from the collective unconscious, superconscious, or beings on a different plane of existence. This knowledge can be about people, places, and things from the past, present, and future.

Necromancy is a term used for divination by means of communication with the dead. The tools of divination have their roots in antiquity. Since the dawn of time, humans have tried to contact and control the spirits of the dead. In this section, we'll discuss the types of divination used for that purpose, rather than those simply used to tell fortunes and predict future events, such as palmistry, card reading, or astrology. Dowsing, which straddles both necromancy and divination, will also be discussed.

Hello, Goodbye

The most famous tool of the necromancer is the Ouija board. The board as we know it dates back to the late nineteenth century. It was made popular during the spiritualist movement, when its widespread use was considered harmless. Today it has come into disfavor, as it is said to open a door to poltergeists and other low-level psychic phenomena. This door, once opened, is not easily shut, so the use of the Ouija board is considered dangerous by most psychic investigators and its use seriously discouraged.

The board's surface has the letters of the alphabet, the numerals 0 through 9, and the words *yes*, *no*, *hello*, and *goodbye*. A triangular device called a planchette, usually made of plastic and about four inches long, has enough room for two people to lightly rest their fingers on. The planchette has three felt-tipped legs that glide over the board's surface to point at letters, spelling out answers to questions asked by participants. In his article "Ouija, Not a Game," writer Dale Kaczmarek of the Ghost Research Society warns that automatic writing and séances are all dangerous for novice users.

FACT

Emanuel Swedenborg was a Swedish scientist and theologian who believed he held conversations with angels, Jesus, and God in which he was shown the true nature of the universe. He alleged that he delivered messages from Aristotle, Napoleon, and other famous people who had passed.

Kaczmarek suggests that spirits from the lower astral plane are the entities most often attracted by these divination tools, and they introduce chaotic and sometimes even dangerous energy into the homes of the naive. If a psychic or medium is present, she can better control the situation, but extreme caution is still needed. Don't be tempted to use these devices without the proper safeguards and training. They have a long history of trouble.

Involuntary Movements?

In 1882, physiologist William Carpenter explained such diverse events as the movement of the Ouija board's planchette, the circular motion of the pendulum, and even the table tipping of the mediums of his day as the result of something he called ideomotor action. This term refers to involuntary and unconscious muscle movements on the part of people participating in these activities. Carpenter argued that these unconscious muscular movements could be involuntarily initiated by the mind and then interpreted by participants as paranormal.

As plausible as this explanation may sound, there have been many documented cases of table tipping so extreme that the idea that small muscle movements caused them is simply ludicrous. And if the Ouija board spells out answers to questions that none of the participants knew the answer to and are later verified as true, what are we to think of that?

I Scry Something Wicked

Scrying is another form of divination, often used to foretell the future and communicate with the spirit world. Scrying was used by ancient cultures from Persia to Greece to Egypt as a tool for prognostication, or predicting future events. Spirits were thought to have a hand in conveying the messages. Nostradamus, arguably the most famous psychic of all time, was said to have used a small bowl of water as his means of seeing into the future. From the Middle Ages to present times, scrying has been widely used by wizards, witches, clairvoyants, and psychics.

Scryers most often use crystal balls or black mirrors, although any reflective media, even ink, water, and crystals can be used. Most people are familiar with the image of the gypsy fortuneteller gazing raptly into a crystal ball to relate the fate of her gullible clientele.

The premise behind scrying is that when the person gazes into the reflective surface in the proper state of relaxation, she will see images that unfold either before her or in her mind's eye—glimpses of a future time, a far-off place, or a past event.

E-QUESTION

What is a necromancer?
A necromancer is a person who uses divination to gain information from the world of spirits. He can use tarot cards, crystal balls, or séances and Ouija boards. Necromancers have been known to use the mummified hands of corpses or paws of animals. They open themselves up to paranormal influences and all the dangers inherent in that process.

The cave at Tassili Najjer in the Sahara, where the earliest picture of dowsing was found.

Art copyright Melissa Martin Ellis, 2006.

Water Witching

Dowsing is another form of divination used since ancient times to seek answers to questions. The first recorded use of dowsing may be a cave painting at Tassili Najjer in the Sahara, dated to approximately 6000 B.C.E. It shows a crowd gathered to watch a dowser at work. Ancient people frequently used dowsing rods to locate water.

Probably used initially to determine the will of the gods or find answers to questions about the future, dowsing is used widely today to locate things. Whether they search for water, oil, or precious metals, dowsers use a forked L-shaped rod or a straight rod to find the material they are looking for.

It has long been debated whether dowsing is an electromagnetic phenomena or an actual paranormal ability. Regardless, the process has withstood the test of time, despite its many detractors.

Map Dowsing

Sometimes pendulums of metal or crystal are used to dowse, particularly when the dowser is hoping to locate something on a map. Controversial psychic Uri Geller has stated on many occasions that the bulk of his income comes from dowsing to locate oil fields for the petroleum industry.

In the 1970s, Geller underwent double-blind tests in which he was asked to locate either a ball bearing, water, or a magnet concealed within identical metal containers. A third party placed the items in the containers, and scientists filmed Geller as tests were run repeatedly. Geller used a form of dowsing and correctly located the items in almost all of the tests. The scientists determined that the odds were a trillion to one that he had obtained his results by chance.

No one really knows how the dowsing process works. Is the subconscious moving the pendulum, or is a spirit or higher force doing it? Is it biofeedback and bioenergy? Theories and speculation continue.

Perhaps the simplest way for beginners to learn to dowse is with a pendulum. You need a pendulum, metal bobber, or crystal and a chain or string to suspend it from. Make sure you're comfortable with the dowsing tool and are away from any noise, distractions, or electronic equipment.

1. Determine a system for yourself—for instance, clockwise may mean "yes," counterclockwise "no."
2. Relax by taking three or four long, deep breaths.
3. Begin the experiment by holding the chain or string of the pendulum in your dominant hand about two inches away from the dangling object or bobber.
4. Break the east-west motion by making a deliberate movement either clockwise or counterclockwise. Hold the pendulum over your other hand.
5. Ask yourself how the movement feels; does it feel natural? If not, hold the string or chain a bit higher and keep on going until you find the position that feels right to you and allows the weight on the chain to rotate freely.
6. Mark that place with permanent marker or a straight pin.
7. Ask simple "yes" or "no" questions and start your dowsing session.
8. Be sure to make note of the answers and the day's date on the paper.

What sort of questions should you ask? Don't get into dark areas, and try to keep the questions simple. If you're looking for employment, you can start by asking, "Will I find work in the next three months?" If the answer is "yes," then narrow it down even further. "Will I get work in the next month?" Don't ask complex questions with an open-ended response that can't be answered properly with a simple yes or no, such as "How much money will the job pay?"

Predicting Events

In dowsing, as in so many things in life, practice makes perfect. Inevitably, people who have some luck at dowsing begin to ask for information about the future. Be aware and guard yourself against the influence of negative responses. There is a real danger to those who are sensitive to negative news. Remember that the answers that you get about future events are only possibilities of what is to come and are not written in stone. Remember that free will and corrective actions in the present can change what is still to come. In other words, if you don't like the answers you get, use your free will to make choices that will change the outcome.

CHAPTER 4

Are They Kindred Spirits?

A strong dose of healthy skepticism is a good place for any investigator of the paranormal to start. If you don't try to debunk potential paranormal experiences, you won't make a good investigator. However, you must also believe paranormal experiences do occur. You must also be aware of the different types of spirits that may remain in this world after death.

Ghosts, Apparitions, and Demons

Although it might at first seem irrelevant what we choose to call the entity sighted at a haunting, a strong case might be made that it is important to be able to classify these sightings.

What Are Ghosts?

The *American Heritage Dictionary* defines a *ghost* as:

1. The spirit of a dead person, especially one believed to appear in bodily likeness to living persons or to haunt former habitations
2. The center of spiritual life; the soul
3. A demon or spirit
4. A returning or haunting memory or image

Photo copyright Melissa Martin Ellis, 2006.

The shadow people appear as a dark silhouette, usually with no discernible features.

The first definition is the one we are all most familiar with, but it is perhaps a bit surprising to see a ghost referred to as a demon. The appearances of ghosts are as varied as their observers. People may only catch a glimpse of a partial image of the entity. This can mean they only see a pair of legs scurrying away. Or a legless torso and upper body floats about, perhaps absorbed in some activity and oblivious to the observer. Occasionally, semi-transparent figures will appear.

What Is an Apparition?

The *American Heritage Dictionary* defines *apparition* as:

1. A ghostly figure; a specter
2. A sudden or unusual sight
3. The act of appearing; appearance

Though the terms *ghost* and *apparition* are often used interchangeably, they are actually not the same type of entity at all.

Shadow people, also called shadow men or shadow beings, are a type of apparition. They are often described as black humanoid silhouettes, usually without any details, although they are sometimes reported as having red or yellow eyes. Their movements are often reported as being very jiggly and abnormal, or extremely slow and slippery, like a liquid shadow.

If you are visiting a historic site and glimpse someone in period garb, you would naturally assume you've seen a tour guide, or that there is some other plausible explanation for the person's odd clothes. But if you saw that same person walk through a solid door or wall, or if no one else noticed him, you might begin to suspect that what you had seen just might be a ghost.

If you see a figure that is misty or partially transparent, it is obvious that what you have seen can be called either a ghost or an apparition. But what if you see something dark, so dark it looks as if it is made of shadows? Perhaps what you have seen is most appropriately called a shadow person. Or perhaps it is a demon.

What Is a Demon?

The *American Heritage Dictionary* defines a *demon* as:

1. An evil supernatural being; a devil
2. A persistently tormenting person, force, or passion: the demon of drug addiction
3. One who is extremely zealous, skillful, or diligent: worked away like a demon; a real demon at math
4. Variant of *daimon*

Now we are introduced to a category of entity that is quite distinct from either a ghost or an apparition. We also have the added component of evil—a being that takes delight in tormenting the living. It implies a malicious and active type of haunting, which is quite different from something like a residual haunting, which is defined as being almost like a taped version of the event that plays and replays over decades or even centuries. The entities in a haunting of this type do not seem to be aware of onlookers and don't interact with them in any way.

Demonics, on the other hand, seem to want to interact; indeed, they seem to derive a lot of pleasure from doing so. Reports of these creatures predate the Bible and accounts of them have existed in one form or another in every civilization of which we have a record. They were often simply called evil spirits. The word *demon* is derived from the Greek *daimon*, and in ancient Iran and India they were called *daewon*. These malevolent spirits were perceived in the Christian tradition as fallen angels. Whatever you call them, they are bad news. Dealing with these spirits requires preparation, an abundance of caution, and most definitely some outside help.

Ectoplasmic Mists and Fogs

The whole concept of *ectoplasm* began in 1894, when French physiologist Charles Richet coined the term to describe the misty substance associated with the formation of ghosts and believed to be the actual physical substance created by the energy manifested by mediums. Richet, a winner of the Nobel Prize for Physiology or Medicine in 1913, was also the first to use the word *metaphysics* to describe what, up until that time, had been called *materialization*.

This rubbery, milky substance could appear either as a solid or a vapor. Extruded from the body of the medium, it would subsequently materialize limbs, faces, and even entire bodies. These manifestations were reportedly warm, flexible, and even dough-like. They emerged from orifices such as the mouth, ears, nose, and occasionally less convenient locations.

Ewwww! What Is That?

Forms of ectoplasm vary widely—anything from mists to thin tentacles or full bodies. This substance disappears when exposed to light and snaps back quickly into the medium's body. It was believed that touching the ectoplasm or exposing it to light might cause injury to the medium. This was one of the main reasons mediums insisted that séances take place in almost total darkness, as any attempt to touch or approach the mediums or ectoplasm could cause severe bodily harm. Daniel Dunglas Home was one notable exception to this rule; he conducted séances and manifested spirits in full daylight. The fact that these ectoplasmic manifestations occurred in semi-darkness and that some were obvious frauds has cast a negative pall over the whole issue. Of the hundreds of shots of ectoplasm in existence, about 95 percent are less than convincing.

Do My Eyes Deceive Me?

Occasionally, cameras capture spectral mists and fogs during an investigation. Experienced ghost hunters know these mysterious mists are often the fog caused by exhaled breath on a cold day or a shot of someone's cigarette smoke. Since no one should be smoking during an investigation, hopefully the latter can be ruled out as the cause of the fog during a professional investigation. For the most part, when these eerie mists appear in photos, they were not visible to the naked eye when the pictures were snapped.

So what are we seeing? By following good paranormal investigative protocol, you will perhaps have enough other evidence to help understand what has transpired if such a picture shows up during one of your investigations.

Do you have a record of the room temperature at the time the photo was taken, or EMF or infrared DVR readings? If the ambient temperature

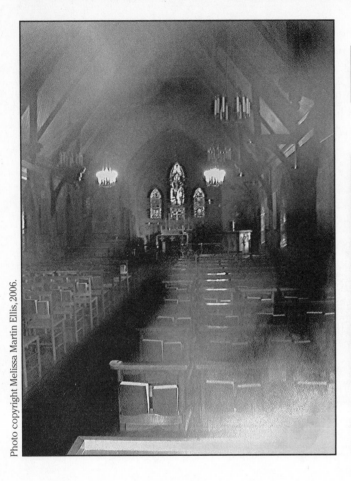

Photo copyright Melissa Martin Ellis, 2006.

There was no fog or mist visible when this photo was taken (*left*).

Photo copyright Kym Black, 2006.

Kym Black was tracking these orbs with her camera as they went up the stairs at the Sprague Mansion (*above*).

in the room remained constant but you encountered cold spots or sudden temperature drops, then there is an increased likelihood that something paranormal has been captured in your photos. If you have no other supporting evidence, whether such anomalous images represent genuine ghosts or anything paranormal will very likely be in dispute.

E-QUESTION

What are orbs?

Some investigators insist that orbs are nothing more than a side effect of the flash going off too close to the lens and bouncing off dust, bugs, or other particles in the air, such as raindrops. Others counter that they can indeed be evidence of paranormal activity or even entities themselves.

Anomalous Images

In metaphysical photography, shots that show fogs, mists, and odd-looking lights are often intriguing. Even before the advent of digital photography, these images were turning up on film, so their cause cannot be attributed to the flash being too close to the lens. In these cloudy shots, it is nearly impossible to tell what the vapor and mists represent.

Perhaps some can be dismissed as ordinary light pollution, reflections, or cigarette smoke, but when all these things have been eliminated, there still remains an impressive number of cloudy images and foggy forms caught by photographers. The fact that they seem to happen more frequently in allegedly haunted houses and sites with some religious or spiritual significance is a pertinent observation.

One of the best examples of alleged ectoplasmic mists was in a video shot at the Civil War battlefield in Gettysburg, Pennsylvania. In it, a DVR recorded what appear to be spirits on the battlefield. It can be viewed at *www.disclose.tv/viewvideo/672/Gettysburg_Ghosts*.

A Close Encounter

A few years ago, after a visit to the chapel in St. Columba's Church in Middletown, Rhode Island, an unusual photo turned up. Founded in 1884, the Berkeley Memorial Chapel is one of the most beautiful stone chapels in New England. It looks as if it has been transported by magic from the English countryside to nestle amongst the old beeches in the churchyard.

On impulse, an interior shot was snapped inside the old chapel. The shot of the chapel appears to be filled with a swirling mist, although the photographer saw nothing like mist when the shot was taken. The same is true for the gravestones and memorials in the churchyard. They appear to have streamers of smoke or fog trailing off them.

Poltergeists and Elemental Spirits

A poltergeist is a noisy spirit that makes its presence known primarily by way of sound. Physical manifestations follow, beginning as scratching noises from within the walls and escalating to more frequent banging or thumping sounds. Objects begin to sail through the air, usually narrowly missing the unfortunate inhabitants. It is often the case that there is an adolescent or teenager in the house where the manifestations occur.

It is also possible for adults to trigger the manifestations. All that is truly necessary is that the person be troubled emotionally. One theory is that this person may be unconsciously manipulating the items in the house by means of psychokinesis, which is the power to move things with an energy generated by the brain. Although largely unexplained, psychokinetic energy has been demonstrated to exist. Usually, people have no idea they are causing the poltergeist activity, which is happening all around them, and they are surprised to find that there is any possibility they themselves could be making the chaotic events happen.

Picture This

To be fair, not all cases of poltergeist activity involve troubled individuals. These hauntings aren't always so easily categorized. It is vital that the paranormal investigators involved be observant and not jump to conclusions too quickly. The three most famous cases of poltergeist activity in the United States were:

- The Amityville haunting, which became the basis for both a book and a movie (*The Amityville Horror* is generally considered to have been blown out of proportion for the sake of a story.)
- The case upon which author William Peter Blatty based *The Exorcist*
- The nineteenth-century Bell Witch case

All three hauntings have ended up as movies, with many dramatic additions to the story. *The Exorcist* is the best known of these three, and perhaps one of the most interesting aspects of this story is that Blatty based his book on a diary kept by a priest who assisted at the exorcism. He changed the lead character from a fourteen-year-old boy to a twelve-year-old girl. He has stated that 80 percent of what appears in the book is fact according to the priest.

The typical poltergeist disturbance does not usually last long. Disturbances usually subside after just a few weeks, although the malicious entity that tormented the Bell family between 1817 and 1821 was certainly a notable exception. The problems started for the Bells when they began hearing sounds on the exterior walls of their house. These noises sounded as if someone was pounding on the walls. Soon the Bells began to hear other sounds, such as scratching and knocking.

There wasn't actually a witch involved in the Bell Witch case, at least as far as we know. Benjamin Batts had a dispute with John Bell over a slave. This later became the source of a rumor that Kate Batts created the Bell Witch to get revenge on Bell.

This is a classic example of poltergeist phenomena. But instead of building to a crescendo and then diminishing, the phenomena increased. Soon physical attacks began; people were scratched, slapped, had their covers ripped off, and were thrown out of bed.

Although almost everyone in the household suffered similar treatment, the focus seemed to be on the Bells' daughter Betsy. The terrifying activity in the Bell household went on for so long that it is very well documented, and local legend has it that even General Andrew Jackson had an encounter.

It's Really Elemental

The common conceptual framework that underlies the perception of these beings is that elemental spirits are believed to be comprised of what the ancients perceived as the building blocks of the world—earth, air, fire, and water. Elementals are often described as primitive and malevolent beings or forces that attach themselves to a particular location. Magicians and sorcerers believed they could use these spirits to do their bidding through a process called binding, which protected the person doing the spell from harm and allowed her to control the spirit as it did whatever task she assigned it. Sometimes this can backfire, as many dabblers in the occult can attest to.

An instance of this is well represented by the story of the elemental at sixteenth-century Leap Castle in Ireland. Leap has a long and bloody history of strife, discord, and murder. The local people have always believed it to be haunted and avoided it when possible, particularly at night.

By the late nineteenth century, an English couple, Jonathan and Mildred Darby, had inherited Leap. Like so many other people at that time, Mildred Darby was interested in the occult. She held several séances at the castle with unwelcome results. When she began to dabble with the occult, she had apparently awakened a terrifying elemental.

In the journal *Occult Review*, in 1909, Mildred describes her experience with the creature she summoned: "I was standing in the Gallery looking down at the main floor, when I felt somebody put a hand on my shoulder. The thing was about the size of a sheep. Thin, gaunt, shadowy . . . its face was human, to be more accurate, inhuman. Its lust in its eyes, which seemed half decomposed in black cavities, stared into mine. The horrible smell one hundred times intensified came up into my face, giving me a deadly nausea. It was the smell of a decomposing corpse."

Residual Hauntings

If the same apparition is seen over and over again, doing exactly the same thing, if the same sounds are heard at the same time of day, if the same scene plays out over and over again over a period of years or even centuries, it is a residual haunting. Also called energy remnants and memory imprint, the apparition in a residual haunting never interacts with onlookers, but rather seems totally oblivious to them.

What Are Residual Hauntings?

Perhaps residual hauntings are simply playbacks of past events. The apparitions involved may not even be actual spirits but just impressions or recordings of events that were so traumatic that they have become imprinted on the very materials of the space in which they occurred. There are many theories regarding residual hauntings. One of the first to offer a possible hypothesis of how residual hauntings occur was Thomas Charles Lethbridge, in his 1961 book *Ghost and Ghoul*.

His theory is that just as audiotapes and videotapes record sounds and images, certain materials used in the construction of older structures may record impressions of events. If a traumatic, emotionally charged incident occurs, these materials record it for future playback. The event can suddenly occur and play out without an apparent cause. Sometimes there is no visual component to the event, only repetitive sounds, such as footsteps, breathing, or smells that have no apparent cause. No one knows what triggers the playback of these recordings.

It could be anything from the observer's own emotional state or sensitivity to weather conditions, such as high humidity or barometric pressure. Whatever its cause, the residual haunting is intriguing. In the Tower of London, people have seen the ghosts of Anne Boleyn and many others who were held within its walls before their executions.

FACT

There is a theory that the building materials of the haunted site may have recorded the energy of the event in the case of residual hauntings. Older structures often have quartz, iron, and slate in them, and these are thought to hold an impression of the event.

Europe has many ancient structures made of porous stones, which might function like batteries to store energy. This could explain why there are so many instances of haunted sites in Europe.

American Residual Hauntings

How then do we explain the many residual hauntings in America? Indeed, many of these take place in old buildings as well. New England, as one of the oldest settled regions in the country, seems to be particularly prone to hauntings. When several different witnesses report seeing the same repetitive event, you can be fairly sure they are reporting an energy remnant from another time. Moreover, whether this event is triggered by the environment, the sensitivity of the observer, or a window into the past, the phenomena is totally fascinating.

Battlefields where many fought and died, often in agony, are the perfect settings for residual hauntings. Gettysburg, Pennsylvania, was the scene of a horrific battle during America's Civil War. On the battlefield, men have been seen charging downhill, people have heard troops singing Irish folksongs and the sounds of battle—swords clanging, thundering hoofbeats, the cries of the dying. Devil's Den was the site of heavy fighting on the second day of battle, July 2, 1863. Even before the three-day battle that took place there, the site had earned its name from reports of paranormal activity.

After the battle and up to the present day, visitors have reported seeing an apparition that may be the ghost of a Texas infantryman, sometimes gesturing or motioning but never speaking or interacting with onlookers. Some say that he is the ghost of a sniper who held the Northern troops at bay on Little Round Top.

Intelligent and Human Hauntings

Ghosts who have not yet crossed over, have unfinished business, or are too emotionally attached to a person or place and can't move on are classified as intelligent human hauntings. They linger for a reason. They are trying to get your attention. These entities can interact with humans and sometimes do so in a spectacular fashion.

SIGNS OF AN INTELLIGENT HAUNTING

- Objects disappear, then reappear in impossible places
- Cold spots and the strong sense of a presence or someone watching
- Strange, unexplained sounds
- Furniture and small objects are moved—sometimes even thrown
- Doors and windows open and close
- Lights, televisions, radios, and faucets turn on and off on their own

These apparitions have a mission to complete and they are looking for assistance—possibly, your assistance. If the ghost is interactive and trying to communicate, it is most definitely an intelligent human haunting.

Reasons for an Intelligent Haunting

Sometimes this sort of haunting occurs shortly after a friend or loved one dies. It is as if he is trying to comfort or communicate with those left behind. In this sort of paranormal investigation, a certain protocol should be followed to ascertain the true circumstances of the case. We'll explore this more fully in the next section.

The highest concentrations of paranormal activity can be found where there has been a great deal of human suffering and pain, trauma, or any other strong emotion, such as fear or desperation. Surprisingly, cemeteries aren't that high on the list, but prisons, sanitariums, and hospitals are.

How to Proceed

Talk to the witnesses. Listen carefully and take notes. The witnesses' reports of what has transpired will quickly determine whether you are dealing with a residual haunting or an intelligent one.

Intelligent hauntings without a human component have been documented. These types of hauntings would most accurately be termed poltergeists. They are not human, but they still seem to have an agenda they wish to accomplish and they are most definitely interactive—in fact, most of the time far too much so. Animals that become attached to a location or person can also be interactive and thus termed intelligent hauntings. This is particularly true of pets, such as cats and dogs.

In intelligent hauntings, the entity retains the personality and appearance of the deceased person or animal. Sometimes, strangely they even appear wearing the same clothing they were wearing before passing over.

When an entity is strongly attached to a specific site, person, or object, it may try to protect it. This is a common occurrence. After all, when a person dies, he may not even realize it. If he has lived in a house for years, he may refuse to leave it even after he has passed on. He may think the new residents are trespassers and may naturally try to scare them into leaving.

Dangerous Entities

You should steer clear of demonics, intelligent hauntings with a score to settle, and sometimes even elementals. It is widely believed that ghosts can't harm you, but even paranormal investigators who have taken every safety precaution and prepared themselves in every way should be prepared to meet an entity that will cause them to retreat. The Sci Fi Channel's *Ghost Hunters* are known for a phrase that pretty well sums it up: "When in doubt, get the hell out!"

It is possible to sustain physical, mental, or emotional harm in the course of an investigation. Be cautious, careful, and respectful. Be aware that on rare occasions, bad things can happen to good investigators. In a later chapter, we will discuss steps you should take to protect yourself and safety procedures you should follow.

The entities in inhuman hauntings, also known as demons or elementals, are powerful forces of unknown origin. One thing we do know is that these entities may try to harm or possess humans. They can be a serious threat and have caused harm and even death. They are not in the same class as the entities of intelligent human hauntings, commonly called ghosts, or the memory remnants of the residual haunting. They are far more powerful and dangerous.

CHAPTER 5

Playing Psychic Detective

The classic definition of a psychic detective is a person who investigates crimes by using paranormal psychic abilities. Today's definition has been expanded and in the last few years, television viewers have been bombarded with programs about this sort of paranormal investigator. Recent advances and breakthroughs in the field today are attributable in great part to the fact that we use the tools of science to unravel the secrets of the paranormal. This is revolutionary, because at last there is a way to independently and scientifically verify subjective phenomena.

Laying the Groundwork

Most parapsychologists believe ordinary people can increase their innate psychic powers. The best way to learn about anything is to actually do it. If you have read everything you can get your hands on about paranormal events and ghost hunting, if you have talked to people about the supernatural and have joined in discussion forums online, you may be ready to start doing a little investigating on your own.

Joining the Hunt

Ask around your community about paranormal groups that meet regularly. Try to find individuals who have developed a reputation as psychic or paranormal investigators.

Call or write and introduce yourself. Set up an appointment to meet them and see if you can arrange to go on a ghost hunt. Most people in the paranormal field are very friendly souls. They are in the business of helping other people in trouble, usually at their own expense, so they are likely to be receptive to sincere overtures.

Most groups that perform paranormal investigations have a form they ask prospective members to fill out. They do this to be sure you understand the responsibilities, possible danger, and/or legal issues involved in paranormal investigation. This form frees them from legal liability should anything happen to you in the course of the investigation. You will also be briefed and made familiar with the group's procedures and investigative techniques. It is likely you will be put on probation until the training is completed. This is to ensure that you understand all the possible ramifications of your actions should something unexpected occur.

FACT

Many small businesses that sell ghost hunting equipment are booming, reporting brisk and steady sales in electromagnetic field detectors, white noise generators, and infrared motion sensors. The rise in paranormal equipment sales has increased to the point that some ghost hunting related businesses now offer "ghost counseling" consulting services.

Paranormal Protocol

These groups do actively screen out people with mental problems and those who abuse drugs and alcohol. Smoking is not allowed during investigations for several reasons. It can be a fire hazard in old structures, and smoke can be mistaken for paranormal mists or fog.

People are also trained to keep their religious opinions to themselves. It is inevitable that people on an investigation may begin to discuss the afterlife and the question of life after death. This sort of discussion is acceptable, but when it crosses the line into a discussion of an individual's religious beliefs it can lead to discord and dissension in the group.

Training and Probation

A good organization should expose you to, and train you in, the tools of the trade as they are defined today. You may show an affinity for one particular tool, say a dowsing rod or digital camera. If you find that you're particularly adept at something, try to develop your expertise in it; the group will appreciate having someone who is highly skilled and motivated. No two researchers are the same, and everyone's skill levels will vary.

A calm demeanor and good observational skills are essential. If you can remain objective and are very keenly aware of your surroundings, you will be an invaluable asset to any group you join. If you have any natural psychic ability, you can work on developing your sensitivity and skills in that area. A sort of natural on-the-job training in this area occurs as a result of the feedback you receive on an investigation.

Collecting Eyewitness Accounts

Are you a good listener? Do you have an easy rapport with people, an empathic and sympathetic nature? If so, you are in luck. These skills are in demand for ghost hunters. A very important part of the process is talking to eyewitnesses and gathering as much information as possible about the haunting.

People who are dealing with a poltergeist or haunting will often be in a highly stressed state. They may feel as if they are going crazy or that they will be labeled as unstable or worse if they disclose what they have seen. They often fear ridicule and want to feel that their anonymity will be protected.

The last thing people want is for their location or names to be disclosed. Part of a psychic investigator's job is reassuring clients that their experiences are not unique. This is where your extensive reading on the paranormal and self-education in all things supernatural can be extremely helpful. You must also project an air of professionalism that reassures clients that the investigation is in good hands and will be conducted with the proper professionalism and competency.

The last thing in the world the victim of a haunting needs is to feel jeopardized by the investigation. Clients are owed respect, for both themselves and for their property. Particular care must be taken in households with children. Don't scare them or talk too much about the investigation in their presence.

On-the-Job Training

Initially, you will probably work with an experienced investigator to gather eyewitness accounts. Carefully observe the sorts of questions that are asked. Just as important, note the way they are asked.

Some organizations do a preliminary interview to see if a full-scale investigation is warranted. An experienced team member usually evaluates the information the potential client supplies. A walk-through of the property may be done at this time as well. Some groups bring a psychic along to the preliminary interviews to see if any paranormal activity can be detected, particularly if the person who contacted the group mentions that there may be poltergeist or harmful activity that may threaten the safety or well-being of the people who occupy or work at the site.

ALERT!

Some so-called paranormal investigation groups are actually scammers. Their primary goal is to frighten the client into believing that certain items in their home are haunted or possessed and must be removed immediately. These items are usually antiques or other valuables that are then sold or pawned.

This holds especially true if there are children on the premises. Every effort must be made to speed the investigation along if the well-being of children is at stake.

The Client's Statement

Before the team arrives at the site, the potential client should be asked to organize the information about what he has witnessed and to prepare at least a rough chronology of events. Some groups ask for a report to be written before they come out to do the investigation; others will bring a form with them and interview the person or persons involved in the incidents.

If more than one person has seen or experienced something paranormal, each person should be interviewed separately. Investigators should compare the interviews to catch discrepancies or find points of congruency. These reports should be as detailed and comprehensive as possible; they will help you understand the chronology of the phenomena. They should contain the approximate date of the onset of the activity, with a full description of the paranormal events.

Digging Deeper

Investigators should ask for further details about sounds heard and things seen, smelled, or even sensed. People will sometimes mention a feeling of being watched, or a feeling of extreme fear. Often, they will mention cold spots or extreme temperature shifts. Investigators should question individuals about any event that might have triggered the activity. The following questions can be used as a starting point:

- Was a séance held, or Ouija board used, before the disturbance began?
- Did someone die in the house recently? Did someone die in the house at any time in its history?
- Has anyone been physically harmed: scratched, bitten, or slapped?
- Has anyone had disturbing or frightening dreams?
- Are there reports of unexplained fires or disappearing objects?
- Do any pets live in the household? If so, are there any areas they avoid or growl at consistently?

Gathering Background Data

As much information as possible should be gathered about the case once the decision has been made to proceed with the investigation. Know what you are getting yourself into; find out all you can about the history of the house or building. Your clients are your first source for information about the property, but sometimes they don't know the complete story. Particularly in the case of older buildings, the full history may take some digging to uncover.

What shape is the property in, and are there any areas that should be avoided due to safety issues? This could be anything from quicksand on the property to weak floorboards, walls, or ceilings in the building. Safety issues should be discussed with the property owner at the initial interview, and the team members should be briefed immediately prior to starting the investigation. Always be aware of your surroundings. Most investigations are done at night, but a walk-through done under good lighting conditions offers you the opportunity to find and note safety hazards that might go unnoticed in the dark.

Permission Granted

You must have permission to explore a site. If it is necessary to trespass on someone's property to gain access to the property you're investigating, or if you are investigating an alleged haunting in an abandoned property or cemetery, be sure to get the proper permissions before setting foot on the site in question. You don't want to get in trouble with property owners or the law.

ALERT!

The popularity of ghost hunting has led to property damage and personal injury in some areas. In an allegedly haunted house in Worthington, Ohio, a homeowner fired shots to scare off a group of self-proclaimed teenage ghost hunters and shot a girl in the head. Trespassing ghost hunters have been arrested in many states.

You most certainly don't want to be arrested for trespassing. There are legal repercussions, and it will tarnish your professional reputation.

Permission is usually not hard to obtain, and team members work better when they know they have every right to be there.

Institutional Resources

The researchers should visit the local library and the local historical society, if there is one in the area, to check on the background of the property. Because hauntings often occur in older properties, it may be necessary to dig quite far back into the property records.

Allot enough time to do this part of the investigation properly; it may take several long days of research to follow the paper trail. There is often red tape to be cut through at historical societies, so contacting them ahead of time is a good idea, particularly if they are only open a few days a week or have membership requirements to search their records.

Place a call to public libraries and ask pertinent questions about their hours and procedures for researchers. They will often have records on microfiche, and most have the local newspaper on file going back to the early days of the community. You can check records to see if anything newsworthy happened in the vicinity of your site. If a murder, suicide, or any other traumatic incident occurred on the premises, a search of newspapers may turn up something that verifies potential paranormal activity. It can also verify names of people or facts involved in the case.

You can search census records, court records, and birth, marriage, and death records at most county courthouses for a nominal fee. Once you've found out who lived in the house during a given time frame, these records can yield a lot of background information. State historical societies are a good place to access information if you have the last name of the person for whom you are searching. This can yield the birth and death years and possibly the names of other family members buried nearby.

FACT

Famed stage magician Harry Houdini was probably the first well-known psychic investigator. After his mother's death in the 1920s, Houdini turned his energies toward debunking spiritualists and so-called haunted houses. This activity cost Houdini the friendship of Sir Arthur Conan Doyle, who was a staunch believer in spiritualism.

This sort of record checking can be time consuming, especially in big cities where the higher population will mean sifting through a lot more data. Checking online to see if some records might be available through the city or county's Internet site is one way of saving time during this phase of the investigation. Cemetery records are sometimes listed in a database online.

Land Data Research Resources

Land data records can be a rich source of information about the history and owners of the property in question. These records are kept by the county or city in which the property is located and also include the tax records.

In order to access the records, you may need to provide the legal description of the property; be sure to get that before heading out. Another source of land data information is the tax assessment data, which can often be accessed online if you have the property address. These records are kept differently in each locale, but mining them for data can be easy if there is a record of each time a property changed hands, whether through inheritance or sale. Sometimes they contain such important data as the names of co-owners or even floor plans or photos of the house.

Accessing Databases

Outbuildings and the condition of the property can sometimes be ascertained online. Most online databases do contain the current property owner's name, the year the property was built, the lot size, the construction material the house is made of, the number of bedrooms and bathrooms, the type of heating, and square footage.

Armed with the knowledge of when the structure was built, a history of residents and any potential past paranormal activity can be scrutinized. Occasionally your research will turn up something significant in the history of the place.

Geographical and Geological Data

Another factor that must be considered is the geography and geology of the area. Some people suspect that haunting activity takes place more

Art copyright Melissa Martin Ellis, 2000.

A painting of spooky stone gates in Newport, Rhode Island adjacent to a mansion dating back to the nineteenth century.

readily near running water. If the building where activity is being investigated is near a running stream or brook, or if water runs under the structure, it may help explain what is going on.

In the famous case of the Pontefract Poltergeist in Britain, the activity all took place near a small stream. In fact, the property had originally been located practically on top of the site of an old bridge crossing the stream.

Thomas Lethbridge, who was an archaeologist and historian, spent most of his working life as the keeper of Anglo-Saxon antiquities at Cambridge University Museum. He was one of the first people to theorize that moving water generated a faint magnetic field, which might supply sufficient energy for paranormal entities to manifest. He also thought that lava and quartz rocks could generate mild fields from which entities could draw energy.

E FACT

Thomas Lethbridge was one of the first researchers to postulate the existence of ley lines, the hypothetical alignment between underground watercourses and various ancient holy sites. Ley lines are believed by some to possess a mystical energy, which would explain why so many paranormal events occur in their vicinity.

Local Sources of Information

After searching for records on the Internet, looking through microfiche in the library and historical societies, and investigating records at City Hall, what else can you do to research an active haunting? Small communities may not have a historical society, but usually there is still a local historian. Ask around, but don't be discouraged if no name comes up. The local newspaper or library may be able to give contact information for the local historian, who is often an amateur history buff or a retired history professor.

Advertising and Canvassing

Running an ad in the local newspaper or posting a query to message boards for the area may turn up leads to events in the past. It doesn't have to be a large ad or even refer to ghosts directly. You merely need to say you want to talk to someone who has knowledge of a particular address at a particular time.

Neighbors and former neighbors are often happy to come forward to tell you what they have heard about a haunted location. Sometimes they will know how to reach former occupants of the house who may have experienced something during their time at the property.

FACT

As interest in the paranormal has increased, the competition between different ghost hunting organizations has heated up as well. Many groups compete with one another for publicity, giving rise to rivalries and feuds. TAPS and the International Ghost Hunters Society have frequently questioned each other's methods.

These days, people seem more relaxed and tolerant of the paranormal. There is more acceptance of it by the mainstream, so many people are actually eager to speak of their experiences. Interviews with these people should be conducted with the same care and courtesy as those with the primary residents who called you in.

Use What You Have

If a number of years have passed, memories will often be hazy. People may not remember the details or may make things up to fill in the gaps. The information obviously isn't as fresh as that you obtain from people who were more recent residents or neighbors, but there should be enough to draw some parallels between the older reports and the newer ones. If any of the witnesses have children, be discreet around them. It can be quite scary for children to have to deal with talk of ghosts and hauntings, and they should be sent out of the room before you begin the interview.

Dealing with Curious Neighbors

Occasionally, neighbors or former residents will want to know what is going on and why you are investigating. Discuss this possibility with your client before you cast a wide net to interview others. The client may not want any publicity and may not want anyone else to be brought into the case. Always honor their wishes regarding confidentiality. Those who don't put any restrictions on the investigation may find that by not limiting the research they are giving themselves a better chance of resolving the case satisfactorily. Although finding the history is important, it may not actually be relevant to the case you're investigating. Do not assume that connections exist until the facts support it.

Using the Internet

The Internet presents a wonderful smorgasbord of supernatural sites for eager paranormal investigators. There has been an explosion of interest in all things paranormal, the likes of which haven't been seen since the Victorian era. You can access background and land data information via the web. Online parapsychology classes are available, and all sorts of free educational resources exist. Many paranormal investigators have created their own websites.

Proceed with Care

Because there is so much information so freely available, you must proceed with caution. There are organizations on the Internet whose integrity is unquestioned. Appendix D includes many recommended sites.

Some resources you can access are:

- Ghost hunting groups
- Paranormal/supernatural sites
- Ghost and haunting photo galleries
- Free educational sites
- Marketplaces for ghost hunting technology and supplies
- Online paranormal investigation classes
- Online paranormal bookstores

Shadowlands (*www.ghosthunting101.com*) has some great links for finding paranormal investigative groups in your area. It also has a list of recommended groups. This list is made up of paranormal investigators throughout the United States. The Rhode Island Paranormal Research Group site (*www.triprg.com*) has a great deal of information and hosts an online forum.

CHAPTER 6

Psychic Practice
Makes Perfect

Not all ghost hunters use sensitives in their investigations, but a significant number continue to do so.
There has been a growing tendency to rely more on
the use of technology rather than psychics in investigations. However, that doesn't mean psychics are no
longer important in investigations of the paranormal.
Their expertise can be valuable on its own; when it
is paired with the data gathered by high-tech tools, it
can present a well-rounded picture of a haunting.

The Knowledge

Psychics, sensitives, and intuitives have always been with us. They have become part of our culture and it is generally accepted that there are certain people among us who have unique access to knowledge through supernatural means.

In Chapter 3, we discussed the different types of psychic abilities—clairsentience, clairaudience, claircognizance, and clairvoyance—and how individuals with these abilities might be helpful in the course of an investigation. Different sensitives experience the situation based on their own gifts. For some, the experience is auditory. For others, it is visual. Others may feel a presence, a sensation known as kinesthesia.

FACT

Many psychics' perceptions combine in the mind's eye to convey a sensory image experienced as a haunting. At this point, the observer believes the image to be three-dimensional, although it may be semitransparent or look superimposed onto the environment.

Tarnished Reputations

It is very unfortunate that the spiritualist's movement of the nineteenth century and some flamboyant fame-seekers and TV psychics in the twentieth and twenty-first centuries have tainted the psychic community. Because building credibility is so important to ghost hunters, it is obvious why some organizations have steered away from evidence that smacks of chicanery or that cannot be verified independently.

Some groups, however, feel that including psychics on the team adds so much to the investigation that they simply cannot be excluded. The knowledge and insights psychics intuit may play a huge part in the investigation and may bring closure to a situation when nothing else will.

Asset Versus Liability

Those groups with sensitives on their team feel that they are a huge asset to the investigation. Their contributions to the gathering of evidence are often integral to the case, and they have the ability to bring closure to the restless spirits that created the haunting. However, many groups draw the line at using mediums. A medium who becomes possessed during the course of an investigation is a definite liability to the team.

ALERT!

Some parapsychologists feel that so-called spirit possession is often a two-way street. Wanda Pratnicka, author of *Possessed by Ghosts: Exorcisms in the 21st Century*, theorizes that ghosts may come back and possess people repeatedly. "Emotional bindings between people and ghosts are like rubber bands," she says, "that draw the ghost back into the patient's body."

The Commitment

The mediums and sensitives on the case must make a commitment to communicate seamlessly with other members of the team. They must understand that they are not the focus of the team. Their goal must be helping others, so the main thrust of the investigation should always be uncovering the facts and maintaining a high standard of professional behavior. The psychics should be experienced, seasoned investigators in their own right. They should not be prone to melodrama or attention-getting behaviors but should report what they are experiencing as simply and truthfully as possible. They must be adaptable so that no matter what situation arises, they can remain poised and ready to take the appropriate action.

Just One of the Guys

Ideally, mediums and sensitives should be trained in normal investigative skills and be able to function as a regular team member, trained to use the equipment and follow proper protocols. It should be obvious to everyone that all jobs on an investigation are of equal importance. Cases are turned on their heads when the investigation revolves entirely around the medium and little verifiable data is gathered. If there is too much emphasis on one area of the investigation, the other aspects suffer as a result.

Career Advancement

Psychic and investigator Maggie Florio has been with the Rhode Island Paranormal Research Group (T.R.I.P.R.G.) for about five years. For the last three, she has worked as a sensitive for the group. Her role grew out of the notes she kept during the course of her early work with the group. When the investigative panel reviewed her notes, they noticed that most of her speculations, observations, and assumptions were quite accurate. In fact, it was estimated that about 75 percent of her observations on the case hit the mark. Her first experiences with receiving impressions and information came to her aurally, when she would hear phrases or just snippets of voices.

Further Growth

Eventually, Florio's talents evolved further, to the point where she was seeing and hearing what was transpiring as if in a movie. This is not surprising, as Florio had seen apparitions as a child and there is little doubt that her latent psychic abilities were further enhanced by the situations she encountered as a ghost hunter.

It is apparent when speaking with her that Florio is extremely empathic and sends out very comforting, caring vibes. This is not always a good thing. In the course of her investigations, the entities must have noticed that, too. Some have become very attached to her—literally.

It is interesting that churches and Christian institutions such as Salve Regina University still use the terrifying symbol of a gargoyle in their architecture.

Just Leave!

In the past, despite Florio's cleansing ritual after a case, an entity has followed her home and caused minor disruptions. At no time did she feel threatened, but she did not want to have to deal with the spirit on a daily basis. In vain, she tried asking it to leave and even smudged her home. It was only after she figured out where it had come from and politely and firmly asked it to go back that was she able to get rid of it.

FACT

Famed turn-of-the-century journalist Ambrose Bierce wrote of a haunted plantation known as the "Spook House" in Kentucky, so named because the owner, his wife, and their five children disappeared one night, leaving no clues as to their fate. A local judge and army officer went to investigate and shared a vision of dead children behind a wall. They fled; the army officer fell into a delirium and the judge vanished.

The Ghost Team

How does a team that includes sensitives or psychics interact and function? There may be as many answers to that as there are paranormal investigative groups.

Some investigators have expressed concern about a phenomenon that sometimes occurs in the presence of very strong psychics, whose perceptions of the spirits or haunting can be so overwhelmingly strong that they can actually help it manifest for onlookers. Dubbed the observer effect, it is almost as if a very faint signal is boosted by the sensitive's mind. In effect, the observers on scene can influence the outcome of the investigation by their very presence, and more phenomena than usual can be observed.

These effects can be a help or a hindrance to the case, depending on the circumstances. They may confuse the team's investigation of the haunting if they are attributed solely to the ghosts.

I See Dead People

Often, the perception of spirits by psychics and other investigators at the scene can be quite startling. They may perceive an entity walking through a doorway, where there is now no doorway to be seen. In these instances, the apparition might seem to walk up to and pass through a solid wall or climb an invisible staircase. However, it is not always necessary to have a sensitive participate in the investigation to have a life-altering experience.

I Dare You

Andrew Laird of T.R.I.P.R.G. had an amazing introduction to ghost hunting. Laird's friend Ray was a true believer in ghosts who was forever trying to get the skeptical Laird to accompany him on ghost hunts. Laird's typical reply was "Leave me alone! I'll do it on my own!" One night, Ray succeeded in convincing Laird to come along.

There was a $20 bill and a case of beer riding on the outcome of their impromptu investigation at the abandoned Danvers Asylum. Ray said that if he didn't experience anything that night, he would never bring it up to him again. Ray was sure that Laird would see something that would shake him out of his skeptic's stance; Laird didn't think so, because he "just wasn't into it."

Ghosts and spirits may communicate through symbolic language, by moving certain objects that have meaning for the percipient. They often make use of a physical environment to draw attention to themselves, changing the temperature of a room or rapping on a wall.

Unexplained Cold Spots

After securing permission to enter the asylum, the two men entered the location and went to the second floor "excitable ward." As they approached the nurse's station, they saw that the double doors adjacent to it were chained open.

A sign reading "No Objects Beyond This Point" caught Laird's attention and he began to feel really uneasy. His first thought was that his friend had set the situation up very well by bringing him into a place where he was front-loaded to expect something to happen.

Ray assured him he would get the same apprehensive feeling in any similar situation. As they talked and walked down a corridor, Laird felt the place growing very cold and thought to himself, "Wow, this is just weird; it isn't that cold out. This is cold—shiver cold!" As they walked down the hallway they approached the cells—small rooms with one doorway, no windows, and padded walls. These cells were used to detain violent inmates who might hurt themselves or others.

The Persistent Patient

When they were about twenty feet down the corridor from the first cell, they heard a door opening and saw a person step out. The man was wearing patient garb. He stopped and looked at Laird, looked at Ray, walked into another room, and closed the door behind him. Laird laughed and looked at his friend. "You gotta be kidding me!"

Ray said, "Andy, look, we got him now. We both know there's only one way in and out of that room, right? You owe me a case of beer, bud."

Laird walked to the door and pushed it open. There were no knobs on the door, since all of the locks had been struck off the doors after the asylum closed. He pushed it open. There was nobody in the cell.

Although ghosts can manifest anywhere, they appear most often at night in an isolated area because they cannot manifest around many people. The energy required to materialize physically may be more quickly depleted when one is in contact with the bioelectric fields of other people.

I Just Saw a Ghost

Laird thoroughly searched the room with his flashlight. He said it only took him "two seconds to see that there was nobody in there, nothing in there but the old padding on the walls." He turned to his friend and demanded to know how he'd done it.

Then it hit him. He looked at Ray and said, "I just saw a ghost." Ray answered, "Yeah, you did. We both just saw a ghost." Right after that, all the open doors along the corridor banged shut in quick succession, "Bang, ba-bang, ba-bang."

So Ray got his beer and Laird was left with the age-old sensation of "feet, don't fail me now!"

What Is Real?

This is a blunt reminder that what is experienced as "real" in any haunting may or may not be taking place only in the minds of the onlookers. Often there may be actual physical phenomena to capture on camera or record on tape, since there are actual light or sound waves involved. Mysteriously, we're not sure why this sort of phenomena at hauntings sometimes does have an actual physical component, as shown by evidence of apparitions and EVPs that are often captured in photographs, sound recordings, and videotapes.

E-QUESTION

How do I know if I've encountered a ghost?
First, rule out all other explainable phenomena. If the event is truly paranormal, then trying to find an ordinary explanation may seem more ridiculous than considering a supernatural reason. However, the human mind has a tendency to create situations that seem paranormal, so a rational approach is the best tool in determining if the sources of the events are paranormal.

Misperceptions and Misidentifications

Whether or not the team doing the investigation witnesses an apparition, the anxiety and expectations of the clients at a haunted site can sometimes trigger another sort of observer effect. These effects can be a combination of misperceptions and misidentifications of ordinary events, or the unusual movement of physical objects at the scene. This attitude can set other activities in motion, quite literally. Unusual physical activity observed on-site may actually be a result of psychokinesis (PK), the power of the human mind to move matter. In this case, the events are very hard to classify. You could be dealing with a real haunting or just an instance of PK that is not caused by the originating phenomenon.

The Equipment

In T.R.I.P.R.G., there is an expectation that all members of the group, even the sensitives, must function as regular investigators as well. They train on the standard ghost hunting equipment but usually find they have developed a particular affinity for one or two of the technologies.

In T.R.I.P.R.G., although all members must be trained in the use of paranormal investigative tools, sensitives may often bring their own specialized tools along to the investigative site. These tools must be portable enough to be practical in a field investigation and can be anything from a pendulum to a dowsing rod.

An Ear for Sound

Maggie Florio is particularly good with EVPs and has very good luck with her digital tape recorder in capturing spirit voices. She has found as many as eighteen separate EVPs from a single one-night session. She is also good at spotting them when the data is reviewed after an investigation, even though she suffers from slight hearing loss. She thinks the fact that she has to pay stricter attention may have something to do with her talent for EVPs. At one of her favorite investigative sites, the Paine House Museum in Coventry, Rhode Island, Florio has become so comfortable with the entities in residence that she often catches EVPs of them commenting about the investigators and interacting with one another.

ALERT!

Professor Ernest Senkowski of the Bingen Technical University in Germany claims he stumbled across a method of two-way voice communication with the dead through a combination of radios, white noise, and tape recorders. He says the spirits talk of a beautiful afterlife of happiness and no one is lonely.

Spirited Comments

The ghosts of Paine House sometimes make very personal remarks about the investigators. Because the team has been there so many times, the ghosts often even refer to them by name. Florio admits that she and her fellow sensitive Kym Black find this all rather amusing and enjoy the interaction with the fascinating presences in the old house. She and the team have been investigating there for about four years, and new situations and phenomena continue to arise.

About EVP Work

Florio says of her EVPs, "I use a digital voice recorder. Sometimes I carry it around with me and sometimes I place it in an area that is active. I usually ask a few questions like: 'What is your name? Did you live here (work here, play here, etc.)? How old are you? Can you see me? Are you aware that you are no longer on the earthly plane?' I wait about thirty seconds in between questions for any answers that may come. I try not to record longer than one hour, because it is tiresome to review. I sometimes play one section a half dozen times if I think there is an EVP. I write down the time and what I think the EVP says."

The Paine House in Coventry has long been the object of investigation for Rhode Island paranormal research groups.

Photo copyright Melissa Martin Ellis, 2008.

Cleaning Up the Talk

Most people who use digital voice recorders upload their files to a computer to tweak the sound quality and boost the signal. Most also use some sort of audio software program to clean up the recording for optimal quality. Florio uses Wavepad and a regular computer microphone to review her tapes. "I don't mess with the EVP very much," she says. "If I can't hear what is being said, I may amplify it to eliminate the hum and hiss, but that's about it. If I want to play something backwards to hear a message, I'll dig out the Beatles *White Album* from my collection."

My Favorite Things

Both Kym Black and Maggie Florio are big fans of the K2 meter. They are very comfortable with their EMF meters and have even used the meters, which are equipped with flashing lights, to interact with the entities. They use T.R.I.P.R.G.'s paracode system—two flashes for yes, three flashes for no. They have been able to have many two-way communications using this method at psychic sessions they call sit-downs. These sessions are held when they get the sensation that the entities wish to communicate. They are also comfortable with more traditional technologies, often using pendulums or dowsing rods as tools to facilitate communication. Florio's favorite tool is a pendulum, and she has found her abilities with it have increased over time.

E-QUESTION

What is an energy pendulum?
It is a device suspended from a cord and is popularly called a radionic pendulum, relating to instruments used for healing at a distance. It is most often used for pinpointing health and medical problems.

The Resources

How do sensitives develop their talents and learn to do their jobs? Again, there are many answers. In Maggie Florio's case, she says, "I didn't receive any formal training in the group (T.R.I.P.R.G.). I have read and taken a mediumship class on my own. Now, we mentor our sensitives and they have a six-month training period." Many groups have established psychic development educational programs for their members.

On-the-Job Training

Hands-on training is a great way to develop latent psychic abilities and benefit from the tutelage of seasoned investigators. The experienced investigators have made their own mistakes and can help a novice steer clear of them. The neophytes who observe the more experienced psychic's handling of delicate situations can learn what to do and, perhaps more importantly, what not to do.

Knowledge Quest

For those looking to advance their knowledge and expertise, there are many resources available on the Internet, including online classes. Private classes and personal instruction can also be helpful. How does an individual who wants to learn more and develop her own innate talents differentiate among the available resources to figure out where to start?

Most experts agree that you should read a lot and talk to people with a background in the area in order to put a reading list together. After several weeks of research and reading, you should be able to discern your proper course of action. The important thing to remember is that you have to trust your instincts and approach the topic with a certain healthy skepticism.

Getting personal recommendations from friends or reliable sources is usually the best way to proceed. If you seek out personal instruction, check references and pick someone who has a proven track record of reliability.

When paranormal researcher Ben Radford investigated the Santa Fe, New Mexico, courthouse ghost, he was amazed when the spirit seemingly showed itself on the film of a surveillance camera as a glowing dot drifting in front of a police car. Upon close examination of the footage, he found the glowing dot was actually a ladybug crawling across the lens of the camera.

The Access

Though the use of psychics and sensitives may expose them to criticism from the skeptics and more technologically minded investigators, the traditional investigators feel that it would be counter-productive to exclude sensitives from their cases.

Shielding the Sensitives

Many groups have developed procedures and protocols to ensure that any prior access to information about the case is concealed from the psychics and sensitives involved. Most never allow the sensitives to book locations or conduct the preinvestigation interviews.

If a sensitive booked the location or even sat in on an interview, it would compromise any future information provided by the psychic or sensitive. It is imperative that the sensitive does not know the facts underlying the case. This could compromise the entire investigation.

Therefore, many groups tell the sensitives nothing about the location until they are en route to the site. This protects the sensitive from any appearance of impropriety, especially in the case of famous haunted sites.

E-QUESTION

Did the Amityville Horror really happen?
According to recent revelations, the Lutzes—the family involved in the so-called "horror"—claim they made up the story "over many bottles of wine." When the paranormal investigators involved in the case realized they had been the victims of a hoax, they were too fearful of damage to their reputations to publicize it. The investigators denied this.

On the Road Again

Maggie Florio says sensitives in her group are given only the sketchiest idea of where they are going, sometimes only knowing whether they are staying in the area or going farther away. The exact location is divulged after they are already on the road to the site. If the case sensitives do learn any information they shouldn't, they must immediately inform their team leader of it so there will be no issues later.

Sensitives know that if they are informed ahead of time about the destination, skeptics could easily make accusations that they had researched information about the site or the case. The team's goal is to bring an open and unbiased approach to the case, so it is vital to maintain the utmost integrity.

Credibility Protection

Some groups may even go so far as to cover up anything that may offer clues to the site's history or former occupants—house plaques, grave markers, historical signage, photos, and so on. This is yet another means of making sure the information gleaned by the psychic remains pure, unsullied, and uncontaminated by outside knowledge.

Also, sensitives are usually isolated during the set-up phase of an investigation, which often means they are left sitting in a vehicle while the equipment is set up and walk-throughs or interviews are done. These steps are not so extreme when you consider that the integrity of the entire investigation may be at stake.

CHAPTER 7

Who Ya Gonna Call?

The concept of the paranormal investigator is definitely not new, but putting a team of specialists together to look into supernatural events is of recent vintage. The idea of approaching investigations in this way is thoroughly modern, the outgrowth of our industrialized, scientific society's methods of solving problems. The multifaceted approach has lent a much-needed balance to the field.

Tech People

Not all paranormal investigation organizations are fortunate enough to have a full-time tech person on staff, but those that do find their investigations function much more smoothly. Today's ghost hunts are very technology dependent, and practically all the equipment is innovative technology. The equipment can be bewildering to the nonprofessional; therefore, it makes sense to have at least one team member who can figure out where to deploy and how to interface the digital camcorders, electronic field meters, infrared cameras, and motion detectors. This specialized knowledge takes a big responsibility off the shoulders of other team members, who might otherwise waste valuable time and resources trying to figure it all out.

E-QUESTION

What are ghosts made of?
A recent theory is that ghosts are composed of so-called quantum matter, a form of plasma energy that would appear to the observer to exist for only a few seconds at a time. According to this theory, ghosts actually blink in and out of the range of our perceptions continually.

The Tech Guys and Gals

Keeping track of all the equipment and their batteries, cords, and accessories is a daunting task. One person should be responsible for making sure that equipment is field-ready and all batteries and accessories are in good working order.

At the end of the investigation, all equipment must be gathered up, checked in, and put away properly. Without a clear division of tasks and responsibilities, things get lost, left behind, or damaged. Most of the equipment is expensive, so it should not be handled carelessly or without the proper training.

Where Did I Leave It?

Remember, investigations can go on for many hours late at night, and everyone is fatigued when the time comes to gather the equipment and pack it away. There should be one person in charge of double-checking and supervision of equipment. This ensures all equipment is efficiently checked back in.

Those who have watched the *Ghost Hunters* TV series have probably seen Jason Hawes yell at his tech people numerous times for mishandling or losing expensive equipment. Excuses that the ghosts took it don't cut it.

Psychics and Mediums

Many paranormal groups have psychics, clairvoyants, or sensitives on their teams and often let them set the course of the investigations of possible hauntings. In the early days even Jason Hawes and Grant Wilson routinely used clairvoyants in their investigations.

Apparently, that changed after they decided to shift the emphasis over to science and technology in their investigations. Occasionally, they will work with psychic consultants such as Chris Fleming, who is ready to validate the team's readings. But their main thrust is to bring credibility through scientific proof.

Setting the Stage

Even investigators who are very technologically oriented sometimes have intense experiences that give them a glimpse into a psychic's involvement in the world of spirits. Gloria Young is one such ghost hunter; she has been a paranormal investigator for more than fifteen years and founded the paranormal research group Ghost Trackers (*www.ghost-trackers.org*). She has co-produced two documentaries on ghost hunting and wrote the book *Faces of a Ghost Hunter.*

FACT

According to some sources, the first historical mention of something resembling a Ouija board was found in China around 1200 B.C.E, a divination method called *Fu Ji*. But the first use of the Ouija board, named for the French and German words for "yes," occurred during the spiritualist movement of the nineteenth century.

Young was invited to attend the videotaping of a séance for the Biography Channel. She hoped it would be a typical séance, where the medium would try to bring someone through. After settling in at the restaurant where the séance was held, she opted to sit across from the medium and cohost. She liked the man at once and felt quite at ease—until the séance began. Young attempted to join in and be interactive, but she felt an awful churning beginning in the pit of her stomach, which came and went.

Unwelcome Guest

The strange sensation slowly built until it felt as if something was trying to move up from Young's stomach to be expelled from her mouth. She wasn't nauseous but said she felt like the character played by John Hurt in the movie *Alien*, who had an extraterrestrial tear out of his torso. She felt as though something wanted to come out of her mouth so badly that she could barely speak.

She began to tremble, although only her hands were cold. She felt a terrible anger that welled up within her.

It seemed to be directed at the medium seated across from her and she could feel her eyes narrow into slits as she looked at him. Young didn't know why her anger was aimed at him or why she was feeling it. The urge to spit words at the medium was almost uncontrollable. After an internal struggle, she managed to get control of herself and didn't allow it to happen.

All through this extraordinary experience, Young could hear the medium talking to her, but his words were incomprehensible. She struggled in the grip of her anger, then heard the medium say that her face looked like it was changing.

Becoming Dispossessed

The medium began a cleansing ritual for the people at the table and ordered any malevolent entity to depart and go about its business. After what seemed like hours, Young's stomach calmed, although she felt the beginnings of a headache. Her muscles began to relax. The uncontrollable shaking stopped and she managed to speak a few words. The thick, oppressive air in the room began to dissipate. Young admits it was an amazing, mystifying experience that she probably wouldn't have believed if it hadn't happened to her.

A recent theory about ghostly activity suggests that spirits have a degree of control over local magnetic fields. The shaking and levitation of objects and interference with electronic equipment could be attributed to the spirit alternating the magnetic field from positive to negative.

Researchers and Investigators

Most ghost hunters are just average people who have developed a healthy curiosity and respect for the supernatural. Jason Hawes and Grant Wilson of TAPS are still plumbers, but they are also the cofounders of TAPS, the stars of the Sci Fi channel show *Ghost Hunters*, and hosts of a three-hour radio show every Saturday on Beyond Reality Radio online (*http://beyondreality radio.com*).

Clash of the Titans

In 2007, Hawes and Wilson interviewed Yvette Fielding from the popular television show *Most Haunted*. The three paranormal investigators clashed repeatedly over techniques, procedure, and authenticity. The interview can be accessed on the Beyond Reality Radio website.

It Is about Emotion

Part of the discussion centered around the differences between their investigation philosophies. Fielding asserted that emotion was the key to paranormal investigation, while Hawes and Wilson emphasized the scientific method. The exchange got quite heated, with both sides questioning the other's professionalism. The interview raised questions every paranormal investigator should consider. What are the goals of paranormal investigation? What are the proper methods for investigating the paranormal? Can both science and emotion be part of the answer?

Clergy and Shamans

The late Dr. Malachi Martin was a theologian who spent thirty years as an exorcist. After leaving the priesthood, Dr. Martin wrote several bestselling books: *Vatican, The Final Conclave, Hostage to the Devil, The Jesuits, The Keys of This Blood*, and *Windswept House*.

A Priest and a Scholar

As a scholar who studied at the Catholic University of Louvain in Belgium, Oxford University, and Hebrew University of Jerusalem, Father Martin received doctorates in the Semitic languages, archeology, and Asian history. In 1958, Father Martin was in Cairo to study a newly discovered collection of Hebrew writings from the time of Abraham. The trip had a profound impact on him. While he was there, he was asked to assist in an exorcism. A young Egyptian man had become so involved in Satanism that he was suspected of being complicit in sacrificing his own sisters.

Fighting the Devil

What Father Martin saw in Egypt convinced him that he had to fight the powers of evil, no matter the personal cost to him. Some have speculated that Father Martin may have been the inspiration for the older priest in William Peter Blatty's *The Exorcist*.

Before his passing, Father Martin said, "Every exorcism takes something out of you that cannot be put back. The demon goes, but it carries a part of you away with it. A little of the exorcist dies each time. It's a permanent mental fight against a powerful, dangerous enemy."

E-QUESTION

What is a shaman?
In tribal cultures, shamans served as healers, psychological counselors, and spiritual ministers to their people. Their presence was central to the health and well-being of the tribe. Many shamans claimed they were only as powerful as the number of helpful spirits who acted as their allies.

Keith and Carl Johnson

The Johnson brothers, identical twins Keith and Carl, grew up in a house in Rhode Island where paranormal phenomena would occasionally occur. Those events triggered their extreme interest in the supernatural world.

In the early 1970s, when they were just teenagers, Keith and Carl attended a lecture featuring paranormal investigators Ed and Lorraine Warren at nearby Rhode Island College. Subsequently, they developed a friendship with the Warrens, which lasted for decades.

They joined a paranormal research organization at Rhode Island College, known as the Parapsychology Investigation and Research Organization (PIRO), and as it turned out, Keith's first major investigation turned out to be a case of demonic infestation. In October of 2004, Keith and his wife, Sandra, founded New England Anomalies Research (NEAR). Their website can be visited at: *www.nearparanormal.com*. Keith says they founded NEAR after the *Ghost Hunters* series, with which they were involved for the first two seasons, became so successful, because their involvement with the show made it difficult to focus on their clients' cases—especially those of a confidential and sometime even demonic nature.

Keith often officiates when house blessings and exorcisms need to be performed for both TAPS and his own organization, NEAR. Keith still consults with TAPS as a demonologist, as well as working with fellow demonologists and associates at NEAR to help people who believe themselves to be the victims of hauntings, possession, or demonic oppression in New England. NEAR is comprised of many former investigators from TAPS, and they have stayed true to their goal of investigating and analyzing phenomena that is suspected to be of paranormal origin. Keith and his wife Sandra co-produce a weekly cable television show called *Ghosts R Near* in Providence, Rhode Island, which explores the topics of ghosts, the paranormal, and hauntings.

Keith's twin brother Carl is a demonologist, too. He is also NEAR's senior investigator and alternate co-host of *Ghosts R Near*. He continues to explore the paranormal with his colleagues, Father Bob Bailey, who is frequently seen on the A&E television show *Paranormal State*; Greenville Paranormal founder Andrew Lake; author and investigator Thomas D'Agostino; mediums Pamela Patalano and Paula O'Brien; and his girlfriend, paranormal investigator Dina Palazini.

The two brothers combine their mutual love of history and the paranormal in the tours they conduct at Slater Mill in Pawtucket, Rhode Island. Using their extensive knowledge of both Slater Mill and the Blackstone Valley area, plus their unique love of all things ghostly, they host tours in this old, allegedly *very* haunted mill in their Paranormal Pawtucket Ghost Tours.

Photographers and Videographers

With the advent of affordable digital technology, advanced camera equipment is available to more and more people. Therefore, it isn't surprising that some strange photographs are coming out.

At Ghostvillage.com, photographer Jim DeCaro writes of his initiation into ghost photography, of which he was highly skeptical. At the repeated urging of a psychic friend, he went to a graveyard one night with his digital camera and took several dozen shots of headstones. When DeCaro returned home and reviewed the photos, he was astonished to find orbs and glowing three-dimensional objects in several shots. Looking closely at them, he discovered that five or six had some sort of anomaly in them. DeCaro e-mailed the files to his psychic friend, who told him he believed his camera had caught the playful ghosts of children that night. DeCaro immediately retraced his steps to the spot where he had taken the shots and found that, unbeknownst to him, he had been shooting within twenty feet of the graves of no less than six children. Though elated to have his proof, he was still saddened at the realization that the ghosts of children were trapped there in the cemetery.

Photo copyright Melissa Martin Ellis, 2007.

Although this seems to be an example of orb activity in a cemetery, the orbs are actually lights in the background.

There's No Place Like Home

DeCaro decided to try doing spirit photography in his own yard. By his seventh week, he found discernable human shapes in the pictures. Sometimes there were even smiling faces with an amazing amount of detail. Animal shapes and skeletal figures were occasionally discernible. He also captured streaks of light, three-dimensional orbs, and colored orbs.

At one point, he was alone in the middle of a field at 2:00 A.M. and heard a voice calling his name. When he snapped a picture and looked at it, he saw a large cloud of wispy smoke only an arm's length away from him.

A Sort of Mediumship

DeCaro believes photographers can establish a rapport with the spirits that significantly increases the odds of attracting paranormal activity. He also believes that spirit photography is an instrument-aided type of mediumship, since the photographer is literally using the camera to communicate with spirits, or, more accurately, using the camera to let spirits communicate with him.

To try some ghostly photography, visit DeCaro's website (*www.ghoststudy.com/photography_class.html*). It features a step-by-step guide and good tips for would-be ghost photographers. Always remember to be respectful of the rights of others, living and dead, during the shooting process.

Careful Reviewing

When you take pictures, it isn't always apparent when you have captured an anomalous image. More often than not, orbs, mist, and peculiar lights aren't visible to the naked eye. It is only when you review the photos that you realize what you've captured.

Perhaps even more amazing than ghostly still photos are ghosts caught on videotape. The TAPS team caught an apparition by using their thermal imaging camera in a morgue. Although they made an effort to debunk it, they could find no explanation for the image, which they captured about three feet away from them.

Parapsychologists and Demonologists

Although Ed and Lorraine Warren were parapsychologists and demonologists by trade, you would never have guessed to look at them that they would become involved in such high-profile cases as the Amityville Horror.

It is estimated that from the time they began their work in the 1950s until Ed passed away in 2006, the Warrens investigated more than 4,000 cases. They are considered true pioneers in the field of parapsychology.

In their early married life, Ed and Lorraine would stop to check out any haunted areas they heard about when they traveled. Lorraine didn't believe in ghosts, but Ed remembered some experiences in his childhood home, and Lorraine went along with him.

Getting in the Door

At the time, the Warrens looked so young they weren't taken seriously. Ed would make a sketch of the allegedly haunted house, even putting ghosts coming out of the windows in the drawing. Lorraine would then knock on the door and give the sketch to the owners, who more often than not would invite the Warrens in.

When the Warrens first began their paranormal investigations, they were merely trying to help people who needed somewhere to turn when something they could not understand began to disrupt their everyday lives. As demonologists, the Warrens specialized in the phenomenon that surrounds inhuman spirits—demons and devils.

Demonics—nonhuman, malevolent entities that never walked the earth in human form—are always dangerous. Their intent is never ambiguous; they are out to injure and cause pain by whatever means they find at their disposal.

FACT

Ed and Lorraine Warren were staunch Catholics who saw their faith as protection from demonic elements, as do many ghost hunters in the twenty-first century. Even non-Catholics will sometimes carry holy water. If it works, it works.

John Zaffis

Demonologist John Zaffis, the nephew of Ed and Lorraine Warren, has been studying and investigating the paranormal for more than three decades. Under his Uncle Ed's tutelage, John learned to detect the signs of the demonic in cases that were far more intense than normal hauntings. He also learned how to successfully confront and deal with these situations.

John became involved in cases of possession and exorcism and worked with other leading exorcists of many different faiths—Catholic priests, Buddhist monks, rabbis, and ministers. He assisted and worked with well-known exorcists Bishop Robert McKenna, Father Malachi Martin, and Reverend Jun. His work and research have taken him throughout the United States and the United Kingdom. Because of his many years of working with other investigators and clergy, John Zaffis has earned a reputation as a very knowledgeable authority on all things paranormal.

In his early investigative years, his association with the Warrens gave him access to some amazing paranormal experiences, including numerous encounters with ghosts, poltergeists, and frequently even the demonic and diabolical. He is also a founder of the Paranormal Research Society of New England (PRSNE; *www.prsne.com*), a group that exists to help people who are having unpleasant or alarming paranormal experiences.

The Bangs sisters of Chicago were two of the most notorious fraudulent mediums in the history of the field. They used a variety of techniques to fleece the gullible, from spirit trumpets floating on wires to spirit type-writing and spirit slate writing. They were most famous for their ghost-rendered paintings.

Dr. Ciaran O'Keefe

In October 2005, the British newspaper the *Daily Mirror* printed a piece about the enormously successful United Kingdom show, *Most Haunted*. They alleged that the show's resident skeptic and parapsychologist, Dr. Ciaran

O'Keefe, had blown the whistle on the ghost hunters, claiming that the public was being deceived by "showmanship and dramatics." In his words, "I was put in the show to give a professional slant to it, to give it an element of credibility, but the skeptical argument is just swept away. In my opinion, we're not dealing with genuine mediumship."

The Demon Hunter

Nathan Schoonover has been interested in the paranormal since he was a kid. After experiencing two full-body apparitions as a young man, he studied with demonologist John Zaffis to learn the trade. Schoonover acts as a consultant to paranormal groups in the New York and New England area. Sometimes the calls come in from all over the world and he helps find another demonologist to take the case.

The East Coast S.C.A.R.E. Society uses his services when they suspect the case may involve a malevolent. He screens clients before making the drive and says the job is "all about talking to people; you have to help them deal with the situation while you are trying to get rid of it. You act as a counselor half the time. You really have to look for signals." Formerly, Schoonover worked as a counselor for emotionally disturbed teenagers, so he understands what is required to handle people in distress.

Many ghost hunters would not dream of heading out without holy water, rosaries, and scapulars. These symbols of faith work best for those who believe in them. Every professional paranormal investigative team should have a specialist within their group or on call who can deal with demonic attacks that are extreme enough to require the use of these holy symbols.

The Methodology

In the preliminary investigation of a malevolent haunt, Schoonover conducts interviews with the client, preferably while being videotaped. He wants an audio recorder running elsewhere in the house to gather EVPs, too. "If something is going to happen, it is likely to happen while we are talking about getting rid of it. We might expect EVPs, a disembodied voice, or a picture falling off a wall."

Schoonover believes that demonologists are dealing with entities that are truly malevolent, beings that rebelled and are separated from the grace of God. Schoonover and his friend and partner Shaun Burris host a podcast every week, Ghostman and Demon Hunter, where they have some laughs and interview paranormal investigators and demonologists. Episodes can be downloaded online at *www.ghostanddemon.com*.

CHAPTER 8

Paranormal Investigation Gear

The most important paranormal investigative gear you will ever use is your own common sense and judgment. However, for those who are determined to approach the field of ghost hunting in a scientific way, commercial markets and Internet stores are loaded with specialized devices that can help you detect and document paranormal phenomena. Although many researchers say poltergeists are notoriously difficult to capture using the new technologies, their shenanigans can sometimes be captured with video cameras.

Purchasing the Gear

You do not need all the gadgets listed to carry out a paranormal investigation. Individuals who are into ghost hunting as a hobby and are not into advanced research and investigation can begin their investigations with as little as a light source, a compass, a voice recorder, and a camera.

What Do Pros Use?

T.R.I.P.R.G. lists this equipment as being helpful in an investigation:

- Compass
- Gauss multi-detector
- Gauss meter
- Air ion counter
- K2 EMF meter
- ELF meter
- TriField Natural EM Meter
- Infrared motion detector
- Remote sensor wireless thermometer
- Magnetic field sensor
- Infrared thermometer
- Digital thermal hygrometer
- Hardwire thermometer
- Two-way radios
- Ionizing radiation meter (Geiger counter)

- Closed-circuit TV
- Night Vision equipment
- Microcassette recorder
- Four-channel multi-headphone amplifier
- Dust mask
- Sound level meter
- Black light
- Video camera (night vision capable)
- Jacob's ladder
- Laptop computer
- Physiological tools/software
- Mini-strobe light
- Thermal imager
- Facial composite software program

Should you decide to shop online, check out *www.ghostvillage.com* or *www.ghosthunterstore.net*.

Many paranormal researchers believe that solar activity has an effect on electronic equipment and even ghosts themselves. Geomagnetic field disturbances may damage power systems, cause false readings, or even give a boost of energy to spirit manifestations and interactions.

A Word of Caution

Equipment malfunctions far more frequently at some allegedly haunted locations. Batteries drain, monitors go dead, and all sorts of equipment problems occur. When equipment is removed from the site, their functionality usually returns.

Video and Still Photography

A picture is worth a thousand words. That's never more true than when it is applied to pictures of the paranormal. Although in the digital age people may tend to be suspicious of all images in general and ghost photos in particular, it is still truly stunning to see video or still photos of apparitions or ghosts. A controversy rages in the paranormal community over the use of the new digital photography.

Researcher Troy Taylor argues that camera images of more than five megapixels have sufficient resolution and clarity to be used by investigators. He has admitted that the technology has evolved, and newer models are no longer plagued by problems with false orbs. Some models also offer other important features, such as a night shot mode.

According to paranormal investigator Kenneth Biddle, digital cameras with a flash often give the photographer a false positive result. Items with reflective qualities such as brass, chrome, silverware, and even highly polished wood will return a reflection if a flash is used. "If the surface is close enough," says Biddle, "you get an 'apparition' in your photograph."

Authenticity

More expensive digital cameras offer a format known as *raw*. These files are uncompressed and any anomalous raw image that is examined using this format can be easily authenticated.

Complete Data

A bonus feature of digital files is that vital information is embedded within them. They can tell you about the camera make and model, the date and time the image was shot, what camera settings were used, whether flash was used, and the ISO settings. If an attempt is made to manipulate the image, the EXIF data records this information as well. You can easily analyze a digital image to see if it has been manipulated.

Audio Voice Recorders

Small devices that pack lots of investigative punch, recorders can be extremely useful and inexpensive investigative tools for ghost hunters. The technology is advancing so quickly that it is a good idea to check back frequently at online stores to see if prices have dropped or capabilities have grown. The sound quality of digital recorders is excellent and digital files are easily copied and transferred.

FACT

Nikola Tesla was an electronics genius whose early radio receivers picked up organized, intelligent signals during a time when the only functioning radio transmitter was Guglielmo Marconi's. Tesla studied the phantom signals and speculated they might originate from another planet—or even the spirit world. There were claims that he invented a Teslascope for the purpose of communicating with spirits or extraterrestrials.

Audio and Electronic Voice Phenomena

Using tape and digital voice recorders is standard practice in paranormal investigations. They are used both to tape interviews with witnesses and to record voice messages from the spirit world during investigations. Electronic voice phenomena (EVPs) are of particular use to serious investigators. EVPs are unexplained audio events, which can sometimes be heard as they are happening but more often go unheard until the recording is played back during evidence review.

Capturing EVPs

The EVP voices on the recordings are often distinctive, taking in regional accents and dialects. Sometimes they have such an eerie quality that it is barely tolerable to listen to them. Some seem to struggle to get the words out, as if they are communicating over vast distances. They often call researchers by name. Some may even answer questions or queries about their names or history. That sort of exchange is very exciting for investigators, particularly if they can substantiate some of the information.

Three types of these devices are commonly used in investigations:

- **Microcassettes.** These analogue recorders have micro audiotapes.
- **Digital voice recorders.** Tiny and inconspicuous with no tape, these digital recorders have great sound quality. Files from DVRs can be uploaded to computers for analysis and audio cleanup. Files can also be emailed or posted on websites.
- **Wireless microphones.** An often-overlooked tool for paranormal research, these devices are growing in popularity. The wireless microphone allows users to record audio straight to the hard drive of a computer, virtually eliminating background noise. Most kits include a microphone, transmitter, and receiver.

E-QUESTION

What is a PCFTD?
A phenomena related to EVP is known as PCFTD—phone calls from the dead. For decades, people have reported receiving telephone calls from deceased family members and friends. Many of the reports are similar—a person receives a phone call late at night, and although the connection is bad, they can recognize the caller's voice. When the recipient of the call makes a reference to the person being dead, the call abruptly ends.

Thermometers and Chilly Spirits

Sensing cold spots and recording sudden temperature fluctuations is an important part of ghost hunting and is of major interest to investigators. One hypothesis is that when there is a sudden drop of temperature in a given area, something is drawing energy in an attempt to manifest.

A Remote Sensor Wireless Thermometer

This type of thermometer uses wireless technology and a remote sensor. The device should be placed in a remote area that needs to be monitored. It shows temperature changes and will alert investigators if there is a sudden shift in temperature.

FACT

Triggered by a motion sensor, a security camera in Sydney, Australia, switched on and taped a glowing, vaporous apparition moving along a stairway. Although some skeptics have dismissed it as a cobweb, others claim it shows an object solid enough to have registered on the camera's motion detector.

Infrared Thermometers

Infrared technology, commonly called IR, is used to measure a type of EMF we don't hear much about—but you know it when you feel it! An infrared thermometer is a pistol-grip meter, equipped with a laser pointer that will measure temperatures from 0°F to 600°F at a safe distance for the user. It is incredibly accurate and has a backlit LCD readout for ease of use in dim lighting conditions. It can be used to quickly measure the IR temperature of corridors, rooms, basements, or attics.

Hardwire Thermometer

This is a high-tech thermometer used primarily to back up readings found with IR thermometers. They use an extremely sensitive wire probe, which is hard-wired into an equally sensitive meter with a digital read-out. The probe is then placed in the target area to record the temperature.

Infrared Cameras and Motion Sensors

Infrared technology may hold the key to getting results during the investigation. However, some ghost hunters scoff at this notion, believing it is better to see and record in the full spectrum of light, rather than limiting oneself to just part of the spectrum.

Night Vision Video Cameras

Prices vary depending on the features you want, but these devices are not too expensive. Most modern handheld video camera models have all the bells and whistles that a paranormal investigator would want, and they are quite durable. They are a sensible alternative to the super-expensive Night Vision devices because they are considerably cheaper and many come with some form of their own Night Vision technology.

FACT

Ghostly images, faces, and even hands have appeared on television screens over the years—when the television sets are turned off. In one instance, the face of Prince Albert, who died in the 1890s, appeared on the screen of an unplugged television set. Some people have reported their television sets turning on in the middle of the night, with strange smoky shapes swirling across the screen.

Infrared Motion Detectors

Easily available and cheaply purchased, these instruments can detect anomalies in a controlled area in two ways:

1. The device's passive infrared motion detector sweeps the zone and compares the area's thermal makeup to the reading it took upon activation.
2. The device's infrasonics detect noise in the sweep area and any sudden disturbance in the room's air mass. Small objects, even on the molecular level, will displace enough air within the room to trip a warning signal.

EMF and ELF Meters

These meters are widely used by ghost hunters today because they can be so helpful in finding paranormal activity. However, they all require a certain amount of familiarization and training. Remember that any equipment, no matter what model or brand, can give a false reading in the presence of the following:

- Poorly grounded or unshielded structural wiring
- Microwave ovens in use
- Dimmer switches
- Cellular phones in use
- FM, FRS, GRS, and CB radio transceivers in use
- Air conditioning and power system/stations
- Television screens, plasma screens, and LCD screens
- Computers
- Power lines within 100 yards, especially high voltage (tension) towers and transformers
- Fuse boxes

K2 EMF Meters

As in other fields of serious scientific study, one tool may be better suited for a situation than another. K2 meters have five LED lights that alert the user to different levels of electromagnetic field activity. These lights make using the meter in the dark a whole lot easier. The ghost hunter's theory about EMF activity is that manmade EMF will stay steady, while paranormal activity will produce peaks and spikes in the reading, because spirits emit a pulsing electromagnetic field. As soon as the meter goes to the second light, it is a definite indication of a higher than normal level of electromagnetic energy.

The Ghost Alert

We know that electromagnetic fields are always around us and that even humans are surrounded by electromagnetic fields. This meter compensates for this ambient field and will only give an alert when the field is above the human threshold or is significantly higher than normal. Manifesting entities

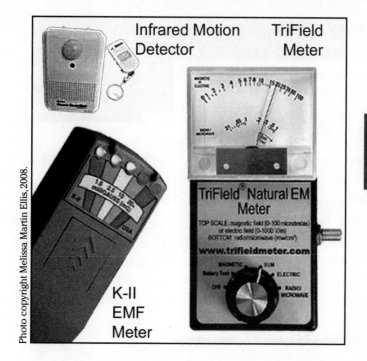

Photo copyright Melissa Martin Ellis, 2008.

Infrared Motion Detector

TriField Meter

K-II EMF Meter

The infrared motion detector and two types of EMF detectors are very popular with ghost hunting groups.

will typically cause the meter to go all the way up to the highest level and make the meter readings spike. That's pretty exciting to witness.

Gauss Meter

Use these meters when sensitivity, ultra-fast reactivity, wide detection range, and audible tones are needed on an investigation. They are precision instruments designed for specific situations, and their unique qualities make them a great asset to the team. A single-axis gauss meter detects paranormal activity within an area by showing the "electromagnetic smog signature" such activity generates. These instruments are very accurate and fast. They respond twice as fast as their closest cousin, the CellSensor. A color-coded graph helps indicate the level of a field's intensity at a glance.

Gauss Multi-Detector

The gauss multi-detector also detects gauss fields, and this moderately priced meter is far more sensitive than most. It measures values in both electrostatic and electromagnetic scales independently and with high accuracy. Using a corresponding colored bank of LED lights and a field strength rating capability ranging from .00001 to 1.0 on both the electrostatic and electromagnetic scales, this device is a necessity for most serious investigators. Some models come with a built-in audible signal feature as well.

EMF/Gauss Meter, ELF Meter

This device detects electrostatic (Tesla) and electromagnetic (gauss) fields with extremely high sensitivity, and it has a very high range and accuracy of measurement. A frequency filter allows different frequency fields to be monitored separately, so both VLF/RF (very low frequency/radio frequency) and ELF can be measured. It features lights that give the user the ability to read results in dark areas. Both the RF and gauss meter portion provide audible sound and large flashing lights, which correspond to abnormal spikes in field strength.

TriField Natural EM Meter

These instruments are relatively expensive, sensitive, and easily damaged, so they are not feasible for many paranormal investigators. Designed to detect only what we would consider paranormal activity, they take most of the guesswork out of situations where the gauss, ELF, and ION detectors may leave investigators otherwise unsure of their findings. They are fairly simple to use and have the audible warning tone so necessary in dark areas.

Flashlights, Lanterns, Compasses, and Watches

Sometimes the simple low-tech tools are the ones people underestimate. If you have a limited budget, some of these devices can replace their high-price counterparts in the short-term. Sometimes batteries drain and electronic devices fail; when that happens, even those who have the high-tech gear may be glad they brought along backup.

Flashlights

Flashlights really are an essential, basic item for any investigator. Naturally, most investigations occur after dark, and when it is time to cut off power the flashlight becomes one of the few light sources available. The investigator should have a red filter fitted to the lens or a red bulb. The red-tinted light keeps night vision intact and eyes adjusted to lower light levels. Lots of extra batteries are also essential.

FACT

Intense emotional events, such as a murder, suicide, or the tragic loss of a loved one, might leave an electrical imprint on the surrounding area. The human brain constantly releases small electrical discharges that may be powerful enough to imprint themselves onto objects in the immediate area. These imprints contain a sufficient EMF charge to be detected by electronic devices.

Lanterns

Flashlights have their place, but batteries can drain quickly and it is good to have backup. Kerosene lanterns can provide light when flashlights die, and although they are more cumbersome and expensive than the average flashlight, they can be enormously helpful.

Compasses

Simple in both its construction and function, the compass is probably the most overlooked yet dependable paranormal tool in existence. The humble compass is a highly dependable electromagnetic field sensor. It has largely been replaced by more accurate and sensitive electronics, but this paranormal tool is still used by many investigation traditionalists and those who wish to have a dependable backup to their modern-day electronic equipment. Compass needles can be moved by entities with a strong EMF that may well be paranormal in origin.

Watches

A reliable timepiece is an essential bit of equipment for keeping track of time spent during the investigation and to help coordinate the team's efforts.

Miscellaneous Equipment

These items are not necessarily widely used in the field by all investigators. Some can be quite helpful but may also be quite costly. Some are superfluous in the sense that their function is similar to cheaper equipment in more widespread use. Only big-budget investigators can afford some of them. They are worth a look, nonetheless.

Thermal Imager

Designed so the user can easily see and then analyze heat signatures and remnant heat signatures, this device analyzes hot and cold atmospheric anomalies instantly. A thermal imager is considered one of the most sophisticated, ultimate tools for paranormal research, and it's probably one of the most expensive, too.

Magnetic Field Sensor

This high-end device can detect, monitor, and document even the slightest change in a magnetic field through computer software enhancement. T.R.I.P.R.G. has used this device to successfully confirm the presence of entities when its sensitives are trying to communicate with them. These magnetic field sensors are so sensitive they can detect even the slightest shift in Earth's gravitational fields.

Digital Thermal Hygrometer

This is an invaluable tool to record temperature and humidity data. Investigators say it is worth its weight in gold, particularly when investigating orb activity and determining whether an orb is natural or paranormal.

Ion Detector

The air ion counter is used for the detection of both positive and negative natural and artificial ions. It is standard paranormal theory that when a ghost/spirit is about to manifest, a certain amount of energy is drawn from the surrounding environment or from nearby sources. These meters measure the resulting change in the positive or negative ions (electrostatic energy) in the air. It is a fascinating tool in the paranormal investigator's arsenal. This particular instrument has the following features:

- Audible notification of activity
- Visual notification of activity
- Long battery life (up to eighteen hours continuous use on a single battery)
- Telescopic antennae for maximum signal gain

Two-Way Radio

Handheld communication is a must for responsible and safe paranormal investigations when normal speech isn't possible. Groups that are spread out need to maintain communication with all members at all times to ensure their safety during investigations and to coordinate their efforts. These handy little devices make that possible. Most of today's handheld transceivers have a two- to five-mile range and are powerful enough to transmit through walls and obstacles to allow clear communications in all kinds of weather.

Geiger Counter

If you're serious about your research, this sort of meter most often associated with atom bombs and radiation may be a good choice. These meters are tough, durable, portable, and powerful. They're also very affordable. Paranormal energy ionizes the air and this meter detects that change instantly. These simple meters detect changes in the number of negatively and positively charged ions on-site at investigations.

Closed-Circuit TV

A monitoring system of this sort is of huge assistance to paranormal investigators, but its cost usually puts it out of the reach of most groups. A closed-circuit television with Night Vision capability (CUT/IR) allows an investigative team to monitor one or more areas simultaneously without risking direct exposure to any paranormal activity. If there is suspicion of the presence of inhuman entities or poltergeists, investigators may find this system well worth the cost.

Night Vision Equipment

If you have plenty of cash to throw into your gear, quality night vision devices are durable and incredibly useful. They eliminate the need for flashlights to light the way, which enables investigators to travel through completely lightless areas in total safely. Military surplus stores are a good source for this sort of equipment.

Sound Level Meter

Enhanced sound level meters are widely available on the Internet through specialty stores and merchants. They are used in paranormal investigation to detect ELF (extra-low frequency) and EHF (extra-high frequency) sounds.

With slight modification, the meter will easily pick up the sound of a tape recorder in operation, or a video camera's mechanical signature. If hoaxsters have set up equipment in a building to try to trick investigators, this device will help find that equipment by locating the sound of it in operation. Since it is so sensitive, it is extremely useful to the EVP-seeking investigator and very helpful when determining the quietest location to place microphones and recording devices.

Black Light

Inexpensive and portable, a black light or UV light is an interesting multi-use tool for investigators. It can be used to detect airborne particles in a room or building, and it also allows investigators to distinguish between true orb phenomena and non-paranormal airborne contaminants.

FACT

Some paranormal investigators theorize that you can use a black light to "push" spirits out of an area and herd them toward another space, where they can then perhaps be photographed or contacted. Many of these very affordable devices also come with a flashlight feature.

Gear and Weather-Appropriate Clothing

Most ghost hunters in northern regions talk about the benefits of layering and wearing thermal underwear on hunts during the colder months. It is important to be practical. An investigator will be out late at night, in a dark area, often without heat of any kind. Comfort and protection from the elements become very big priorities during overnight hunts. Comfortable shoes or sneakers are a must, too.

Make sure you have clothing with lots of pockets to stash your ghost hunting paraphernalia. Many researchers wear fishing vests, but now you can actually find online stores that sell clothing designed for ghost hunters.

CHAPTER 9

Prepping
for the Paranormal

If fools rush in where angels fear to tread, what shall
we call the ghost hunter who does the same? All kidding aside, proper preparation makes a great difference in the type of experience you take away from
investigations of the paranormal. To get the most out
of it, the investigator must put her best into all the
various phases. Ensuring that proper procedures and
protocols are in place before beginning the investigation should always be a priority.

Protecting the Client's Privacy

The client who has reached a decision to contact a paranormal investigator or a team of ghost hunters is very likely a person who has undergone very unusual or even inexplicable experiences. Very often, clients feel as if they may be losing their grip on reality. They may have already been ridiculed when they conjectured that something supernatural was taking place around them.

When a client finds you, he may be emotionally vulnerable. It is part of your job to reassure him that you will do everything in your power to safeguard his privacy. You must also assure him that while an investigation is taking place at his home or business, the people who are involved in that investigation will protect and respect his property, treat it with consideration, and, most importantly, let the client retain his anonymity, should he want it. Most do. T.R.I.P.R.G. estimates that 95 percent of their clients want them to maintain client confidentiality.

What does "client confidentiality" mean, in practical terms? Many groups and investigators approach it differently, but to most, it means:

- The identity of the client and the client's family are not disclosed.
- The location of the investigation is kept secret, especially in a small town.
- Facts about the case that could eventually lead to the deduction of the identity of the site or the person(s) are suppressed.

This means training investigators to watch their tongues when talking about their activities. Several pieces of information casually sprinkled though a conversation that can lead someone to deduce the client's identity or reach a conclusion about the site's location is the most common form of slip-up. People mean no harm, but it is very unprofessional and may result in actual legal liability if the client can prove he was damaged as a result.

The Confidentiality Agreement

Most teams sign a confidentiality agreement to reassure clients that their information will be kept confidential. The documents vary in length and complexity, but they all have one thing in common: They warrant that information gathered in the course of the investigation is treated as privileged and private. All team members are asked to read it and sign it, just to reinforce the idea that the responsibility and liability to the client are on the shoulders of the investigators.

There are even CDs available that offer the various forms investigators may need. You can purchase the Paranormal Paperwork CD from Vanderworker Todd Paranormal Research online. Profits from sales of the CDs help fund the group's investigations. These are simple forms that can be adapted to the needs of the purchaser.

A bare bones agreement should contain the following information:

CONFIDENTIALITY AGREEMENT FORM

We respect your privacy rights. We guarantee that your confidential information will remain so. We treat as confidential any information divulged during the course of the investigation, as well as any information that may be inadvertently obtained during the course of the investigation. These facts include the names and identities of all parties, clients, and witnesses, as well as the physical address of the investigation or any other feature that may make the site readily identifiable.

THE AGREEMENT

On occasion, this organization may ask to use information and evidence collected during the investigation for educational or publicity purposes, or possibly for inclusion on our website. Please check the level of confidentiality you would like to request and with which you would feel comfortable.

You have our assurance that your information will remain confidential unless you choose to release it. Please place a check mark beside your choice and draw a line through the options you reject.

❒ Full disclosure, including the identity of witnesses, clients, and the site location
❒ Partial disclosure, including the identity of witnesses and clients, but the site location is changed and the exact address of the location is undisclosed
❒ No disclosure of any of the pertinent facts of the case whatsoever

continued

SPECIAL REQUESTS

_____

_____

_____

_____

Signed: _____ Date: _____

No Confidentiality Required

There are those rare times when investigators are not required to conceal information about the case. These usually arise in instances where the allegedly haunted site would actually benefit from the notoriety the investigation would bring, such as the Lizzie Borden Bed and Breakfast in Fall River, Massachusetts, which has only benefited from the exposure it has received from being featured on _Ghost Hunters_.

These cases are a delightful breath of fresh air to investigators. They can free the group to break loose from the constraints of confidentiality and discuss the case with other team members or their fellow paranormal investigators. The nonconfidential cases allow the ghost hunters to freely discuss their fascinating experiences and dissect the phenomena with other groups. It also gives the team a chance to post its findings about the case, along with EVPs, photos, and other evidence online.

Making an Honest Assessment

Determining what is actually happening is the first responsibility of the investigator, and an honest assessment of the situation, phenomenon, activity, and people involved may not always support further investigation. Are there ever times when a case is dropped after the preliminary interview?

Absolutely. Seasoned investigators realize that it is a big drain on resources to pursue a case when there is little likelihood that the disturbance is paranormal. They also will not continue an investigation if:

1. There is obviously a natural explanation for what is occurring.
2. It is apparent the investigators are being lied to or set up.
3. The situation is in a state of flux, and the malevolent energy present actually requires the services of a demonologist.
4. One of the parties involved objects to the investigation.

Following Scientific Protocols

More and more groups are adopting strict protocols to their methodologies. It is rare to find a group today that completely ignores the scientific approach in favor of the barging-around-an-old-house approach of yesteryear. Groups who do so quickly find themselves without clients and are faced with genuine credibility issues. Beginning with the assumption that they will try to debunk or find an organic explanation for the allegedly supernatural phenomenon, researchers gather hard data that they can use to prove their assertion that paranormal events do occur.

With the scientific approach, the investigators seek to gather and follow the evidence, only declaring the incident paranormal when all the natural explanations have been discarded. Sometimes this is at odds with investigations that seek neither to foster nor debunk mysteries but only to solve them. The methods may vary slightly from group to group, but those seeking hard evidence of a haunting must necessarily follow similar rules to achieve their ends.

- They obtain permission to access the site, clearing it with whatever agency or person controls access before entering the site.
- They investigate in teams. Investigators buddy up so no one is on her own.
- Strict records are kept of the equipment in use and electronic equipment is checked before being used in the field to ensure its reliability.
- The phenomenon that has been reported is analyzed for reproducibility by natural means.

- Evidence is carefully screened and reviewed with an aim to debunk it.
- Evidence that cannot be debunked is properly archived and preserved.

The goal is to gather credible, reproducible evidence of life after death, communications from those who have passed on, poltergeist phenomena, or even malevolent hauntings. If any evidence is in doubt, it is discarded. This practice sometimes causes discord in a group. Some members may argue that the evidence is credible when others believe it is not. Groups will often set up evidence meetings where all members can examine evidence and vote about whether or not to keep it.

TAPS first came into the public eye when Jason Hawes declared on the web that all orbs were dust. Later, he admitted that this was a publicity ploy, but it is true that many orb photos, particularly those taken in the early days of digital photography, are not very credible.

Helping or Hurting?

The scientific approach is a hard discipline to learn. Not all investigators see it as a good thing, especially when it emphasizes gathering evidence over helping the people who are being disturbed.

The best ghost hunters are the people who do not lose sight of why they got into the field in the first place—simply to help people. If tons of evidence is gathered on a case but the family has been driven out of their home, the case does not have a happy resolution.

Personal Evidence

Some of the most compelling events occur when an investigator has a personal encounter, like the one Andrew Laird had at the asylum or Nathan Schoonover's encounter with the full-body apparitions in his bedroom.

Unfortunately, if these personal experiences are not backed up by physical evidence in the form of a photo or recording, it is not considered hard evidence, even if another person was there to witness it.

Information should be gathered using the scientific method:

1. Define the question.
2. Gather information and resources.
3. Form a hypothesis.
4. Perform experiments and collect data.
5. Analyze the data.
6. Interpret the data and draw conclusions that serve as a starting point for a new hypothesis.
7. Publish results.
8. Always retest.

ALERT!

To even minimally document evidence, the investigator needs a camera, an audio recorder, and a watch and notepad.

Integrity and Accountability to Clients

The client has invited you into his home and trusted you with access to the minutiae of his day-to-day life. He is virtually at the mercy of the team who is conducting the investigation, not only in terms of his privacy but also in respect to property damage and misappropriation. Every attempt should be made not to violate his trust in any way.

Case files should be locked and inaccessible to anyone but authorized team members. Confidentiality agreements should be reviewed before public relations work or media interviews. If case files are no longer needed, they should be shredded. Professionalism and objectivity in the course of an investigation refers to the following:

- Careful record-keeping
- A sense of responsibility to both the client and the team
- Never fudging data or attempting to support bad data by suppressing evidence
- Discarding any evidence that could be explained by natural means
- Careful coordination of experiential and technical data

A brief list of rules of conduct should be reviewed as a reminder before the investigation. Make the language plain and unequivocal. Suit it to the needs of your team, and be sure they have all read and agreed to it before the investigation starts.

- Do address the client by name in a respectful manner when introduced. Make eye contact. Shake hands.
- Do listen to any special requests or concerns the client mentions. Honor them.
- Do maintain a pleasant, professional demeanor.
- Do respect private property and the client's personal belongings.
- Do tie back long hair.
- Do bring along a signed form granting permission to investigate.
- Don't smoke in the area being investigated.
- Don't drink alcohol or use drugs before or during an investigation.
- Don't wear perfume, cologne, or after-shave.
- Don't be disrespectful in any way to the client or contradict her as she relates her experiences.
- Don't interfere with personal belongings or open drawers in private areas of the home, such as bedrooms.
- Don't comment about the condition of the premises, particularly if they are messy or in disrepair.
- Don't remove anything from the site without express permission of the client.

Professional Deportment

Unfortunately, it isn't possible to know what to expect from a new team member until she is field-tested. Members should be briefed on what is expected from them as far as their interactions with clients and the client's property.

As guests in the client's home, they should conduct themselves as such. It isn't good procedure to flip though personal papers, read diaries, poke through drawers or medicine cabinets, or even to make personal comments about the appearance of the premises or clients, unless it has a direct bearing on something pertinent to the case.

When Problems Arise

If a new team member deliberately or inadvertently violates one of the rules, he should be taken aside and warned that he has committed an infraction of the rules and should be more aware of his actions. The warning should be handled in a low-key and sensitive way. If the team member argues or proves disruptive, he should be asked to leave the site and a review of his membership status should take place as soon as possible.

When a veteran team member violates the rules, it can be more serious. As long-time members, these procedures should be ingrained, almost second nature. Again, the team leader should draw the member away from the investigation and talk with her to discover why the infraction occurred. Some-times, there will be a good reason, but the team member may have grown sloppy in her approach and needs to have a refresher course in proper protocols.

If the team leader cannot break away from the premises to follow up, he should ask the person to leave the site until they can have a talk about what has transpired. Never argue in front of the client and try not to embarrass or humiliate the team member in front of his or her peers.

Photo copyright Melissa Martin Ellis, 2007.

The Chinese believed that these figures, called Foo Dogs, were guardian spirits who could keep evil from entering a doorway. They were often placed at the front entrances of temples and palaces.

Accountability to Team Members

Team leaders who organize investigations have a lot more responsibility than the rest of the team. They should have gained confidence in their leadership abilities over time and feel sufficiently motivated before being put in charge of an investigation. A certain level of maturity must be evident, because the team depends on the decisions the team leader makes and they must have implicit faith in her judgment.

Just as the team leader is responsible to the members, the members are responsible to one another, the team leader, and the client. They should never argue with one another while on a case or speak ill of one another to clients or the media. If they have concerns about a fellow member that are pertinent to the case, they should resolve it within the group by requesting a meeting.

The Team Leader's Responsibilities

If an investigation is characterized by chaos, confusion, and ineptitude, the person in charge of the investigation is going to bear the brunt of the responsibility for it. If he cannot delegate authority and responsibility properly, it will soon become apparent.

Ideally, in larger, better-established organizations, the role of the team leader rotates as cases demand. This role may fall to the older investigators who have been on many cases and know the ropes, but they should be supportive when a novice investigator becomes a team leader for the first time.

The team leader must be responsible for the following areas:

1. Responsibility to the client
2. Responsibility to conduct an ethical, fair investigation
3. Responsibility for fellow team members' safety
4. Responsibility to supervise personnel and property in a professional manner that does credit to the organization

All are important and interconnected, but it should be apparent that client confidentiality and safety issues are paramount.

The Client's Responsibility

A lot has been said about the paranormal organization's responsibilities to the client and to its own team members, but we must remember that the client has responsibilities, too. When a client calls an organization to investigate unexplained phenomena in her home, there is usually no charge for the service and the investigators bear the brunt of the expenses.

Therefore, it behooves the client to keep this in mind when requesting help. She should attempt to be as cooperative and helpful as she can be. What should the client do?

1. Be truthful about the phenomena she has been experiencing. This means no exaggerations, equivocations, or withholding of evidence.
2. Allow the investigators full access to areas where activities have occurred.
3. Try not to place too many restrictions if full access can't be granted.
4. Be courteous and hospitable.

Follow-Up Investigations

It is not unusual to have a case that continues far beyond the scope of a preliminary investigation. If the evidence that is found during the initial investigation proves promising, the team may return again and again to gather evidence.

A prerequisite, of course, is that the haunting is not causing problems for the client and that he has decided he can live with the situation. When people understand that the ghost(s) are not trying to harm anyone, they often accept the situation and decide to peacefully coexist. This allows investigators the opportunity to delve deeper into the case and gather more evidence.

The Paine House Museum in Coventry, Rhode Island, is an ongoing investigation site for T.R.I.P.R.G. They have returned repeatedly, and even though one of the entities present has caused some distress to the sensitives, they find the site to be too active to leave alone.

This is often the case for paranormal investigators. Some cases are so active that the team can barely scratch the surface in just one visit, and it may be possible to do an investigation that stretches out over the course of days. If the site is secure the investigators have the added advantage of leaving the equipment set up and in place.

Repeat Offenders

Another reason to follow up on a case may be that the entity that was bothering the client has returned. When this happens, the team has to return to the site and try to evaluate the situation. Is it really the site that is haunted, or is it the people? This has to be determined first and may take a great deal of work to uncover. Sometimes it is clear that the client has personal issues that are far graver than dealing with a few ectoplasmic entities.

If a client believes she has been the victim of a demonic oppression, she may very well be emotionally and physically exhausted and should be referred for appropriate follow-up treatment by mental health practitioners. Investigations can continue while this is going on, but extreme caution and consultation with a demonologist or person who deals with malevolent entities regularly is highly recommended.

Some of the most spectacular evidence of paranormal activity has been witnessed during this type of case, but the well-being of the client should always take precedence over evidence gathering. The safety of the team also comes into play during this type of case.

Hard Evidence

Sometimes the team may return to a site that was promising at first but that produced no hard evidence. If a team refuses to use any sort of metaphysics to document paranormal activity, or even an investigator's own personal experience, they will need to return to gather evidence that can be verified through technological documentation. Although some think modern ghost hunting relies too much on science and prefer the experiences of sensitives and psychics, many groups now stick to the hard-evidence protocols.

What are these ways of gathering hard evidence? They usually coincide with other methods of evidence gathering, such as photography or digital videotaping. But they can also mean the use of more instruments, such as mobile weather stations, which are used so that data such as humidity and air movement can be recorded. They can also identify potentially ordinary explanations for reports of activity, such as drafty windows and old radiators.

Ruling Out Natural Causes

Infrasound is low-frequency sound, and although it is audible to the human ear, it may not register on a conscious level. It can sometimes cause people to believe they are seeing things out of the corners of their eyes, or to experience the creepy sensation of being watched. Infrasonic sound is now believed to be one possible explanation for why some people experience quickly moving shadows as a haunting.

Small motors produce these sound waves, which resonate around eighteen or nineteen cycles per second. The human eyeball has a resonance frequency of eighteen cycles a second, so the theory goes that the sound wave produced by the motor sets up a sympathetic resonance in the eye, triggering the impression of fleeting images.

CHAPTER 10

Having the Right Spirit

Developing the proper protocols and approaching the paranormal with an attitude of respect and responsibility should be standard for all investigators. As people add to their knowledge of the supernatural realm, they should also be more careful in their procedures. Knowledge is power when dealing with the unknown; the more investigators know, the better researchers and ghost hunters they become. Aspiring investigators put themselves and others at risk when they don't bring a sense of seriousness and responsibility to their research.

Interviewing the Witnesses

People who contact ghost hunters and paranormal investigators are some-times quite desperate. They have reached the end of their rope emotionally; in some cases, they really fear they are losing their minds. They may have had no experience with the supernatural before, so they have no context for what is happening. They are often referred by clergy and will be desperate to tell their stories to the investigators in hope of finding some relief from the chaos and fear that accompanies paranormal situations.

When interviewing, different protocols are required for different cases, depending on the urgency of the situation. Many groups will drop everything to come to the assistance of families with children, or if there seems to be a risk of imminent harm to the occupants of an allegedly haunted home.

The Process Begins

When a call comes in, the case manager will take down the information about what is happening. Other pertinent data, such as the address where the activity is occurring and the degree of urgency, is weighed before the case manager books a time for the investigators to interview the witnesses.

If there is sufficient time, a researcher might visit reference libraries and historical societies to look into the history of the house or site. Every little tidbit of information may be of importance in figuring out exactly what is happening at the allegedly haunted location.

Some groups have all of their prospective clients fill out questionnaires or conduct telephone interviews, asking for as much background informa-tion as they can get, such as the age of the site, what sort of sounds have been heard, and what abnormalities have been seen. Perhaps the most important question of all concerns how the client feels about what she is experiencing. Does she feel threatened? Based on the client's answers to these questions, the case manager will decide whether the respondent is sincere and cred-ible. If she seems to be, then an investigation is planned.

Meeting the Client

The interviewers proceed to the site and meet with the clients. Occa-sionally, another in-depth interview takes place on-site, and team members are thoroughly briefed on the case. Pertinent follow-up questions are asked simply to verify the witnesses' first account of the phenomena. Before much time and energy are invested in a case, be sure that something real is occurring and that the ghost hunting team is not being set up or tricked.

FACT

Paranormal investigators went to a house in Colorado that was reportedly haunted by demon eyes—red glowing orbs. After witnessing a manifestation of the red orbs, the investigators realized that the demon eyes were a set of reflections of reflections. The brake lights of cars stopping at a nearby intersection were reflected through a window into a wall mirror.

Hoaxing the Hunters

Andrew Laird was urgently summoned to a location to do an investigation only to discover that the client had set him up by concealing devices around the premises to simulate a haunting in order to "test" the group. Apparently, this sort of thing has happened to many groups, and investigators should be aware that it might eventually happen to them. Laird's group discovered the chicanery through the use of listening devices, which detected the sound of the equipment in operation.

All people in the household should be present as the interviewers talk to the client. Everyone who is in any way a participant—either a victim of or a witness to the activity—should be interviewed. If young children are present, they may be very disturbed to hear what is being said, so investigators must exercise a great deal of discretion.

An investigator who is both skilled and gentle can interview children later. A great deal of information can come out during these sessions, and clients are relieved to be able to talk freely about their experiences to people who will believe them and may really open up.

Noted and Logged

Notes on the interview must be made to record all the pertinent facts. These are useful for reference later. Occasionally, some clients may at first deny, then reluctantly admit, that they have been involved in some sort of experimentation, such as using a Ouija board or holding a séance that opened the door for entities to walk through. Sometimes the clients are reluctant to make the admission in front of other family members or house-mates and this is where follow-up conversations by team members are quite helpful.

ALERT!

There are some reports of ghosts that slap and bite. Christina Foyle of Essex, England, had a terrifying experience at Beeleigh Abbey. She slept in a room supposedly haunted by Sir John Gates, who was beheaded in 1553, and awoke the next morning with tooth marks on her shoulder and a serious bite mark on one finger.

Let the Investigation Begin

As the investigation begins, clients generally either go off-site or get out of the team's way. Each team member makes his own preparations, part of which is doing preliminary readings and keeping notes of his individual experiences during the investigation. In their diaries or work logs, the individuals involved in the investigation will record which pieces of equipment were used and make careful notes of any unexplained phenomena they may have personally experienced.

Assessing the Threat Level

The threat level can be assessed after the client interview. Sometimes, investigators may suspect that there isn't a threat at all. In most cases, the activity being investigated does not turn out to be paranormal but can be debunked as a normal occurrence that has been mistakenly perceived as supernatural.

The team will assess what is happening and will confer about the information gained from the interview and during the preliminary research. They design a plan for conducting the investigation and attempt to make an initial classification of the entities that might be involved.

No two cases are the same and they can range from merely annoying and puzzling to genuinely frightening.

A Haunting in Philadelphia

The General Wayne Inn in Merion, Pennsylvania, has a long history of bizarre events. Built in 1704 in a Quaker village called Merioneth, just outside Philadelphia, it is rumored to be haunted by such legendary figures as Ben Franklin, George Washington, and the Marquis de Lafayette, the French aristocrat who helped the Americans fight for their independence. It is believed that Edgar Allan Poe revised "The Raven" there.

During the Revolution, the inn was captured and recaptured alternately by British and American troops. Because of this, many deaths occurred in its vicinity. Soon, the rumor spread that a young Hessian soldier was buried in an escape tunnel that had been dug under the foundation.

At the inn, a hostess claimed to have seen a man in a Revolutionary War uniform on the stairs. She also heard someone calling her name, but when she whirled around to see him behind her, he vanished.

The owner reported an occasion when he opened up the cash register to find its drawer full of water, as were thirty wine decanters across the room and glasses on a shelf behind the bar. An insurance inspector could find no leak in the roof and fought the owner's insurance claim.

At other times, when there were young women seated at the bar, someone or something would playfully blow on the back of the neck of each one in turn, making them think their husbands or boyfriends had done it.

According to paranormal researcher Paul F. Eno, ghosts use electromagnetic fields, including those around the human body, to gain access to the ability to create a brief tactile sensation. This is how ghosts are able to touch people even though they have no bodies.

Malign Spirits

The Bell Witch haunting began in 1817 when a Tennessee family heard scratching and rapping noises in the walls of their home. Over a period of months, the activity accelerated and became increasingly violent. Bell family members were kicked and had their hair pulled. The Bell's daughter Betsy was singled out for special attention. She was kicked, pinched, punched, and tormented. Some of the ghosts appeared in human form and were seen not just by family members, but also by neighbors and visitors as word spread of the haunting. Before long, the Bell Witch was notorious, making trouble throughout the county.

The witch had a deep and abiding hatred for John Bell, the family patriarch. When John became sick, the witch could be heard lingering near his bed, badgering and insulting him, even as he lay dying. After his passing, a bottle of poison was found on a shelf in his room, and the witch told John's son she had tricked her victim into drinking it. After his death, the witch even made an appearance at Bell's funeral, alternately cursing and jeering as he was laid to his final rest.

A Spectrum of Spectral Events

Paranormal activity can range from harmless residual hauntings to more interactive types like poltergeist activity and malevolent entities. In very rare instances, there are reports of elementals or fairies.

In 1878, Esther Cox of Amherst, Nova Scotia, was the target of violent ghostly attacks. Throughout her teenage and young adult years, she was choked, slapped, and bitten, her hair was pulled, and sewing pins were jabbed into her face. The incidents only stopped when she was released from jail after being arrested for arson.

Protection procedures are discussed in Chapter 15, but the best way to prepare the team for their first encounter with malevolent or inhuman spirits is to thoroughly research the topic and use whatever spiritual protection they deem appropriate.

Understanding Site Layout

When interviewing clients, it is a good idea to have them show the investigators around the site, pointing out areas that may be of particular interest. In small homes and businesses, the setup and floor plans may be so simple that there is no concern whatsoever about team members tripping over obstacles or getting lost in a maze of interconnected rooms. But in large older buildings such as the Paine House Museum in Coventry, Rhode Island, even seasoned investigators easily lose their bearings.

The Paine House was built in 1669, and the interior rooms are like a maze. The wooden-shingled structure is an extremely active site with a perplexing interior layout. Andrew Laird says that it is possible to become very disoriented or even temporarily lost when conducting an investigation at this site. With no electricity or heat in the building, investigators find themselves faced with a very challenging set of circumstances. Maggie Florio, a sensitive and an investigator who works with Laird, found the site a challenge but was also thoroughly intrigued by it. It became her favorite place to investigate, and she revisits again and again.

Although Laird and Florio are extremely familiar with the site, they still experience moments of confusion in the rat's nest of room leading into room leading into room. Site layout becomes a real issue when it comes to setting up electronic surveillance equipment, with cords and power lines snaking through doorways and corridors. The best locations for the equipment must be planned quite carefully, both to keep the team safe and to optimize the possibility of catching the most paranormal activity.

Mapping Power Sources and Natural Anomalies

Determining the locations of power lines and wiring within a building can save investigators many problems and false readings later. Remember, the team is there to debunk the haunting, so eliminating the natural explanations for unusual readings is the first step. Once known sources of EMF spikes and other environmental anomalies have been eliminated, what remains is probably paranormal. It is in the best interest of the investigation to try to rule out all geomagnetic and geothermal explanations for events. Although instruments that measure electromagnetic fields and

Cemeteries make good training sites when learning to do EVP and digital photography work. Do get permission before entering.

Photo copyright Melissa Martin Ellis, 2008.

temperature fluctuations are considered reliable means of detection, they should be used with caution. Too often, alarmingly high positive readings are only the result of interference from electrical wiring, conduits, or appliances in use in the building. When using any sort of EMF meter, interference from power sources must always be ruled out before drawing any conclusions that readings may be of paranormal origin.

Powerless Site Locations

Fortunately, some investigative sites are in old, abandoned locations that have no power sources and are consequently free from any artificial, man-made electrical interference. This simplifies the analysis of unusual EMF readings because it is easier to rule out electrical sources.

What generates EMF? Most household appliances, actually. Electricity is the most common source of power and it is easily generated and transmitted. As electricity moves through wires and appliances, an EMF field is generated.

Electromagnetic Interference

What is not generally known is that any large concentration of metal, such as old iron pipes, fuse boxes, or radiators can cause magnetic fields that will affect the equipment. Even cell phones can cause small magnetic fields that will affect sensitive equipment.

FACT

Occultist Dion Fortune suggested in 1936 that many haunted sites could be attributed to having "ley lines," geomagnetic lines passing through them. Other scientists theorized that ley lines followed lines of energy running throughout Earth and could be detected using dowsing rods.

Tracking Site Conditions

During investigations, environmental conditions should always be recorded in an attempt to identify noticeable trends or fluctuations that may possibly correspond with paranormal activity. Whenever possible, sites that are open to the elements should be avoided, as there are so many conditions that are uncontrollable. Good investigators try to take baseline readings at the beginning, middle, and end of an investigation, no matter what else is going on. For comparison, further readings are taken as investigators explore the site and encounter situations or activities that are out of the ordinary.

Educating and Comforting Clients

In investigating cases that are self-generated, such as reports of apparitions seen along the roadside, paranormal investigators have the luxury of being able to put the investigation first, as there are no clients to deal with. They may proceed with the ghost hunt without having to consider the impact the investigation may have on their clients, so they can experiment with new equipment and techniques. But this sort of investigation happens rarely; most often the team will be called in to investigate when there is paranormal activity that is affecting people's lives.

The first vampire case in the United States was that of Mercy Brown in Exeter, Rhode Island. This is her crypt at the Brown plot.

Photo copyright Melissa Martin Ellis, 1980.

Sadly, sometimes investigators who embark on challenging cases are so wrapped up in the thrill of the hunt that they forget the human aspects of the job. If an investigative team is called in to discover the reasons behind paranormal activity, it is usually because truly disturbing or threatening events have disrupted the lives of the clients. Although every client will be different, one constant seems to be that the situation will have reached a stage that is disturbing to the people in the environment. Paranormal investigator Nathan Schoonover asserts, "With me, it is never about the proof. It is about helping people." Schoonover primarily consults on cases of malign hauntings.

ALERT!

Many paranormal investigators in New England have made the pilgrimage to visit the grave of Mercy Brown in Exeter, Rhode Island. Dubbed the first vampire in America, the body of Mercy was disinterred in 1892, three months after her death, by her family and neighbors after many other deaths in the community. It is said her body was unblemished and there was blood on her mouth.

Establishing Rapport

Even if the clients seem to be maintaining their composure, they may be putting up a brave front for the investigators. A good approach to take is to reassure the person that she has made the right decision to call the team in. Act as professionally and calmly as possible during the execution of the interview and investigation. This is reassuring to the client, and that is particularly necessary if she seems to be at the physical or mental breaking point.

Unless you have someone with a psychology or counseling background on the team, clients who appear extremely agitated or on the verge of a mental breakdown should always be referred immediately to a health care professional.

E-QUESTION

Can animals come back as ghosts?
The ghosts of animals, particularly pets, are sometimes reported. Spirit cats are the most common. Feline ghosts are generally friendly, except for the so-called demon cat that haunts the Capitol Building in Washington, D.C. According to researcher and author Dusty Rainbolt, the cat guards the ceremonial platform on which the coffins of dead presidents rest—ferociously, if necessary.

Reviewing the Evidence

After the team members complete their various inquiries and feel it is time to evaluate the evidence, they will wrap up the investigation for the night and remove their people and equipment. The photos, taped footage, and audiotapes must all be reviewed by team members and thoroughly sifted for any possible paranormal activity. This is a very time-consuming process.

The team members' activity logs and notes on personal experiences are also thoroughly reviewed, and the lead investigators may use all the information from the investigation to draw conclusions about possible natural explanations. If a local group has the option of returning to the site to gather more data, they may decide if it is warranted. If a conclusion can be drawn based on the evidence, the investigators set up a meeting with the client where the results of the investigation are revealed.

Revealing the Evidence

Next the ghost hunters meet with the client to show all the evidence that supports the haunting. If there is none, that is revealed, too.

If there is clear evidence of a haunting, the investigators state what sort of situation they feel the client is facing. They will then offer their professional recommendations for dealing with it.

This can range from advising the client to ignore the activity to calling in sensitives to clear the space of any negative energy. This phase often requires educating clients about the threat level and the various sorts of hauntings. Clients are often relieved that their claims have been validated and feel that they can live with the spirits, as long as they are benign. Sometimes clients are very disappointed if nothing has been found.

Lorraine Warren feels that too many paranormal investigative groups focus on trying to prove a location is haunted without taking into account the human element. She thinks that the closure aspect is too often ignored. "This is what is missing with so many groups," she says. "That's what takes time, that's what takes effort, that's what takes knowledge."

Remaining Objective and Professional

Perhaps the biggest challenge the novice ghost hunter faces is remaining objective about the phenomena he is called in to observe. He should try to bring as much professionalism and objectivity as he can to his evidence gathering. Ghost hunters who conclude that most of the sites they investigate are haunted are doing something seriously wrong. Professional investigators say that only 10 percent of their cases show any proof of paranormal activity; others assert that even that number is rather high.

Scientific Methodology

As long ago as the nineteenth century, the Society for Psychical Research (SPR) began trying to debunk activity or explain it by natural means. Today's investigators have developed this approach toward the paranormal even further. It is a good one to follow.

In reality, ghost hunting is a subject that is open to enough ridicule and criticism already, so scrupulous investigation is absolutely required. That attitude builds not only the team's credibility, but it also brings higher standards to a field that really needs them.

Building On the Past

As this field matures, more and more is learned about the limits of the technology used in investigations. Teams using the TriField Natural EM Meter discovered recently that this meter is so sensitive it can be affected by lightning within seven miles of the site. Investigators now have to double-check weather reports before going on an investigation to ensure that they aren't getting bad readings. It is extremely important to learn as much as possible about environmental conditions before gathering evidence.

During the course of a professional investigation, good record keeping and cross-referencing information by each individual team member gives perspective and depth. If technology is used, the data from the equipment must be carefully recorded for analysis later or it is useless.

Hard Evidence

Personal experiences that are not independently verifiable by written or recorded means become just that—merely personal experiences, not hard evidence. In *Ghost Hunting: How to Investigate the Paranormal*, Loyd Auerbach gives advice on maintaining the proper procedures and objectivity to meet professional standards. He maintains that the investigation of ghosts and hauntings is all about the concept of consciousness that exists independently of the physical body. In order to obtain evidence about something that is so hard to quantify, investigators have to come up with procedures and methods that ensure something virtually unquantifiable is quantified— a tall order indeed.

Auerbach feels that there is a lot of validity in parapsychology, augmented by the careful use of the tools modern science has given us. This opens up many interesting possibilities, such as the use of sidereal time.

Sidereal Time

This way of measuring time does not use the rotation of the earth or the position of the sun. Instead, it is determined by looking at particular stars and constellations overhead. Since the sidereal day is a few minutes shorter than a solar day, there are windows that allow people to be more psychically active. If this theory is true, investigators may be able to use these LST (local sidereal time) windows in their quest to obtain more verifiable data about ghosts and hauntings.

At *http://tycho.usno.navy.mil/sidereal.html*, you can find the exact sidereal time for your location if you know the longitude. You can determine your longitude by going to *www.astro.com/atlas* and entering a location.

CHAPTER 11

Spectral Sites
Surround Us

Upon a first or even a second glance, a quaint farm-house or a cornfield may seem completely ordinary. Nothing strikes the casual observer as remotely strange. But ghost hunters and psychic investigators who know the history of picturesque antebellum mansions or Civil War battlefields know differently. If ghosts are the spirits of the dead who are emotionally connected to a particular locality, and if the act of passing over was violent or accidental, the chances that the spirit of the departed will linger in some form are much stronger. Obviously, the older the property, the greater the likelihood that ghostly remnants may linger there.

Battlefields and Historic Sites

It's not surprising that many battlefields are believed to be haunted. The trauma and pain associated with such sites may linger as psychic echoes throughout eternity. Battlefields are notorious for paranormal phenomena.

Gettysburg

Gettysburg, Pennsylvania, is reputed to be one of the most haunted places in America—and with very good reason. From July 1 to 3, 1863, Union and Confederate forces fought each other in one of the most ferocious battles of the Civil War.

FACT

Gettysburg was the bloodiest single battle of the Civil War, not counting the 1864 Wilderness and Spotsylvania campaigns as a single battle. The number of killed, wounded, and missing in the two armies combined was 51,000 men. Gettysburg is often considered the turning point of the war.

As the battle raged, Confederate sharpshooters took aim from the attic of a rambling farmhouse on the outskirts of town. Today, the Farnsworth House Inn is a bed and breakfast where guests can study the bullet holes that cover the south wall. On that side of the house, many guests have reported seeing an apparition of a wounded Union soldier at the end of a bed. One woman reported that her infant was lifted by unseen hands and gently placed back down in the crib. Tourists taking pictures around or in the house have been startled when the photographs show transparent figures of men wearing Civil War–era uniforms. One visitor even claimed to have seen Confederate general Robert E. Lee sitting atop his famous grey horse, Traveller.

Residents of Gettysburg mention that during strolls across the battlefield on warm summer nights, it's not unusual to encounter hot spots. It's also common to hear gunshots, screams, and bugle calls.

During the filming of the movie *Gettysburg*, Civil War re-enactors were recruited as extras. While in uniform, one group of men found themselves confronted by a haggard old man, dressed as a Union private. The man smelled strongly of sulfur, a key ingredient of the black powder used in 1863. He handed them a few musket rounds and said, "Rough one today, eh, boys?" Then he turned and walked away into the shrubbery. When the re-enactors brought the rounds into town, local experts authenticated them as original rounds, more than 130 years old.

Built in 1838, Pennsylvania Hall is the central administrative hub and oldest building on the campus of Gettysburg College. In the 1960s, two college administrators rode their building's elevator down to the basement. When the doors opened, they saw a room filled with wounded soldiers and doctors performing amputations. The doctor looked up at the women and beckoned to them. Instead, they punched the buttons to bring the elevator back up to the first floor.

Old Green Eyes

Like Gettysburg, Chickamauga, Georgia, is haunted by the spirits of Civil War soldiers, but this battlefield is unique in that it is haunted by an entity that does not really fit the definition of a ghost. Known as Old Green Eyes, this entity is described as a large creature with fanglike teeth, a hairy body, and burning green eyes. The figure walks on two legs and perhaps wears a cloak. Over the years, thousands have claimed to have seen him prowling about at dusk. Some say the first sighting predates or dates back to the time of the battle of Chickamauga itself, which took place in September 1863.

A number of stories about the origin of Old Green Eyes have been put forth over the decades. The most common is a Native American legend about such a creature that roamed the area long ago, scavenging from the Indian villages. If true, this sounds remarkably like a Sasquatch.

According to some legends, both Confederate and Union soldiers actually saw the creature creeping through the area just after the battle, carrying away dead bodies. Others claim that Old Green Eyes is the ghost of a soldier whose head was blown off by a cannon and whose body was destroyed.

According to this legend, the soldier's head drifts about the battlefield, searching for its body.

Although it is not a battlefield, the USS *North Carolina* saw its share of the horrors of war. The ship served in every major Pacific battle during World War II. Witnesses have reported seeing a young blond sailor in the passageways. Hatches close and open by themselves and there are areas of the ship that are always cold, even in high summer.

Fort Fear

Dale Kaczmarek, the director of the Ghost Research Society (GRS), claims there are more than 100 haunted hot spots in the greater Chicago area. The GRS and independent psychic investigators of the Chicago area know their city is home to just about every kind of apparition and phenomenon imaginable, from sightings of ghost ships on Lake Michigan to singing entities.

One of their most famous "haunt spots" is a Chicago landmark, Fort Sheridan, located north of the city and known to the locals as Fort Fear. Built along an Indian trail connecting it to Green Bay, Wisconsin, Fort Sheridan was originally a French trading post and mission established around 1670.

By the early twentieth century, the fort was all but abandoned and had fallen into disrepair. But for many years afterward, sightings of a lady in an orange dress were reported. Seen during random sunrises around the former officer's mess hall, the lady was rumored to resemble Mamie Eisenhower.

The Alamo in San Antonio, Texas, is a reputed to be hotbed of paranormal activity. During the legendary siege of 1836, 1,600 Mexican soldiers and 200 Texan defenders were killed. Witnesses have glimpsed apparitions of small children in the area of the Alamo's gift shop and seen men in nineteenth-century garb marching across the courtyard.

The Rosewell Ghost

Elizabeth Bissette, a writer, musician, and reluctant psychic, found herself walking through the echoes of a long-gone American family when she visited the Rosewell estate in Gloucester County, Virginia. Constructed in 1725 by Mann Page, Rosewell was the ancestral home of the Page family for more than 100 years. John Page, grandson of the builder, was a schoolmate of Thomas Jefferson. In 1916, a fire swept through the mansion, gutting it and leaving only a magnificent shell, which remained a haunting testament to eighteenth-century craftsmanship and dreams.

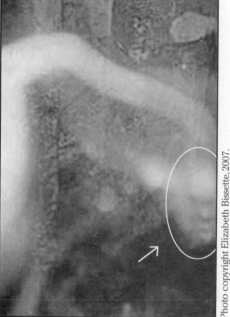

Legends and lore associated with the estate were passed down from generation to generation, written in journals or whispered around fireplaces. Supposedly, Mann Page expired in the grand front hall of the mansion, and the bishop of Virginia proclaimed that God had struck him down for his excesses. Another rumor is that Mann died because he was cursed by the spirit of Powhatan for building the mansion on the site of Werewocomoco, the chief's village.

Elizabeth Bissette's photo taken at Rosewell. He really doesn't look much like Thomas Jefferson.

Photo copyright Elizabeth Bissette, 2007.

Tales of hauntings on the Rosewell grounds cover a broad spectrum, from full-body apparitions to moans. Vintage automobiles have even been sighted. It was into this atmosphere that Elizabeth Bissette, a distant relation of the Pages', turned onto the long plantation road that led to the shell of the mansion.

Parking near the family cemetery, she and a friend wandered the grounds, taking pictures. Nothing untoward happened, except that their car stalled on their way out. "The next day," Bissette said, "I started thinking that there was a good chance the photos wouldn't turn out, because we hadn't been able to get any light." She and her friend decided to return at twilight.

"So, we got there," she continued, "and I'm taking pictures and we're standing around talking and I swear I saw behind [my companion] a man in colonial dress with his hair back in a ponytail. Young, smiling. He winked at me and put his finger to his lips, pointing to my friend. He looked so real, I thought he was a re-enactor, that maybe they'd had an event there that day and he was messing with me and wanted to play a joke on my friend. That is, until he disappeared."

Rather than explain the inexplicable to her companion, Bissette replied jokingly that she had just seen Thomas Jefferson and that she wished he had brought his violin.

Cemeteries and Graveyards

Cemeteries and hauntings would seem to go hand in hand, but in actuality, reports of haunted cemeteries are far less common than those of specter-plagued houses. However, Bachelor's Grove Cemetery in Chicago has been dubbed the most haunted cemetery in America by the GRS. The Grove earned a frightening reputation with reports of a mysterious lady in white, flying light orbs, and even vanishing automobiles.

ALERT!

Smells are often associated with hauntings and spirit manifestations. Odors associated with cooking, flowers, tobacco, perfume, the ocean, and even decomposing flesh have been reported at various haunted sites. A haunted house in Wisconsin allegedly produced a smell so foul that it drove away investigators and made the dog they had brought along violently ill.

Located on the edge of the Rubio Woods Forest Preserve in the suburb of Midlothian, Illinois, this 200-year-old burial ground has been largely forgotten. But almost all Midwestern ghost hunters place the Grove high on their haunted list.

Although the last actual burial in the Grove took place in 1989, the place had been virtually abandoned and forgotten by the mid-nineteenth century. Since that time, many apparitions have been captured on film, the most famous being the image of a woman seated on a tombstone that was taken with infrared film. This spirit is known as "the White Lady" or "the Madonna of Bachelor's Grove." She is rumored to be the ghost of a woman buried in the cemetery next to her infant son. She has been seen on nights of the full moon, wandering about the cemetery with a baby in her arms.

Resurrection Mary

Resurrection Cemetery in Justice, Illinois, is haunted by an entity known as "Resurrection Mary." Since the 1930s, numerous witnesses driving along Archer Avenue have reported picking up a female hitchhiker.

One of the most persistent ghost stories is that of the phantom hitchhiker. The majority of reports follow a basic pattern: a driver traveling at night picks up a hitchhiker, who speaks very little during the trip except to ask to be dropped off at a certain destination. Only when the driver reaches that destination does he realize he is actually alone in the car.

The young woman has blond hair and blue eyes and is wearing a white party dress. Some of the drivers describe her as wearing a thin shawl and holding a small clutch purse. When the drivers get close to the Resurrection Cemetery gates, the woman asks to be let out, whereupon she disappears or floats through the bars of the gates. The bars bear strange handprints seared into the metal—the mark of Resurrection Mary.

Chicago area ghost hunter Richard T. Crowe claims to have collected three dozen substantiated reports of Mary from the 1930s through the 1980s.

Schools and Churches

Illinois College was founded in 1829, and like many other historic spots in Illinois, the events of the past still come back to remind students and faculty members of earlier days. Most claims of paranormal activity are associated with Beecher Hall, a two-story building constructed in 1829. Witnesses claim to hear footsteps and the occasional moan. Years ago, Beecher Hall was a medical building and cadavers were kept in the attic. There are several tales of people following the sound of footsteps up to the attic and then smelling the stench of decaying flesh.

The most famous spirit on campus is that of the so-called Gray Ghost. A female student climbing the curved staircase at the Alpha Phi Omega Hall claimed she saw a man in gray standing on the landing. She quickly realized he was not a student or a security officer—nor did he have a face. Several other students reported seeing a similar phantom over the next few years.

New Hampshire's Colby-Sawyer College

The campus of Colby-Sawyer College in New London, New Hampshire, is reportedly haunted by a man wearing a black frock coat and a broad-brimmed hat. He is usually seen standing inside Colgate Hall. A former student claims to have seen the ghost twice, once in broad daylight and once at sunset. She didn't realize he was a ghost at first. His theatrical garb drew her attention, and she first thought he was a drama student on his way to rehearse a play. When the student paused for a moment and looked again, the man had vanished.

"I didn't think anything of it," the student said. "He'd probably stepped into an office." A couple of weeks later, she encountered him again. She approached him from the library, close to Colgate Hall. As she gazed at him, the man faded from sight. "It was as if I watched him evaporate slowly."

FACT

Tenants in a Greenwich Village apartment reported seeing a figure wearing a black slouch hat and long cloak slinking from room to room. In the 1970s, one of the tenants looked into the history of the building and learned that the haunted apartment had been inhabited by Maxwell Grant, the author of hundreds of pulp novels starring "The Shadow"—a fictional character who always wore a black slouch hat and a long cloak.

York, England

York, England, is one of the most haunted places in all of Europe. It was inhabited by both the Romans and the Vikings, and as one of the most important cities in the British Empire, it has been the site of bloody battles and tragic deaths. At the Treasurer's House, weary Roman soldiers trudge through a basement, cut off at the knees. They are still following the original Roman road that lies beneath the building's foundations. The headless ghost of Thomas Percy, seventh Earl of Northumberland, roams the city, apparently searching for his severed head. He was beheaded in York for treason in 1572 after he led a plot against Elizabeth I.

The apparitions of two women and a child have been reported to appear in a churchyard. One tale is that they are the ghosts of a mother, her child, and an abbess who were killed when Henry VIII's men occupied the church after the dissolution of the monasteries.

And then there are the children. The ghosts of countless children haunt the streets and buildings of York, crying for their mothers, begging for food, and grasping at tourists.

The Borley Rectory, Essex

The gloomy old building on the border between the counties of Suffolk and Essex has been described as the world's most haunted structure. Although the rectory itself burned down in 1939, its legends live on.

Poltergeist activity, full-body apparitions, disembodied voices, and ghostly chanting are associated with the rectory. Some claim that the spirits are those of a monk and a nun who were involved in a forbidden love affair. When they were found out, they suffered from the traditional punishment—the monk was decapitated, and the nun was buried alive.

When the building burned down, several witnesses claimed they saw a gray-clad nun slipping away from the inferno and a young girl standing at an upstairs window. When the ruins were excavated, a woman's skull and fragments of a skeleton were found buried several feet beneath the ground.

Theaters and Museums

Paranormal researchers have often noted that ghosts seem to be fond of theaters, as if they want to enact a drama without a final curtain for all eternity. The famous Adelphi Theatre in London is filled with ghostly activity, much of it attributed to the spirit of William Terriss, a colorful ham actor who was murdered at the stage door in 1897.

Actors and patrons alike have heard mysterious tapping and footsteps running up the aisles and have watched stage settings being moved by invisible forces. Poltergeist activity has been reported, from flying cuff links in dressing rooms to cupboard doors springing open.

Actress Judy Carne claimed to have had an eerie encounter with an eighteenth-century actress who hanged herself in a dressing room. The spirit of the woman was often seen sitting alone in a balcony box. Carne told of a séance arranged to communicate with the phantom actress: "I tried to talk to her but the table we were sitting around rattled and I heard weeping."

The Pantages Theater, Hollywood

One of the last of the elaborate Hollywood movie palaces, the Pantages has been called one of the most beautiful theaters in the world. Eccentric billionaire Howard Hughes purchased the Pantages in 1949, but it fell into disrepair after he sold it in the 1950s. In 1967, Pacific Theaters bought the movie palace and restored it. Staff members who work in the second floor offices often reported feeling a presence, especially in the conference room, which had once been Hughes's office.

Karla Rubin, an executive at the theater, states that twice she has caught sight of an apparition, a tall man dressed in modest business clothes. He has been glimpsed rounding a corner in the remodeled suite where Howard Hughes's original office door was once located.

The British Museum

Given the vast number of historical relics and ancient artifacts housed in the British Museum, it would be a surprise if the huge institution wasn't at least a little haunted. One of the most pervasive tales deals with the mummy of an Egyptian princess who was supposed to have lived in Thebes in 1600 B.C.E. Sneering at the possibility of a curse, an Egyptologist brought the princess's mummy and elaborate sarcophagus to England in 1910.

Shortly afterward, the man's fortunes underwent a swift decline. He presented the sarcophagus and the mummy to the British Museum, and the legend grew from there. A photographer who took pictures of the mummy immediately dropped dead of apparent heart failure. The curator in charge of the Egyptian exhibit was found dead in his bed. Several members of the museum staff reported seeing the figure of a woman floating through the halls.

The board of the museum cut a deal with the Museum of Natural History in New York City and shipped the sarcophagus and its contents off on the first available transatlantic vessel—which turned out to be the *Titanic*. The mummy and the sarcophagus lay in the cargo hold of the unsinkable ship when she struck an iceberg on April 15, 1912.

The Altoona Railroad Museum

This museum in Altoona, Pennsylvania, has been the subject of several investigations over the years. The building holding the museum is nearly 125 years old and once served as the infirmary for the Central Pennsylvania Railroad. Museum staff and visitors have reported sightings of ghosts in the building and around the site.

People hear footsteps coming up behind them when no one is around and have reported harmless poltergeist activity in the museum gift shop. Several employees claimed to have seen a spirit-like figure climb over a steam locomotive exhibit engine only to vanish before it reached the other side. Many visitors reported catching a glimpse of a ghostly figure, freely moving about the outside of the engine.

One evening when a museum director entered an elevator, he saw a man standing in the rear, facing the back wall. The man turned to look over his shoulder at the director and then vanished. Shortly afterward, the director looked at a group photograph hanging on the wall of the first floor of the museum and recognized the man he had glimpsed in the elevator. The man's name was Frank, and he was a railroad worker who had been scalded to death by a broken steam valve. He was brought to the infirmary, where he died of his burns. He is now referred to as "Frank, the Friendly Central Pennsylvania Railroad Ghost."

Private Residences

Independent investigators should deal with clients as though they are interviewing witnesses to an accident. Although many levelheaded people claim to have seen ghosts, the investigator should rule out all other possibilities and find out exactly what they saw or heard, but maintain their own sense of professionalism.

For example, Chicago area psychic researcher Norman Basile became involved in a mission to cleanse a haunted house in the suburb of St. Charles. After interviewing the residents of the house, Basile became personally affected by the sense of gloom that seemed to cling to the house and worried he was falling victim to the subject's delusions. He felt he had lost his sense of objectivity.

Taking photographs of the exterior of the house with infrared film, he noticed that faces appeared in the windows. "One showed a mysterious mist hanging over the whole house," he said.

ALERT!

According to author and psychic investigator Brad Steiger, increasing numbers of people have reported the appearance of Native American ghosts. Some have theorized that the manifestation of these spirits is a reflection of the collective guilt present-day Americans may feel over the shameful treatment of Native Americans. Others claim the experiences are due to the vandalizing of ancestral burial sites.

Basile investigated the history of the house and found the site had been inhabited by Mound Builder Indians, a Midwestern tribe who buried their dead in earthen mounds. Through his research, Basile identified several mounded areas that might have served as burial sites. He suspected that restless spirits resented the presence of the house.

Basile arranged for a cleansing ritual performed by Evelyn Pagalini, a practicing Wiccan. Unfortunately, the owners of the home didn't fully cooperate with the terms of the ritual and the ghostly activity began anew.

CHAPTER 12

Making the
Psychic Connection

Dealing with the many people and situations that can arise during a paranormal investigation is an important part of the big picture. Fortunately, we don't have to reinvent the wheel; there are standards and procedures already in place for most of the challenges psychics face in the pursuit of the elusive world of spirits. We'll explore the different approaches and skill sets that work best.

Site Check with the Client

Once the decision has been made to start the investigation, the case manager should meet with the client and take an exploratory walk-through of the site. This is a good time to set up the option to return after the investigation if it is necessary; follow-ups are often needed. If the client has any special requests or has recent activity to report, this is her chance to share the information.

This is also an opportunity for the investigator to take baseline readings with monitoring equipment. Ideally, this meeting should be done a bit in advance of the investigation so that the information can be coordinated and possibly researched more deeply. It isn't always possible to do a walk-through before the day of the investigation, especially if the site is far away or time is tight.

If the client is able to arrange it, walk through the investigation site in daylight, when anything that may be a physical hazard can be identified. Older and abandoned buildings are interesting to investigate and often have unexplained phenomena associated with them, but they can have many lurking hazards as well.

Ask plenty of questions. You are in the business of seeking answers, so practice asking questions without being too intrusive. Ask about common hazards, including:

- Structurally unsound areas—weak floors, uneven floors with loose boards, unsafe steps or balconies, etc.
- Clutter and debris
- Areas or rooms where hazardous chemicals are stored
- Rooms under construction where nails or sharp-edged tools can be found
- Rooms containing asbestos insulation or other dangerous materials

Other impediments to an investigation could be:

- Antiques and collectibles that cannot be touched or moved
- Areas with high EMF readings
- Areas to which the client refuses access

Photo copyright Melissa Martin Ellis, 2008.

It's a good idea for paranormal investigators to carry their cameras with them at all times; you never know when a spooky shot may present itself.

All pertinent information about the building or site should be noted. Determine the age of the site. The current owner may not know, but a records search will uncover the site's age and ownership history. Never take a building's appearance as a sure indicator of its age; it could have been remodeled and may look far younger than it is, or it could be cleverly designed to look like an old structure, although it was built only a few years before. New buildings do seem to have less ghostly activity than old ones, so knowing the age may help you gauge whether the reports you are hearing are credible. Always check at the local city or town hall for ownership records and building permits to indicate the age of the site.

If you have been told the history of the site, do your own independent verification of the facts. Misinformation and faulty memories cloud the data quite often, so double check everything you can. You can check these records online and do a bit of genealogy research, at *www.ancestry.com* and *www.familysearch.org*. Links to other genealogy sites can be found at *www.cyndislist.com*.

Practical Approaches

Jeff Barnes is a ghost hunter in Indiana (*www.poseycountyghosthunters .com*). In one of his podcasts, he talks about putting together an environmental worksheet for your investigation. This worksheet lists conditions in the home that might adversely impact the client's home and health and even the case. He recommends looking for wiring issues, mold, air quality, and leaks. None of these problems are unique to paranormal investigation procedures, but knowing about them may help you document circumstances that might support or debunk the perception of paranormal activity at an investigation site. Perhaps the reason your client is seeing things might be explained by something as simple as toxic paint fumes poisoning the air.

Structural issues such as cracks in the floors or walls should also be noted, as should basements with bare earth floors, which might be contaminated with industrial waste. Faulty electrical wiring can cause high EMF readings, which in turn can cause paranoia in sensitive people. Mold and plumbing problems like malfunctioning hidden drains can contribute to the accumulation of sewer gas, which can definitely affect the client's behavior.

Getting Fully Briefed

If anything looks as if it is going to cause a problem for the team, make a note of it and/or take a picture of it. This way the team can be fully briefed about any potentially dangerous areas or situations before they get to the site. They should also be alerted if a spot will be virtually impossible to investigate due to high EMF readings or other natural barriers or obstacles.

The walk-through before the investigation is another opportunity to get important information from the client. The client should point out areas of particular concern, or areas where something unusual has been seen, heard, or smelled. Sometimes people remember facts or concerns they forgot to mention initially, and walking around the property jogs their memory.

Equipment Check and Deployment

Ideally, there should be one person in charge of the equipment. In most professional organizations there is an equipment manager who charges and tests the batteries, checks out and packs up the equipment before the investigation, deploys the equipment on-site, and breaks everything down and packs up neatly and safely at the end of the night for the return trip to headquarters. Investigators are so exhausted at the end of a hunt that it is always tempting to cut corners when packing the equipment away. It is a big responsibility to be in charge of a lot of expensive gear, so it is hard to understand why anyone would want to play that role. Fortunately, there is usually someone in the group who volunteers to step up and do the job.

Smaller Groups

Some amateur groups do not have a lot of equipment, and the equipment they do have is owned by the individual team members. In these cases, everyone is in charge of their own equipment.

The equipment manager should also be in charge of evaluating how much equipment to bring along on the investigation. Bringing too much stuff increases set-up time and is also harder to monitor. Each case requires different equipment and a different setup. The theory is, the more gear at

Photo copyright Kathy Conder, 2005.

A full-body apparition caught on film by Kathy Conder at a small family graveyard in Rhode Island.

the investigation, the more likely it is to capture evidence. However, don't bring superfluous equipment.

Small homes require a very streamlined approach. Remember, if five cameras are running, there will be five hours of tape to review for each hour of the investigation. Novice investigators may have less equipment, but they also have a shorter set-up and break-down time. Luggage with wheels is great for hauling equipment into and out of the site, and it is also a great solution for transport and storage problems.

Organizing the Team

The start-up investigator may decide to ask a few like-minded friends to form a paranormal group. It is helpful to set a few rules and create a system for doing investigations early on. Things run more smoothly if everyone in the group understands the basic theories behind paranormal anomalies and has done some of the recommended readings from Appendix D.

Usually, the group breaks down into teams of two and they disperse to various areas that need to be investigated. It is nice to pair people whose investigative styles are similar and whose skills complement one another. This sort of partnership is optimal, and a great deal more can be accomplished if the investigators' personalities mesh well. Nothing is worse than pairing people who get on each other's nerves or bicker about procedures. Team leaders who have to deal with this sort of thing grow very frustrated in dealing with human issues rather than paranormal ones. The energy the investigators bring to a case can affect the outcome and radically change the course of the case, so take care to choose members who are mature enough to put ego aside and work well with others.

Joining a Group

If you are not starting from scratch or would like to join an established group, start your search on the Internet. You can do a search using the name of your town or area and the words *ghost hunters*. You may find that there is an established group not too far away. Joining an established group is really the best way to get the proper training and learn the many skills you will need as a paranormal investigator.

Recording Data and Observations Manually

Keeping track of data is important, and data logs play a vital role in an investigation. The team leader understands this; in an efficiently run organization, so do the other members of the team.

If there is a member who is consistently keeping poor records or isn't turning in records at all, their contribution to the team is going to be compromised. New members should undergo comprehensive training and a probationary period during which they learn the technological side of ghost hunting; keeping track of data and other records should be included in this period.

Modern ghost hunters adhere to the scientific method, so learning correct methodology is critical. Here is the correct record-keeping methodology in a nutshell:

- Take baseline readings.
- Record the date, time, and place.
- Note the site location, client name, and client contact information.
- Record the environmental conditions such as moon phase, outside temperature, inside temperature, humidity, wind speed, weather, and barometric pressure.
- Record initial impressions and comments.
- Use an equipment list.
- List investigators involved.
- Record client data and interviews.

Juggling the Equipment

With a K2 meter in one hand, an audio recorder in the other, and a camera around your neck, it may be a struggle to scribble your notes during the investigation. Lots of investigators jot down as much info as they can initially and then take a break every fifteen to thirty minutes to record what has happened in the interim. You can also hang a small digital audio recorder from a cord around your neck to free up your hands. Most have a simple switch that can turn on the recorder, allowing quick dictation about the conditions, equipment readings, and impressions of the location. Sometimes, investigators actually capture EVPs during this process—talk about multitasking!

Debunking and Natural Explanations

The merits of experiential investigations versus pseudo-scientific ones are hotly debated today in paranormal research. For a while, the experiential, old-school type of investigation was viewed as totally passé. Perhaps it was the influence of shows like *Ghost Hunters*, but it seemed that the field became dominated by the scientific approach, where the main thrust of the investigation is to debunk the haunting through the use of scientific equipment.

The main thrust of the old-school investigation was to prove that something was out there, then to try to find evidence to support it. Secondarily, the goal was to calm the disturbance caused by the paranormal events and to help the client achieve peace of mind. Another objective was to help the entity successfully cross over to the other side.

Noting hot spots and anomalous readings is important. If you get high EMF readings outdoors, you must determine whether there is a naturally occurring explanation for the spike. What gives off sufficient energy to produce this electrical response? If you are not near a power line, car battery, or radio, an EMF spike could be an indicator of paranormal activity. In actuality, almost anything can give off an electromagnetic charge. Surprisingly, even static electricity can sometimes explain such readings if conditions are right. This is where the importance of good recordkeeping comes in. Under certain weather conditions, such as when it is dry (less than 60 percent humidity) and cold, the likelihood of static electricity being an explanation for odd readings should certainly be considered.

EVP Debunkers

EVPs are particularly susceptible to skepticism. Critics say they could be background noise or even random radio signals. Believers counter that background noises and radio waves might account for some instances, but you certainly can't explain some of the most famous EVPs in this fashion, especially when they are too long or when they pick up a recognizable and interactive voice.

Researcher Alexander MacRae designed an experimentation chamber that was both soundproof and surrounded by a Faraday cage, which blocked out electromagnetic signals so that no radio waves could get in. He still managed to record EVPs. More about MacRae's experiments can be found in

"Report of an Electronic Voice Phenomenon Experiment inside a Double-Screened Room" in the *Journal of the Society for Psychical Research.*

A Faraday cage is a space whose perimeter is made of materials that are good at conducting electrical charges. This wall of conductors effectively blocks out external static electrical fields and forms a shield from electromagnetic radiation for anything placed inside the cage.

Parapsychology and Methodology

The application of scientific methodology to psychic phenomena is the approach used by parapsychologists. Of course, this approach sometimes annoys not only the skeptics, but also those who are already convinced of the veracity of supernatural phenomena. The skeptics call it pseudo-science and those already convinced wonder why time is being wasted trying to prove phenomena they have already accepted into their worldview.

Paranormal investigators who follow a scientific methodology seem quite satisfied to keep a foot in both worlds. They feel that in the end, they are doing a real service to believers in the paranormal. They are seeking irrefutable evidence of ghosts, hauntings, and other related events.

Although skeptics loudly proclaim that there is no evidence that any paranormal phenomena is real, there actually is plenty of statistically significant evidence that has been gathered to support the assertion that remote viewing, precognition, and telepathy all exist.

Investigators are invited to ask themselves what an EVP is. Voice recognition software may be able to give us an answer. It can scan files and label sections of a file that fall within the range of the decibels and harmonics produced by the human voice. Voice recognition software also recognizes patterns and will mark them for review. This could be quite handy when reviewing long hours of audio recordings. If the decibel range of a voice at one meter is 40 to 60 decibels and your software identifies an EVP with the proper harmonics within that range, you have probably caught an EVP.

Jeff Barnes recommends a standardized procedure in which the team records the positive element—the voice of the researcher—and the negative element—white noise in the empty room—then compares where the alleged EVP falls in the spectrum between the two. This produces quantifiable data that stands up to analysis and contains within it measurements that can be compared to other data as hard evidence.

Evidence standards for evaluation of the data should contain unfiltered, unedited raw audio files; a negative, white noise sample for background noise; and a positive sample of a voice, preferably that of the investigator, for comparison. These recordings should ideally be made in the room in which the alleged EVP occurred.

In the theory of quantum physics, the universe keeps splitting into separate branches, only one of which corresponds to our perception of reality. If this is true, perhaps other realities can leak into our own or our consciousness may briefly resonate with another reality in a way that affects our perceptions.

Photo analysis of orb phenomena is also an area that is often easily debunked. We now know that digital flash often produces orbs, through reflections off dust or water particles in the air. Turn off the flash and shoot without it or use an external flash to produce images that are not so easily dismissed or debunked.

CHAPTER 13

Ghost Tracking 101

One of the most exciting developments in the field of psychic exploration is the use of technology to capture unexplained human voices or sounds—electronic voice phenomena, or EVP. Other ways of discerning the presence of the paranormal have also gotten a real boost with the latest digital technology and photography. Exciting images and sounds are now being captured, perhaps more than at any other time in history.

Electronic Voice Phenomena

EVPs were first discovered quite by accident by Friedrich Jürgenson as he was recording bird calls near his home in Sweden during the 1950s. He was flabbergasted when he heard a man's voice telling him how to better record the bird songs. Totally intrigued, Jürgenson continued his recordings for many years after that and subsequently published a book, *Voices From the Universe*, that described his method of electronic communication with the dead.

Some claim the discovery of EVPs goes much further back than that. Thomas Edison, the inventor of the telephone, was quoted in the publication *Scientific American* in the 1920s as saying: "Nobody knows whether our personalities pass on to another existence or sphere, but it is possible to construct an apparatus which will be so delicate that if there are personalities in another existence or sphere who wish to get in touch with us in this existence or sphere, this apparatus will at least give them a better opportunity to express themselves than the tilting tables and raps and Ouija boards and mediums and the other crude methods now purported to be the only means of communication."

E-QUESTION

What is "table tipping"?
During the nineteenth-century spiritualist movement, table tipping became a popular parlor game. A group of spiritualists sat around a table with each person resting his hands flat on the surface. After calling on a spirit, the table would vibrate, begin to move, and even levitate.

Recording EVPs

Anyone can try to capture EVPs. It can be done with either analog or digital recorders, though the analog method will probably be phased out very shortly because of the superior quality of digital voice recorders and the ease of transferring files to a computer. Some investigators recommend performing the experiments outside your own home; after all, if something

disturbing is discovered, it may upset you and change how you feel about your personal living space.

Follow these steps to record an EVP:

1. Prepare the equipment and check to see that the batteries are charged and everything is in good working order.
2. Tune an AM or FM radio to the space between channels to generate white noise. Running water and computer programs that generate background noise will also work.
3. State the date, the time, your name, and where you are at the beginning of the session.
4. Ask a question, and wait about thirty seconds for a response, letting the white noise run softly in the background.
5. Ask as many questions as you like, but remember that you have to review the recording. Keep your sessions short at first; thirty minutes will suffice.
6. Be polite. There is no need to provoke anyone out there.
7. Transfer your recording onto the hard drive of your computer and play it back. Audio programs can be used to clean up the files and boost the sound.

Unique Characteristics

How do you know the EVPs you capture are authentic? After all, they are often garbled, full of static, or very nearly inaudible. There have been a staggering number of EVPs gathered in the last sixty years, and some of them have been clear enough for friends and family to recognize the voices as those of their dearly departed.

One of the most interesting aspects of watching the TV series *Ghost Hunters International* is noting that the EVPs gathered in different regions of Europe not only speak with accents that are appropriate to the country, but in some instances the voices on these EVPs have spoken in ancient forms of German or Italian. They often answer questions put to them in an archaic language no longer in use today but totally pertinent to the site being investigated.

Capturing Elusive Images

Images can be captured with digital cameras and thermal cameras. But be sure you know how to interpret images correctly to avoid confusion.

Digital Cameras

Now that almost everyone in the world owns a digital camera, we are bound to see an upsurge in ghostly images, real or imagined. The furor over orbs in the first few years of digital shooting put many investigators off them forever, but if you are serious about attempting to capture paranormal images, your patience may just pay off. New model digital cameras do not suffer from the same technical issues that plagued the early models and caused every speck of dust to look like an orb.

In the book *Ghosts Caught on Film: Photographs of the Paranormal?* by Dr. Melvyn Willin, he suggests that every psychical researcher should ask themselves a series of questions when viewing ghost photos:

- First, is the photo a deliberate fake or fraud? Could the photographer have used props to achieve the image?
- Could anything have happened during the photographic process that might have inadvertently caused this image?
- Did the photographer simply not notice people in the vicinity at the time the shutter was clicked?
- Could some accidental factor have caused the anomaly, such as a light leak or lens flare?
- Does the picture show an anomalous effect that may actually be a natural occurrence? Or does the photo show a paranormal effect that is outside of nature?
- Have you done an objective evaluation, or have you reached conclusions that only serve to reinforce your own beliefs and worldview?

This list of questions, when answered honestly, can really help the serious investigator do a proper evaluation, not only of the images they have captured, but also of the proliferation of anomalous images on the Internet.

Willin's book has a nice selection of black-and-white and color photos, some of which date back more than a hundred years. They are presented as full-page pictures in good quality reproductions. On the page facing them, the author gives the history of the photo and background information, then beneath that, his analysis of the image, including observations of anything suspicious. He does not reach any definitive conclusions, allowing readers to analyze it and make up their own minds.

It is interesting to note that the book also contains frames pulled from video surveillance cameras, like that of the apparition at Hampton Court Palace. In one outtake from a surveillance video, a chillingly pale skeletal figure in cloak and hood strides up to a double doorway, setting off alarms. As amazing as the still photo is, the video is even more so. It can be viewed online at YouTube (*www.youtube.com*); search for the "Hampton Court Ghost" and you'll get several versions of the surveillance tape.

The best approach when trying to capture photographic evidence is to keep shooting. Whenever possible, use the room's own available light and turn off the flash. Then, if the image of an orb is captured, no one can protest that it was the flash bouncing off a dust particle or an insect.

Thermal Imaging Cameras

Thermal imaging cameras are proving to be a very interesting resource for investigators. These cameras, which measure heat signatures, can be used to record interviews as well as the actual course of the investigation.

In an interview with medium/sensitive Carroll Heath, TAPS captured an image that Grant Wilson described as "psychedelic." As Mr. Heath did a reading for Jason Hawes, colors arose from Jason's head area and seemed to reach toward Mr. Heath. When Heath gestured with his hand, the strange colors dispersed. Although TAPS does not usually employ mediums, they allowed Mr. Heath to participate in the investigation because they were in his home.

In another instance of thermal imagery, Jason and Grant captured a full-body apparition standing a few feet away from them in a sanatorium. The apparition was invisible to the naked eye yet showed very clearly in the view screen of the thermal imager.

Investigator's Checklist

Kym Black, a sensitive who works with the Rhode Island Paranormal Research Group, notes that before an investigation starts, the investigators run through a mental checklist of dos and don'ts:

- **Tie back long hair.** Hair that is not tied back can move in front of the lens and produce what appears to be an anomaly. In these shots, the hair strands can actually look like a ghostly blur. Light hair is particularly troublesome; it doesn't block the light as much and the flash burns out all detail. The same is true of wrist straps on cameras. Part of the strap can whip in front of the lens and inexperienced photographers/investigators think they have captured a great paranormal shot.
- **No smoking.** Obviously, smoking on an investigation can make analyzing evidence of ghostly fogs very tricky.
- **Double-check all equipment beforehand to be sure it is working properly.** Batteries in cameras, flashlights, DVRs, and scanners should be fully charged. Keep replacements on hand. Also make sure you have gloves, boots, odor-free insect repellent, an analog wristwatch, and a notebook and pencil.
- **Make sure you have all safety equipment.** Check for your walkie-talkies and/or cell phones, a first aid kit, and perhaps most importantly, an alternative light source such as a kerosene lantern or candles and matches.

The psychological preparation of each investigator should also be taken into account. In the case of regular investigators, this may be a simple prayer for protection or a ritual such as carrying a protective medal or amulet. For some, it is as simple as mentally invoking the powers of light and keeping a positive mindset.

Before she begins an investigation, Black asks her spirit guardian/guide Amalda to assist in the investigation and help protect her from harm. Black also dons her psychic armor after picturing her entire body being cleansed by white light. She mentally hangs mirrors all over her armor, believing that negative entities recoil when they see their true appearance.

Honing Your Skills

Black is a natural psychic who says she learns by experience every time she does an investigation. She also has done extensive reading on the topics pertinent to the paranormal, letting her own interest in the topic guide her reading. Maggie Florio is a largely self-educated psychic, but she has also taken classes in psychic development. She too feels that there is nothing as helpful in developing one's abilities as on-the-job training. New members go through a probationary period during which they learn the basics, which will get them through an average investigation.

One of the most basic skills anyone on a case can learn is grace under fire. Sometimes the atmosphere on a case is so highly charged with negativity and fear that it is uncomfortable for even seasoned investigators to stay near it and persevere. The ability to master one's own fears is the mark of an experienced investigator. However, sometimes it is totally appropriate—even necessary—to get out.

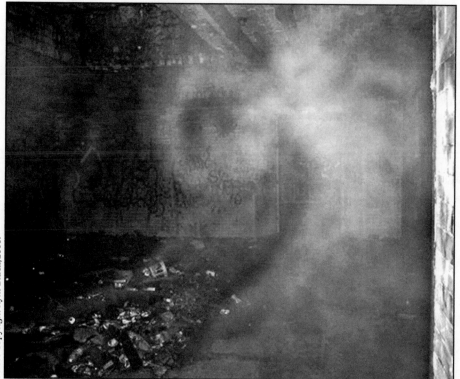

Photo copyright Kym Black, 2006.

A photo taken by paranormal investigator Kym Black during an investigation at Fort Wetherill, in Jamestown, Rhode Island.

Sensitives who have been investigators for a while will sometimes have the sense that if they take a photo or do EVP work at a particular moment they will capture something. Usually, they are right. Reviewing data is a skill that must be honed. Spotting faint EVPs is definitely a learned skill; some investigators like Maggie Florio excel at it. Fortunately for paranormal investigators, technology is more of a help than ever, especially in the area of temperature log analyses. Of particular interest are video analyzers and the new USB temperature and humidity data loggers. Researchers of the future may not have to endure hours of tedium, which is currently just the norm.

Note Taking and Observations

A little-talked-about but important aspect of investigating is the practice of keeping a log during the investigation. These go by different names, such as paranormal investigation log, paranormal investigator's logbook, and paranormal vigil log. These notebooks help keep track of important investigation data and serve as reference points if anything anomalous happens. They also contain the investigators' record of the equipment used and readings from that equipment. A good logbook should have space to record:

1. Weather conditions, temperature, barometric pressure
2. EMF field activity
3. The moon phase
4. Sunspot activity
5. Equipment checklist to help remind you to take all necessary items
6. Equipment used on specific investigations, plus baseline readings
7. Space for documentation of remarkable investigative events
8. Space for documentation of anomalous personal experiences

There should also be a page for personal contact information including emergency contact information, medications, and medical information.

Free Download

The website *www.zdnet.com* has free software called Ghost-Tech Paranormal Investigator that can be downloaded. It is a fairly large Zip file, but it can be downloaded and installed in about five minutes if you have a fast Internet connection.

On the software's home page, you will see a full page with a place for the site location information, the client's personal contact information, a background summary, occupant history, a place for a photo of the location, and a place for special notes. The second page has a place for the date and time, outside temperature, inside temperature, humidity, moon phase, wind speed, weather, and barometer reading. Below that there's space for an equipment list, a record of investigators involved, a media archive, and investigation notes. The third page is for interviews. There is also a place to add more photos of the investigation.

Even the simplest logs should contain a column where the investigators' own impressions, perceptions, and any potential paranormal incidents are noted. If an investigator's hair is pulled, if she smells roses, or if she receives the impression of a voice or sees an apparition, it must be duly noted on this paper so it can be used to correlate data between investigators and locations.

Matrixing Anomalies

Matrixing and *pareidolia* are both terms used for the same sort of perceptual legerdemain, in which random images are perceived as having significance. What is matrixing? No, it isn't a movie starring Keanu Reeves. Matrixing is the human mind's ability to take random sensory data and rearrange it so that it forms an image or sound that is recognizable and familiar to it. It is what we do when we gaze up at clouds in the sky and find a resemblance in them to a face, an animal, or any other familiar image. Artistic people seem to be much better able to come up with images and resemblances, usually faces.

Paranormal investigators must be careful not to fall victim to matrixing anomalies. The images or sounds they see and record must be analyzed objectively, as the human mind always wants to make order out of chaos. One example of this is in photography, particularly digital photography, where images can be manipulated and tweaked to bring out subtle detail.

This ability is a blessing and a curse. Sometimes it makes us see things that really aren't there, and that is a problem when conducting a paranormal investigation. When we see the image of a face leering out from the wallpaper, sometimes it is merely a chance resemblance, with no basis or relationship to the perceived image. These images are called matrixing anomalies.

In this photo of a tree taken outside an old church in Middletown, Rhode Island, you can see what appears to be the head of an old man in the tree near the ground. The man's face is pretty clearly defined; it even bears a resemblance to nineteenth-century naturalist Charles Darwin. Once this observation has been made, the image to the left of Darwin takes on new meaning—it appears to be the face of an ape or a monkey, holding up a hand as if to say "Stop!" Since Darwin postulated the theory of evolution, this is quite amusing.

Upon returning to take more pictures of the tree, no such matrixing effect was ever captured again, though repeated attempts were made to duplicate the shot in all seasons and lighting conditions. There is some question as to whether this supports or undercuts the matrixing theory of this photo.

Matrixing or the spirit of Charles Darwin having a bit of fun? You be the judge.

Photo copyright Melissa Martin Ellis, 2003.

This natural tendency for the human mind to interpret sensory input—what is perceived visually and audibly as something recognizable—is just a mental filling in of the blanks. Usually, matrixing is useful. It allows us to interpret data quickly and organize it into coherent messages. It also lets us distinguish subtle nuances in similar patterns.

We've all heard of the cinnamon bun that looks like Mother Teresa or the water stain on a wall that resembles Jesus. Everyone has seen cloud formations that appear to be animals or faces. Finding meaning in random images is not at all unusual and is harmless enough, except when it misleads paranormal investigators.

The biggest problem for paranormal researchers concerns matrixing anomalies that happen during the evidence reviews, when someone spots an image or sound that appears to indicate paranormal activity. Careful review by several individuals is sometimes necessary to disprove that the image is of supernatural origin. Remember, whenever a natural explanation for a phenomenon is found, the paranormal explanation is thrown out.

Grant Wilson of TAPS has spoken and written about this topic, and the gist of what he is saying boils down to some very useful guidelines investigators should keep in mind:

1. **Is the photo you're analyzing mostly trees, fields, and cluttered areas, or reflective surfaces, such as mirrors and glass?** If the image is made up of complex shapes and patterns, there is plenty of raw material for the mind to use in fabricating images, such as a face or silhouette.

2. **Zero in on the face or figure.** Is it made up of its own unique material or of the components of the picture? If it is truly paranormal, the face or figure should be made up of its own separate materials, not the material that comprises the rest of the image. Take the example of a face in the forest. If it is made up of branches and leaves, it is matrixing. If not, you may have something truly paranormal.

3. **If you are satisfied that the two previous criteria have been met, closely examine the anomaly.** If it is a face or figure, are the proportions correct or are they disproportionate? If the proportions are distorted, that is a problem. The image you have found is probably naturally occurring.

Pareidolia can occur with EVP work as well. As soon as a sound is iden-tified as being anomalous, it must be played over and over again until the listener is eventually able to discern what is being said. If you have to listen to a sound clip dozens of times, artificially boost it a great deal, or play it backward, you are probably dealing with a naturally occurring sound.

CHAPTER 14

I Put a Spell on You

Anyone can experience psychic attack. Mediums and sensitives are often the targets for this sort of attack because they are such open channels for energy and they often find themselves in circumstances involving disturbing phenomena. If they are wise, they learn to take psychic countermeasures to stop these threats, which can take the form of any number of terrifying visions and feelings.

Psychic Attack

Nelia Petit, a psychic, medium, and paranormal investigator, has been the target of psychic attacks many times in the course of her work and has helped people escape supernatural oppression. Petit has a spirit guide who shields her from the worst aspects of the attacks, but she is still vulnerable. She has seen horrible visions of her dogs and even her mother lying slaughtered in her home. Petit usually ignores such things but also finds that anger is a helpful response. It seems to drive the entity and its negative influence away. Once she even heard an entity whisper, "I think I'll go for a little ride, I'll be back." She resisted the urge to pick up the phone and call her husband, John. She didn't want the entity to know that it had successfully pushed her buttons with its implied threat.

Petit has been plagued by a shadowy figure who lingers outside her door. She claims that after weeks of harassment, she decided to go into a trance to confront the entity. Petit grappled with the figure and dragged him toward the light, where someone helped her by pulling the entity through and into the light. Because the transition has to be voluntary, this being was able to escape and has returned to continue harassing her.

In her experience, Petit believes that psychics are vulnerable to attack and can even be physically hurt when they attract the attention of entities on the other side, both good and bad. All psychics agree that allowing yourself to be intimidated is the worst possible response, as fear opens a point of vulnerability that can be further exploited. Once the primal emotion of fear is triggered, the entity has a handle it can use to do further damage.

As in other areas of paranormal investigation, rule out the natural explanations before jumping to the conclusion that you are under attack. A tummy ache or a creepy feeling aren't necessarily paranormal. Warning signs of a psychic attack include:

- **Tiredness and fatigue.** In this frequent form of psychic attack, energy is drained from the victim. He may even have a strange sense of detachment, as if the things that are happening around him are unreal. Feeling drained and exhausted without good reason is an indication that something strange may be going on, and a psychic attack may be occurring.

- **Physical ailments.** Headache, stomach ailments, and unexplained pains may be symptoms of psychic attack. If a person, place, or thing consistently causes a negative physical reaction, consider the possibility that a supernatural situation may be the cause.
- **Persistent or recurring bad dreams.** If you have never been prone to nightmares and suddenly you dream of being hunted or oppressed, you might be experiencing psychic attacks in your dreams.
- **Physical sensations.** Strange physical sensations in the solar plexus may be a sign that someone or something is interfering with your energy field. The warning signs start as a tightening in the abdomen. Shaking or trembling, coldness in the extremities, and an unbearably anxious feeling of panic may also be signs of psychic attack.

Largely unknown to the public before the premiere of the 1973 film *The Exorcist*, possession cases have been around for millennia. Although there are many recorded instances of benevolent possession, most of the cases that require treatment by an exorcist are of an extremely harmful and alarming nature. There is a rumor that cases of possession are on the rise globally in the new millennium. Some psychologists attribute this to the stress of modern life and drug use; others point to increased diagnoses of disassociative disorders.

It seems inevitable that many so-called cases of demonic possession are in actuality merely graphic examples of autosuggestion or hysteria. This is where today's ghost hunters must exhibit their expertise. If someone is behaving very oddly, it must first be determined if it is a case of possession or mental illness. Only after all the logical explanations are dismissed can the occasional valid case of possession be identified.

Demons

In demonic situations, horrific damage may have been inflicted by the entities. In these cases of possession, the psychological trauma can be extremely devastating to the victims, their families, and the exorcists involved. Fortunately, the victim often experiences amnesia regarding the most horrific aspects of the incident. The rest of the trauma associated with the case may then gradually fade away over time.

Ghouls

Ghouls are entities that do damage of a different sort. They induce feelings of icy coldness, disorientation, and despair. These attacks eat away at the confidence of their victims until they are so demoralized and frightened that they plunge into a state of deep depression. Although ghosts may be seen, ghouls never manifest, except as a horrible feeling of evil and despair. This entity's influence has been known to drive people to thoughts of suicide. Oddly, the ghoul seems best able to cast its ghastly influence during warm and muggy weather and seems anchored to specific locations, lingering like a bad smell. The area of its influence can be so clearly defined that one can step in and out of its range within a few steps.

ALERT!

The observed effect of paranormal entities seems to increase in close proximity to water. There are different theories about why this is true, but it has been observed repeatedly. Haunted sites are often near running streams.

Physical Attack

As if psychic attack isn't bad enough, investigators can also find themselves being physically attacked. Nelia Petit, Kym Black, and Andrew Laird all recount tales of coming to physical harm when on an investigation. In the most common type of attack, the person is shoved or thrown against a wall. Black fell victim to an angry spirit in the Paine House who called her a witch and threw her against a wall, knocking her out. Petit has been thrown to the floor, hurled against a wall, and pushed down a flight of steps.

Laird tells of being on an investigation at the Rhode Island Training School when he apparently angered an entity. The 275-pound, 6-foot-5-inch man was picked up and tossed against a wall as if he were a lightweight before being repeatedly hit and punched. He wanted to go to an emergency room but couldn't figure out an explanation for his injuries. As he said, "What are we supposed to tell the doctor? 'We just got our butts kicked by Casper?'"

Amazingly, in none of these cases were any bones broken or any permanent damage done. Petit believes the dark spirits have limits placed on how far they can go when attacking, and the extent of the damage is limited to bumps and bruises.

ALERT!

You can take steps to protect yourself. Petit recommends protecting yourself with the white light of God or the Goddess. Black bathes in white light and dons her psychic armor, replete with mirrors, in a meditation she performs before an investigation.

Sometimes the attacks are not as violent and manifest as dizziness, disorientation, the feeling of bugs crawling over the skin, or a tingling sensation. These weird sensations may also mean a spirit is trying to make contact in the only way it can.

Poltergeists rarely cause accidents that result in serious injury. Though observers may be struck by flying objects and subjected to glancing blows, people are almost never seriously injured. The exception that proves the rule is that rare case that gets all the publicity. These same rules seem to hold true for hauntings, where occasionally the investigators may get punched, clawed, or shoved by an angry entity. In cases of possession requiring an exorcist, claw marks and grotesque swelling may appear, virtually disfiguring the unfortunate victim. If the exorcism is successfully completed, these injuries heal quickly and are soon hardly noticeable. Interestingly, even the fires associated with poltergeist activity are usually quickly discovered and put out.

Client Problems

Although the field of paranormal investigation is made up largely of people volunteering their time and services for free, clients are not always grateful and appreciative of their efforts. In some cases, they can be more troublesome than the paranormal.

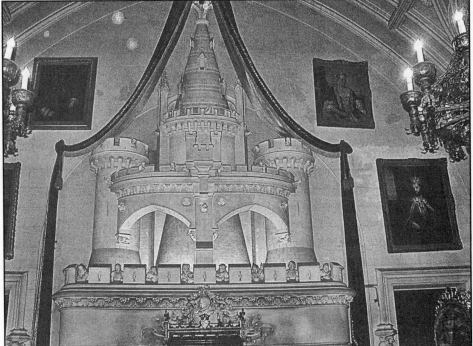

Although the beautiful dining hall at Belcourt Castle has a reputation for being haunted, it was still a surprise to find orbs in this photo.

Photo copyright Melissa Martin Ellis, 2004.

In one instance, a sound engineer participated in a séance at Belcourt Castle in Newport, Rhode Island. The mansion is said to be haunted by a monk who lingers near the chapel and a suit of armor from which weird screams occasionally erupt. There are also forces guarding two antique chairs rumored to be strong enough to throw off anyone who dares sit in them.

The sound engineer reported that the energies in the gothic ballroom during the séance were incredibly violent and his sound equipment picked up the howling and moaning sounds. He found himself wishing that the spirits who were trapped there would just go into the light, and he urged them to do so. Afterward, he learned that the sensitive who conducted ghost tours there had complained that he had affected her bread and butter—all the ghosts were gone. He retorted that she didn't have the right to run a paranormal petting zoo. He has sworn off any sort of paranormal investigation; for weeks after the Belcourt Castle incident he suffered from a lingering malaise.

Equipment Failure

One universal phenomenon observed by ghost hunters is the weird behavior of technology in the presence of the paranormal. Batteries drain and go dead. Audio recorders fail and equipment malfunctions. In a practical sense, this means backup batteries and equipment are always needed to ensure that the phenomena that causes the equipment to fail can be recorded in some way.

If we accept at face value the statement that paranormal activity causes equipment failure, we then have to come up with a hypothesis as to what is actually going on. It also means that you should always bring along some sort of nontechnological means of seeing in the dark, even if it is something as low-tech as matches and candles.

There have been countless reports of appliances, televisions, and computers being turned on by unseen hands, sometimes even when they are unplugged. But sometimes there is a simple explanation for this, as walkie-talkies have been known to act like remote controls and turn on televisions.

Grant Wilson from TAPS explained his theory about all this in one episode of *Ghost Hunters*. When the paranormal activity at a site is really hot, the entities who are trying to manifest will draw energy from the air around them, causing sudden temperature drops or drained batteries. Sometimes the people in the vicinity will also be overcome with great fatigue and tiredness, as if something is draining them.

Another theory goes that increased electromagnetic field activity and positive ionization (static electricity) are present at most active paranormal sites. Most of today's digital devices use nickel-cadmium rechargeable batteries, and the battery manufacturers warn that these batteries are extremely susceptible to both electromagnetic fields and static electricity.

Occasionally, there have also been odd reports of batteries operating for far longer than they should or even cases of electrical meters running backward. These may be instances of entities trying to give energy back rather than take it.

It isn't only battery drain that stops investigators' work. Occasionally, cameras will work, but a strange blurry effect makes all the images look surreal. This is puzzling to experience, especially to seasoned photographers who know what to expect from their cameras under all sorts of lighting conditions.

Jinxes and Hexes

It was once considered a totally radical idea that a consciousness in nature could interact with human consciousness. These days, there are many people who believe this is happening on a daily basis.

Jinxed

We usually associate jinxes as curses placed on an individual by another person, but nature spirits and elementals can bring curses or jinxes down on people, too. In Laurens van der Post's book, *The Lost World of the Kalahari*, the author tells the tale of a jinx being placed on his expedition after they broke a native taboo as they traveled across the countryside toward the Slippery Hills in Africa. They were repeatedly attacked by bees and plagued by inexplicable equipment failures. In general, they had nothing but bad luck from the moment they broke the taboo. When they finally accepted that they had violated a strict taboo, they propitiated the spirits of the Slippery Hills and the expedition proceeded without further incident.

In the literature of the supernatural, there are more stories about cursed objects than about cursed people. It only becomes apparent that an object is cursed after it has passed through the hands of several owners, consistently bringing misfortune and injury to them.

ALERT!

In Hawaii, the goddess of the volcano curses those who remove lava rocks. In Europe, there are cursed castles and moors, and in Ireland there are places called raths and fairy rings where the locals will not build for fear of their lives.

Details of how or why objects carry negative energy vary according to location and time period. One single theme seems to apply in most instances, though. A traumatic event imprints itself so thoroughly on the object or surroundings that its negativity becomes permanently associated with it.

James Dean's Cursed Porsche

After James Dean died in a car crash in 1955, the Porsche he had been driving was sold to a garage owner. It slipped as it was being unloaded and a mechanic standing nearby suffered two broken legs. The car was chopped up for parts and the engine from the Porsche was sold to a doctor who was into racing. Subsequently, the car he had put the engine into went out of control, killing him and seriously injuring the driver of another car in the race, which just happened to have the drive shaft from Dean's car in it.

The Porsche's battered body was sold to be used in a movable display for Highway Safety, and it fell off its mounting brackets and broke a teenager's hip in Sacramento. Weeks later, a transport truck carrying Dean's car was in an accident. The transport's driver was killed when he was crushed by the car, which came loose and rolled over him. A racecar driver who bought the car's heavy-duty tires was nearly killed when all the tires blew out simultaneously for no apparent reason.

In Oregon, a truck carrying the car slipped its handbrake and crashed into a store. On display in New Orleans, it mysteriously broke into eleven pieces. Perhaps everyone breathed a sigh of relief when the car mysteriously disappeared while being transported by train back to Los Angeles.

CHAPTER 15

Spirit Help and Psychic Shields

Astral traveler Oliver Fox, the author of *Astral Projection, a Record of Out-of-the-Body Experiences*, describes a veritable monster he encountered while astral traveling: "I then caught sight of a hideous monster, a vague, white, filmy, frothy formless thing, spreading out in queer patches and snake-like protuberances. It had two enormous round eyes, like globes filled with pale blue fire." With beings like that out there, ghost hunters had better know how to protect themselves.

When the Hunter Becomes the Hunted

Psychics, sensitives, and ghost hunters have existed for hundreds of years in cultures all over the world, so the practices employed to protect them vary according to culture and era. Even some of today's scientific ghost hunters say a prayer of protection before beginning the hunt.

In *Journeys Out of the Body*, Robert Monroe describes his personal experiences of a psychic assault while astral traveling. He describes "rubbery entities" that kept attacking him and attempting to climb onto his back. Eventually, a man in a monk's robe came out and pulled the creatures away, to Monroe's great relief.

Are these non-physical beings ghosts, demons, spirits, or elementals? What do they gain by attacking or preying on humans and what form do these attacks take? The creatures that prey on living humans are characterized differently, but whether these entities are demons or simply the souls of terribly wicked humans, the net effect is the same. Astral traveling is not for the faint-hearted and should not be attempted by people merely wishing to experiment with the paranormal for fun.

FACT

Many paranormal investigators say a simple prayer of protection before starting the night's activities. They ask for protection from anything that might harm them during the hunt and from entities that might become attached to them and decide to follow them home.

People who are interested in the occult must remember at all times that the astral world is filled with all sorts of energies and entities. Just as there are good and bad people, there are good and bad spirits that inhabit the other side. Investigating the occult can be likened to opening a door or leaving your doors and windows open to intruders. Unless you take steps to lock the doors and windows you have opened, you may find yourself playing host to unwanted intruders. This has happened over and over again and is mentioned repeatedly in most literature that deals with the paranormal.

Only very foolish or immature people dabble in the occult without proper preparation and precautions. The classic case is when parents buy a Ouija board for their children to play with, as if it is a game of Monopoly. When problems arise from the opening of a conduit, it sometimes takes a very long time and a lot of effort to shut down that pipeline. Asking for protection and taking proper precautions should be done before any sort of interaction with the spirit realm; this includes reading tarot cards, dowsing, or any sort of divination.

Protection from Psychic Attack

Theologian Henry James (the father of the novelist of the same name) described a horrible event that occurred in 1844 at his home as he was relaxing before his cozy fireplace after dinner one evening: "Fear came upon me, and trembling, which made all my bones to shake."

He reported later that he felt waves of malevolence radiating out from a shapeless form squatting in one corner of the room. He was overcome with a fear so primal that he was reduced to a total wreck. After this experience, he was plunged into a state of total depression and despair. Several years after this experience, he read the work of Emmanuel Swedenborg and he diagnosed himself as suffering from a state which Swedenborg called "devastation" or "vastation," a collapse of vital energies.

Further Investigation

Author Colin Wilson researched this incident and found that James was residing in Windsor, England, at a place with the charming name of Frogmore Cottage. The cottage was near a ley line that ran from the tower of Windsor Castle south through several churches to an ancient Roman building north of Chidingford.

Prolonged depression and anxiety that arises in those who have been around paranormal activity may be a sign that more is going on than is first understood. A state of depression, sometimes bordering on the suicidal, may be triggered by an encounter with demonic or elemental energies. Advise clients to seek medical or psychological help if they are in danger.

Wilson concluded that because of the cottage's proximity to the ley line, whatever paranormal forces were latent there might have been boosted by it. Indeed, that area has been a paranormal hot spot for centuries.

It is possible, according to sensitives, to be on the lookout for psychic attack. They say warning signs may come in the form of a prolonged spell of depression, anxiety, or anger. If the person experiencing the attack suddenly realizes how uncharacteristic her behavior is, steps can be taken to undo the damage.

Dealing with Oppression

Experienced investigators in the field of the paranormal know what to look for and how to counteract the early signs of psychic trouble. Depression, despair, and persistent anxiety are all signs. An effective way of dealing with the situation of psychic oppression and attack is to first ask themselves what could have triggered the feeling they are having or the streak of very bad luck they are experiencing. If there is no logical, natural explanation, what remains must be paranormal in nature.

Most groups have people they can call on for assistance when this situation occurs. It might be a group member or an expert or demonologist the group uses for consultation. Whoever it is, he will be called in to sort out the situation and send the oppressive presence packing. Usually, things are put back in order very quickly.

Protection from Physical Attack

There are hundreds of stories about ghosts who have attacked investigators and done them injury. If they are doing physical or psychic damage, it makes very little difference if these attacking entities are ghosts, demons, poltergeists, or elementals.

Tales concerning physical attack usually seem to deal with ghost hunters, as in the instance when a TAPS cameraman was knocked to the ground, or another case when Jason Hawes was bitten on the back. People who have dabbled in the supernatural are also vulnerable to attack. Casual bystanders or observers don't usually seem to elicit the same active hostility that investigators experience.

Accounts of people being physically injured by entities aren't common, but they do exist—the entity usually manifests a furious energy that blasts people off their feet, causing them to bounce off walls. Most ghosts, like most people, are not violent or angry. But some are. In most cultures around the world, ghosts are thought to have some ill intent toward the living, which they manifest either through inducing a chilling reaction or by doing some sort of physical harm.

E-QUESTION

Are shadow people demonic or likely to harm people?
No one really knows what shadow people are, and although they are truly creepy and frightening to see, they may be trying to annoy us. There aren't any reports of them trying to actually harm the people who have witnessed their eerie presence.

Indirect Damage and Harm

Just as living with the stress and fear paranormal events can induce takes a physical toll after a while, injuries can also occur reacting to an entity; a trip and fall or taking a tumble down a flight of stairs may be accidental, but the trigger was the paranormal event. Entities have been known to trip or push people. When these attacks occur, serious injury is sometimes only narrowly avoided. It seems the beings adhere to unwritten rules and limits. The exception is when they get a little help from their friends, the demons.

Enter the Demons

Researchers pretty much agree that demonic entities can cause serious harm to humans. Demonic encounters are very, very rare. Most entities encountered are human spirits who have passed over. The overwhelming majority of those spirits are benign and even benevolent. Still, if an individual is exploring high-risk areas or is involved in the practice of dark magic or experimenting with decadent and selfish lifestyles, she may attract the demonic. The best way to stop the attack of elementals and demons is not to draw their attention. If you must, conduct a ritual or procedure to protect yourself before each exposure to the risky situation. This can take many forms, including meditation, saging, amulets, prayers, or whatever is congruent to your own belief system.

Territorial Ghosts

There are, however, those rare cases where a ghost has become overly territorial and decided that it doesn't want anyone living in its place. Entities of this sort do everything in their power to attempt to drive the residents away. There are reports too numerous to list of people being struck by flying objects that were propelled through the air by unseen hands. Usually, these human entities can be coaxed and cajoled into the light, or made to stop their activities through other means, such as rituals that invite them to be at rest and which protect the residents of the house. If a protection ritual fails, then it is time to call in the big guns and ask for outside help. Sensitives often get assistance from their fellow psychics on the investigative team. Kym Black underwent psychic attack and enlisted the aid of fellow T.R.I.P.R.G. members to drive the entity away by using a ritual specially designed to break the tie between the entity and Kym, who bounced back from the oppressive presence within days.

Be respectful when visiting cemeteries to conduct an investigation. Respect the departed, take care not to step on graves or lean on headstones, and speak softly and courteously if you are attempting EVP work. This is just good manners, but it also protects investigators from the wrath of territorial ghosts.

Involving Priests and Clergy

When psychic and physical attacks have gotten out of control, most investigative groups will call in help from specialists—the demonologists, clergy, or shamans who deal with these things on a routine basis. The very idea that evil—in whatever form your religion or culture perceives it—can inhabit humans against our will is a terribly frightening concept. It is an idea so alarming that we usually seek protection from it through the representatives of organized religions, and the one most associated with exorcisms is, of course, the Roman Catholic Church.

E-QUESTION

Do non-Catholic paranormal investigators call in Catholic priests?
They do indeed, but they are just as likely to call in an Episcopal priest or a Jewish rabbi. Even though the Catholic Church has a long history of blessing troubled houses and performing exorcisms, many other churches offer these services as well.

Paranormal investigator and founder of T.R.I.P.R.G. Andrew Laird has a friend who is a Catholic priest. He is available to help T.R.I.P.R.G. if the group encounters anything that even smacks of the demonic. Laird says, "Any priest or ordained Christian minister can be an exorcist, so I am told. I have seen both at work and really there is little difference. With that said, I have been with Father John while he has taken part in exorcisms, but he does not consider himself an exorcist per se but an assistant." The *Daily Mail*, a British newspaper, published an article that said Pope Benedict XVI ordered his bishops to set up exorcism squads to address the rise of Satanism and the increased interest in all things Satanic.

The Congregation for the Doctrine of the Faith has been in existence in some form since 1542. Benedict XVI served as its head from 1982 until 2005, when he became pope.

FACT

Every human culture has some sort of belief in ghosts and every culture also has prayers that are said to protect the living from the anger of the departed. There is a long tradition of belief in tormented spirits and demons in the Catholic Church, and special prayers were once said at the end of every mass as a protection from evil.

Pope John XXIII eliminated one Catholic prayer, addressed to St. Michael the Archangel, from the Mass in the 1960s.

Prayer to St. Michael
Saint Michael the Archangel,
defend us in battle.
Be our protection against the wickedness and snares of the devil.
May God rebuke him, we humbly pray;
and do Thou, O Prince of the Heavenly Host—
by the Divine Power of God—
cast into hell, Satan and all the evil spirits,
who roam throughout the world seeking the ruin of souls.
Amen.

This is a brief version of the original prayer, which was composed by Pope Leo XIII more than 100 years ago. In 1888 Pope Leo XIII collapsed after a morning mass and appeared to be dead. After reviving, he repeated a bizarre conversation he said he had overheard, coming from near the tabernacle. Two voices conversed, voices the Pope alleged were those of Jesus Christ and the Devil. The Devil boasted that he could destroy the Church if he were granted seventy-five years to carry out his plan. He asked permission for "a greater influence over those who will give themselves to my service." In response, Jesus reportedly replied: "You will be given the time and the power."

Pope Leo XIII was so alarmed by what he had heard that he composed the Prayer to St. Michael. He gave a papal order that it was to be recited after all Low Masses.

ALERT!

The invocation of St. Michael the Archangel's name as protection against the dark forces is not uncommon among exorcists of all persuasions. He is viewed as a potent symbol of good and the leader of the armies of powerful angelic forces—a key player in the battle of good versus evil.

Wards and Shields

Simply put, wards and shields are selective energy barriers. They can be made of physical substances or they can be forms of thought, like visualizations, or prayers. Whatever their form, they all serve as a wall behind which the investigator can take shelter to ward off physical or psychic attack.

The process of going through a ritual in order to protect oneself or one's home from harm is extremely ancient. Today's investigators draw from many traditions to design rituals that feel right to them and provide the psychic and spiritual strength they need in times of crisis.

Warding and shielding a home can provide protection from negative energies, and many sensitives and paranormal investigators firmly believe that it is essential to protect their own energy fields and homes from the intrusion of negative forces before going out on an investigation. Even

Photo copyright Kym Black, 2006.

A photo taken by paranormal investigator Kym Black during an investigation at the Sprague Mansion in Cranston, Rhode Island.

Christians often invoke the protection of a divine light, which they visualize as a barrier between them and whatever they may encounter in the course of an investigation. The entities and energies they encounter on investigations may not be inherently evil, but frightened and confused spirits can still cause problems. Like confused people, they can lash out and cause harm to innocent bystanders. After a house has been cleared of whatever entities haunted it, a blessing of the house, which acts as a natural ward, should always take place.

Protecting the Home

Some investigators and sensitives feel it is necessary and prudent to protect their own homes as well as their persons. They develop their own unique systems for this, usually involving the establishment of protective shields and wards. These are highly individualistic and should be crafted to fill the needs of the practitioner.

WARDING RULES

- Warding allows positive energy to be retained; it keeps good energy from escaping but also allows it in.
- Warding blocks negative energy and keeps harmful and disruptive energy at bay.
- Selective wards may block certain energies while permitting others to pass; some energy is even transmuted, according to the needs of the occupants.

This sort of warding requires quite a bit of research and a high degree of sophistication to carry out. Some people are able to fine-tune the porosity of their wards to let only the energy they want into their home environment, almost like a strainer. They keep out unwanted energy, and of course, different people will want to keep out different types of energy.

Visualization

After meditation, visualizing shields around the outside or home can prove very effective. An image of armor plates is a very effective protective visualization; people employ it for protection of their bodies as well as their houses. Mirrors, force fields, and thick stone walls are also effective images. These shields should be recharged periodically to maintain their effectiveness. A bubble of white light around the entire body, rather like the one surrounding Glinda in the *Wizard of Oz*, is one of the most common visualizations.

FACT

Charms and amulets many thousands of years old have been found in tombs in ancient Egypt. They were routinely interred with the dead, hidden in mummy wrappings. It is also believed that the living used them both as protection against evil and as a way of attracting good fortune.

Sigils and Charms

In the field of paranormal investigating, it is not unusual to find people carrying lucky charms and other protective items such as sigils that they feel form an energy barrier and protective shield. Sigils can be etched or engraved on a small object and placed in a central location or etched on some part of the house to be protected. Sigils are encoded with intentions and used primarily for defense and protection. They are drawn on the outer walls of the house or inscribed on four pieces of metal and then placed at the four corners of the site.

Simple charms placed around the house, especially at key points like doors, windows, and corners, can be very effective. Little mirrors placed above doors and windows to deflect incoming negative energy work well, too. Wind chimes and other angelic, dangling, or sparkly items can be hung around the home to keep the energy fresh and positive. This is something akin to the principle of breaking up stagnant chi in Feng Shui. Additionally, plants can act like canaries in a coal mine. They absorb negative energy, so placing them around your home can be an effective way of detecting an influx of negative energy. If they seem ill for no apparent reason, you may take it as a warning that something negative is affecting the house.

CHAPTER 16

Is This Really the End?

The conclusion that a site is haunted may not nec-essarily be the end of the case. If the client decides she is happy to live with the earthbound spirits, it may actually be the beginning of long and intense research into that particular property. It is unusual to find a site that is so active that investigators must come back month after month, even year after year. The reliable environment of an ongoing investigation makes it a great training ground for new members.

Cleansing Rituals and Closure

Not all paranormal teams follow their investigations with a ritual. In other cultures, where the belief in spirits is commonplace, it is not a strange concept at all.

In Japanese communities throughout the world, August is a time to celebrate the Obon festival. It is widely believed that during this time, the spirits of ancestors return to the real world to visit their relatives. The Japanese honor their ancestors in various ways, with festivals and food offerings, and by visiting graveyards and cleaning their ancestors' graves. They hang lanterns to invite the spirits into their homes. At the end of the festival, floating lanterns are placed in rivers, lakes, and seas to guide the spirits back to the otherworld.

It is a widespread belief that the spirits of people who were unhappy or met a violent end may linger on in the physical plane as spirits called *yurei*. As is the case in many other cultures, these spirits linger simply to find closure.

We hear this same tale over and over again, from the British Isles to ancient Greece. The practice of ritual cleansing before and after contact with the supernatural is known to many cultures.

Americans Get with It

As a society that was formed from the cultural blending of many nations, Americans have a diversity of opinions and practices concerning the afterlife and ghosts.

In cultures around the world, sage has been used as a cleansing herb for centuries. The dried leaves are rolled into a long bundle called a wand. When they are lit, they emit an incense-like smoke. The smoke of the sage plant can be used to cleanse both people and spaces.

Recently, a cultural consensus seems to have emerged, at least among those in the paranormal community, concerning what is deemed proper procedure after an investigation.

Most groups indicate that they think it is wise to bless the house, its inhabitants, and themselves at the end of an investigation. These rituals can range from the simplest to the most complex and differ widely from group to group and region to region.

THREE TYPES OF CLEANSING

- **Bathing.** A bath with Epsom salts or cleansing herbs serves to remove the last traces of any physical contamination. The soothing scents of the herbs are grounding and make it easy for the investigator to achieve a focused state of mind.
- **Saging.** A sort of bath without water, saging can be done either individually or in a group and has much the same function as a bath in water. The smoke from burning sage provides a physical barrier and the scent provides a mental clarity and relaxation that allow the investigator to erect a barrier of protection.
- **Prayer or spell.** Often preceded by bathing or saging, a prayer or spell provides a clear channel of good intention and integrates the positive energies into a force for good.

House Cleansing Ritual

Rituals of this sort are not to everyone's taste. The supplies you need and steps you should take follow. It is offered only as an example of a typical house cleansing ritual.

- ❑ Incense burner or censer (A censer is a brass incense burner on a metal chain, which can be carried around the house safely. Any other type of incense burner should be placed on a small tray.)
- ❑ Sea salt
- ❑ White candle in a candleholder
- ❑ Broom made from natural, not synthetic, materials (Willow or hazel make good homemade brooms.)
- ❑ Matches or lighters and a candlesnuffer
- ❑ Incense (Frankincense, myrrh, sandalwood, lavender, or sage are good choices, either in stick form or powdered.)
- ❑ Charcoal block (for powdered incense)

- ❏ Plain ceramic bowl large enough to hold the crystal and the incense burner
- ❏ Large crystal
- ❏ Anointing oil (optional) (Frankincense, myrrh, sandalwood, or lavender essential oils are good choices.)

FACT

The most important thing about a cleansing ritual is that the intention of the people doing it is clear and strong. Minor elements, such as an essential oil, can be missing as long as the intention is uppermost in the participants' minds and the goal of the cleansing is positive.

1. Assemble your materials on a table or other flat surface. If several people are participating, gather them together near the table. Nonparticipants should leave the premises until the ritual is completed.
2. Place a few drops of oil on the candle. Light the candle and the incense.
3. Put the salt in the bottom of the bowl. Place a crystal an inch deep in the salt. If you do not have a censer, place the incense burner in the bowl as well. Place these items in the center of the table with the broom in front of them.
4. Concentrate on the broom, bowl, and candle, picturing them all surrounded by a cleansing, bright white light. Let this light expand outward to encompass the whole house. As it does so, it will permeate every corner, nook, and cranny.
5. Pick up the broom and sweep counterclockwise around the entire house, starting at the front door. Continue until you have completed a circle that brings you back to the front door. As you sweep, imagine all impurities being propelled out of the house and repeat, "By the power of all things holy and good, by the sea and the stars, by earth, air, fire, and water, be gone, all unclean things!"
6. Sweep the bad things out of the door and out of the house. Return to the candle and incense. Pick up the incense and walk clockwise around the interior of the house three times, allowing the smoke to pervade each corner. As you walk, offer a blessing: "May this house be filled with light, love, and laughter, so full that all else is driven out. By the power of

all things holy and good, by the sea and the stars, by earth, air, fire, and water, be gone, all unclean things!"

7. An additional prayer may be offered, linked to the tradition of the practitioner, such as, "In the name of Jesus Christ, amen." Or "Blessed be!"

8. Conceal the crystal in the center of the home as a sort of ward against negative energy. Place a pinch of salt in four tiny bowls at each corner of the house. Snuff out the candle.

Analyzing the Evidence

Wouldn't you think this would be the fun part? Well, no, not usually. Those in the field who regularly review evidence from an investigation must have a very high tolerance for boredom. After all, they have to look at hours of video footage and listen to hours of audiotape. Only very rarely do they actually pick up something noteworthy. In addition, they must analyze the still

photos and other evidence from the investigation scene. Some groups have access to so much equipment that they find it a chore to review all of their data. Imagine having to review digital audio and video, thermal images, digital thermometer readings, and the investigator's logbooks.

In most groups, more than one person is assigned to do evidence review duty. Obviously, the more help there is, the quicker it goes.

How to Proceed

The evidence gathered on scene in the form of audio and video files, tapes, and investigative notes are gathered together in one location, ideally a table large enough to set up the computers, monitors, camcorders, and other equipment. The people who will

Photo copyright Melissa Martin Ellis, 2006.

The gargoyles that appeared on churches in the Middle Ages were believed to scare evil spirits away.

be reviewing the evidence sit side by side, with headphones on so as not to disturb one another. When something is found, say an EVP, the investigator who discovered it will ask a fellow investigator to take a look or listen to the anomaly. This is the fun part, and it's the payoff to slogging through the many uneventful hours of evidence review.

ALERT!

Having two people doing evidence review is the best approach. Not only does it go twice as fast, but when one person finds an anomaly, the other can verify if it is actually a significant find or debunk it if it is not.

Now I've Got You

When something is discovered, the time and place is noted and cross-indexed with the other tapes, photos, and notes to see if there may be some correlation or backup verification on them as well. The team's energy level soars if this happens; it is the reward for all their hard work.

The evidence is then copied and archived to be reviewed later by the whole team, which may validate or debunk it. Only credible evidence is presented to the client at the reveal.

Reviewing Photos and Video

People are often better at catching one sort of evidence than another; Maggie Florio is excellent at capturing EVPs and Kym Black is great at capturing photos of anomalies, mists, and orbs. But not only are they better at capturing their specific phenomena, they are also better at detecting it during the evidence review.

What characteristics are necessary to be an effective evidence reviewer when it comes to reviewing videos and photos?

- Patience
- Good vision

- Awareness of matrixing
- Experience

An instance where the client is videotaped as he reports the phenomenon is helpful for investigators to review later. Sometimes the investigator's recollection of what the client reported is wrong and she ends up erroneously thinking she has debunked something.

On episode 63 of *Ghost Hunters*, TAPS investigated the Ruff Stone Tavern in North Providence, Rhode Island. During the walk-through, the proprietress said that she had experienced a strange scent, like that of a woman, in the bar. Grant asked what sort of scent, and she replied, "Musky." Later, when he was attempting to debunk this, he opened some chemicals and bottles in the vicinity, but they were obviously not the source of the odor. Then he opened a drawer and said he thought he had found the source of the odor; it smelled "musty."

Musty and musky are two very different odors, but the words do sound alike. Musk is a scent used in perfumes; "musty" is used to describe the odor of mildew or mold. The two are very different, but no one appears to have caught the distinction. Investigators can catch this sort of error through the use of video or audiotape.

E-QUESTION

What is more important than paying very strict attention during an evidence review?
Almost nothing. Few aspects of the case require as much diligence as the evidence review phase of the investigation. It will not matter if the team has gathered tons of great evidence if the reviewers don't catch and log it.

What to Look For

What do evidence reviewers watch for in photos, videotapes, and thermal images? Anything that is out of the ordinary, but most particularly such things as doors or objects moving with no one in the area; shadows, mists, and fogs that form under strange circumstances; lights or orbs moving through a scene; apparitions; and bizarre temperature anomalies. These are all immediate red flags that something paranormal is happening.

If anything of this sort is captured, the reviewers ask for assistance in assessing what they have found. Then the investigators try to think of any possible reasons to debunk the evidence. For example, investigators might ask themselves whether it was possible for the door to open because there was a strong wind whipping through the house. They would then be obliged to check other data against that suspicion, searching the logs to see if other investigators noted that the wind had picked up at that point. They would also check to see if cameras in other parts of the house had detected something similar occurring at that exact instant. Evidence is always correlated and cross-checked. If there is a possible natural explanation, the evidence has to be thrown out.

EVPs and the Ghost Box

In order to capture electronic voice phenomena, you must have the right equipment. This starts with your digital recorder. There are two kinds—those with the USB option and those without it. The ones with a USB connection allow the digital sound files to be transferred from the recorder directly to the computer very quickly. The recorders without a USB option must actually play the sound into your computer to transfer the files. This means that it takes as long to transfer your recording as it did to record it initially. In addition, there may be a loss of sound quality; this is not the case when you transfer files via the USB connection.

The recorders with USB transfer capability cost about $60, while recorders without it cost about $40. The time you will save by being able to transfer your files quickly makes the modest price difference worth it. If you own a Mac, make sure the recorder and software you buy are compatible with Apple computers.

White Noise Generators

What we don't see when watching television shows about the paranormal is the fact that many investigators like to work with some sort of white noise generator behind the scenes while doing their EVP work. Why? White noise generators are said to give the spirits something to work with, perhaps the raw material out of which to build the sounds that are later discovered on the recordings.

Ongoing EVP work is one of the most exciting things in the field of psychic research. You don't need a lot of fancy equipment to do your own investigations and analysis of your results.

ALERT!

Generating white noise of some sort has become practically standard practice for investigators trying to capture EVPs. Software that generates this noise can be found for free or on a trial basis on the Internet. Spirits are said to manipulate the noise to generate speech.

The electronic voice phenomena researcher simply needs an audio recorder, preferably a digital one, with an external microphone, if possible. To do your analysis and data storage, you will also need a computer and audio software.

It is possible to tune a radio to an unused station to generate white noise, or you may simply go to the Internet to find white noise generator software.

The Ghost Box

The latest breakthrough development in EVP phenomena is the so-called ghost box. This device is said to greatly increase one's chance of recording an EVP. It produces random voltage to create white noise (static) from an AM tuner, which is then amplified, fed into an echo chamber, and recorded. Its fans say the device, which scans through live radio frequencies, allows spirits to pull the words they want to use from the broadcasts in order to string together a message that can be heard. What sets the ghost box apart from simple EVP devices is that the response is audible to the listener. The theory posits that this can lead to the opportunity for real-time conversations. It allows two-way communication with spirits of the departed, a true breakthrough.

The experience is, as one report states, "not unlike chatting with someone by walkie-talkie." A degree of training is required to catch the messages, which are sometimes heavily overlaid with static-filled background noise. But after a bit of experimenting, the responses become increasingly more intelligible, and sentences and answers to questions can be discerned. Voices that are heard over the ghost box can have a very strange quality to them and may sound mechanical. More often than not, EVPs sound like a person speaking, complete with regional accents.

FACT

Frank Sumption was allegedly inspired to invent the ghost box when he read an article in the October 1995 edition of *Popular Electronics*, which asked, "Are the dead trying to communicate with us through electronic means? Try these experiments and see for yourself." Sumption experimented with Stefan Bion's EVPMaker software, with remarkable results.

There are many other versions of the ghost box these days, but most work on the premise that entities can use the radio signals to boost their ability to communicate.

The messages ghost boxes transmit are unbelievably diverse. Just as in the realm of mediumship, there seem to be some entities who are in control and act as gatekeepers, bringing other spirits through to communicate. Notably, ghost box operators in far-flung locations have recorded some of these same guides or controllers.

Go to Frank Sumption's Yahoo Group, *http://tech.groups.yahoo.com/ group/evp-itc/*, to familiarize yourself with the whole ghost box concept. Keyport Paranormal (*www.keyportparanormal.com*) has information on how to make your own ghost box with schematics, examples of audio files captured from a ghost box made from a Radio Shack radio, and links to EVP software.

Showing the Data to the Client

Sometimes known as the reveal, showing the evidence of a haunting (or lack thereof) and the plan for dealing with it is an art unto itself. The client has expectations, and staying professional while you meet the expectations is the whole point of being in the business.

Arrange a meeting time that is convenient for both you and the client. Expect to spend about thirty to sixty minutes on the actual presentation and discussion of the evidence, depending on what you have found. Block out some time after the reveal to answer any questions or concerns the client may have. If you found evidence of a haunting, your suggestions for handling the situation should be discussed with the client at this time. Draw up a plan that is agreeable to everyone.

Evidence Preparation

Digital and analog photos, digital and analog audio recordings, thermal imaging files, and digital video recordings are some common types of evidence that are captured in the course of the site investigation. Sometimes these files can be enhanced through the use of software that is designed expressly for this purpose.

Make sure to follow the two rules of evidence:

- Always make file backups of the original digital files on a separate media storage device, CD, DVD, or flash drive. You should have two copies of both the originals and of the enhanced versions.
- Never alter a file and save over it. Before you do anything to a file, create a copy to work on and leave the original in a pristine state, unaltered. Save digital photo originals as TIFFs. Analog photos should be scanned at 300dpi, at 100 percent.

Evidence Enhancement

Photoshop Elements is a great program for resizing, cropping, and enhancing the contrast and brightness of digital photos. Proper image enhancement isn't hard to learn and can make a huge difference in the perception of the data. There are programs that can be used to clean up digital video, but many investigators choose to send this out to be done.

Audio files can be cleaned up easily enough with programs you can download from the Internet such as WavePad and Audacity. Thermal images are usually so contrasting and bright that they do not require any enhancement.

Where to Meet?

Any place mutually agreeable to you and your client, whether it is your office or his house or office, will do just fine. It should have a space where you can set up a conference-type arrangement, with a table long enough to accommodate two to three team members and the client(s). Having an electrical outlet nearby is a bonus, since most evidence is presented on your laptop, which can run off battery power if need be.

Set up your laptop and evidence files so that everyone can easily see what is happening. Before the reveal, you should load the photos, video, and audio files into the computer. Make a shortcut to the folder; all files should be easily accessible on the desktop. Avoid fumbling through files and trying to locate the evidence as the client watches; it does not send the message that you're professional.

Get the evidence in the best possible shape before going to the reveal to share it with the client. Use an image-processing program to increase contrast and bring out detail on photos and clean up audio files to remove any static and hissing that is too distracting.

The Procedure

Greet the client and thank her again for allowing you into her home. Ask if any activity has occurred since the investigation. Remind her that it is your job to look for any possible natural causes for what she is experiencing. Tell her if you were able to debunk anything and discuss any personal experiences investigators had while there. Then show or reveal the hard evidence—any photos, EVPs, or videos of anomalous events.

Following Up

It is enough for some investigators simply to establish the fact that there is paranormal activity actually taking place. What the client wishes to do with that information is his own concern.

More frequently, if the team finds evidence that a residence is haunted, they will work with the client to find an outcome for the situation that works for him.

Reactions vary. Some people are delighted to find that their suspicions are true. This is particularly common when the reputation as a haunted location can enhance the owner's commercial interest in a property, say in the case of a haunted hotel or restaurant, which can see a huge boom in business as curiosity seekers flock to the establishment to see what all the fuss is about.

When Clients Are Scared

If the haunting is making the client frightened or even just uncomfortable, she may opt to seek a way of ridding the premises of the supernatural pests. It is part of the paranormal investigator's responsibility to try to find a means of bringing closure to this sort of client, either through their own team's efforts or through the help of outside experts in cleansing and closure. In extreme cases, exorcism may be warranted. If the entities can be convinced to leave the premises and cross over into the light, the outcome is optimal for everyone involved.

Never say or do anything to alarm or frighten your client. Be sensitive to your client's frame of mind. Strive to soothe and calm the situation and educate the client as to what is happening without making the situation worse than it was.

Continue to Check In

No matter the outcome of the case, the client's information should be kept on file. Follow up periodically to see how your clients are doing. They really appreciate this, and the team must make sure they are still okay, particularly if you detected evidence of a dark or oppressive presence.

In cases where the client has opted to live with the haunting, check to make sure that nothing has changed for the worse and that he is still comfortable with the situation. Active sites that have an ongoing presence can be a real resource for a paranormal group; if the owner is willing it can become a site for more in-depth investigations and a training ground for new members.

CHAPTER 17

In the Land of Mundania

Those attracted to the paranormal definitely march to a different drummer. So is it any wonder that they shy away from talking about all the mundane day-to-day business that may be involved in their otherwise exciting endeavors? However, if investigators are not able to set up the basic infrastructure to support the team and the investigations, they won't get very far or enjoy the investigations as much as they might have otherwise.

Gaining Access to Sites

It can't be emphasized strongly enough—access to most sites must be obtained and permission granted before investigators traipse around a property. It is just good sense and it protects the team from annoying and possibly expensive legal issues. If a site is on private property, it is privately owned. Graveyards and cemeteries can be either privately or publicly owned, but as vandalism in cemeteries becomes more and more of an issue, police and security patrols may question your presence, especially after dark.

ALERT!

If you have a friend who is super organized and business-like, he might be an excellent candidate to be a case manager if you can get him interested in ghost hunting. The trick will be getting him to go on that first hunt with you; after that you may have him hooked.

Always bring along personal identification and a driver's license when taking part in an investigation. Some sort of business card with the name of the group will also enhance your credibility and professional appearance. Follow these guidelines:

- **Dress normally.** Capes, over-the-top costumes, or anything that makes you appear less than professional is not to your benefit when you are trying to gain access to a site.
- **If you are asked to leave an area, do so immediately.** There is no point in arguing or making a scene.
- **Never go out alone.** Isolated locations can be tricky. Always bring a cell phone.

Exceptions to the Rules

Where can you go to practice and hone your skills without obtaining permission? Try public places to which there is free access during the daytime—for example, parks, museums, and historic sites. If you enter these areas after dark, you should notify the proper and appropriate people or agencies. This may mean alerting the police to the fact that you will be at the location and taking photos. This will save you time and hassles. You can also find out if friends or family will open their homes to you for training.

Be careful if you are investigating in the homes of friends or relatives. Be very considerate of their privacy, and be aware of the consequences if you actually turn up something disturbing. Elderly relatives or friends in poor health are not good candidates.

Another option is the haunted hotel or bed and breakfast. You have permission to be there by virtue of the fact that you have reserved a room, but be discreet if you are investigating in public areas. Ask the management if it is all right to take a few photos; they may be very cooperative. Sometimes they will even tell you where activity has taken place and tell stories of their own personal encounters.

Photos taken during a tour of the Lizzie Borden House in Fall River, Massachusetts, were quite ordinary until one investigator noticed orbs in a photo and took a closer look. One orb is in the doorway where the murderer must have stood when the blows were struck, and one is where Andrew Borden's head would have been.

On the same tour, author Douglas Clegg heard a cat meow in the basement, but there wasn't a cat down there. People standing within a few feet of him did not hear the

Photo copyright Melissa Martin Ellis, 2007.

The Lizzie Borden House in Fall River, Massachusetts, is now a bed and breakfast. Guided tours of the house are available. These orbs were captured at the scene of Andrew Borden's murder.

Photo copyright Melissa Martin Ellis, 2007.

This photo shows Lizzie Borden several years before the murders and scandal.

sound, although there have been numerous other reports of a phantom cat at the Borden House Bed and Breakfast. The website Real Haunts (*www.realhaunts.com*) has a list of haunted houses and sites, some of which are accessible to the public.

Client Release and Permission Forms

It helps to have forms that will cover both you and the client in many different types of situations. Some forms protect you or the client. Others simply spell out the procedures and clarify gray areas. As groups gain experience, they may feel the need to clarify or change their basic forms.

A good form covers you legally and tends to reassure clients that they are in the hands of pros who are looking out for their best interests. Clients in museums, historic houses, or homes with expensive furnishings appreciate the reassurance that furnishings and infrastructure will be handled responsibly.

Types of Forms

There are two basic types of forms—those you use when dealing with clients and those you use within your organization. The forms used by clients should always be in duplicate or even in triplicate.

CLIENT FORMS

- Client Questionnaire
- Permission to Investigate
- Client Interview
- Client Confidentiality Agreement
- Evidence Release or No Release
- Client Summary Report
- Follow-Up Questionnaire

INTERNAL ORGANIZATION FORMS

- Investigation Report
- Location History
- Incident Report
- Activity Log
- Investigators Private
- Evidence Review Findings

When clients are anxious about activities that are going on around them—especially if they feel paranoid, watched, or threatened—the investigator's primary initial role is to calm and reassure the client's fears. His biggest fear may be the thought of being gossiped about or ridiculed in the community. If that's the case, reassure him that the confidentiality agreement means all of his information will remain secret. He may also worry that his home will be damaged if he lets a bunch of strangers run loose in it. Part of any agreement between the client and the investigators should cover what behavior is expected of the team as they conduct the investigation. If the client wants to add something to the contract specifying that personal items may not be touched or duct tape will not be used in certain locations, the client's agreement should contain these requests.

ALERT!

You can make these forms yourself if you're handy on the computer. If you aren't, search for them on the Internet. Be sure to have a copy for the client and a copy for the group. All parties to the agreements should sign both.

Trespassing Is Illegal

Many rookie investigators are stopped cold by the threat of trespassing and feel it thwarts them from pursuing many kinds of investigations. All it really means is that you should protect your own interests by covering your assets. You can be sued or arrested if you aren't cautious.

Usually, obtaining permission to investigate a location is not hard; in fact, clients who call you almost always automatically give you permission. Be sure to have a form prepared for them to sign. The lead investigator should always keep this form with her when on-site.

Vacant Properties

Vacant properties may be seasonal residences or vacation homes that are only occupied for part of the year. Alternatively, a vacant property may be temporarily empty while it is being renovated or put on the market for sale. If an owner recently passed away, the home may be caught up in the process of probate. Check the exterior of the property for signs. If the house is for rent or sale, look for a Realtor's sign on the property.

FACT

It's possible to exhaust your resources looking for a property's owner and still turn up nothing. Total dead ends are uncommon when the research is thorough, but they do happen and you learn to simply move on. If you cannot track down the owner, put the idea of doing an investigation on the back burner until you can find him and get his consent.

There are three other places to do a quick check:

- **Neighbors.** If there are any nearby, they may know the homeowner's name and have her contact information as well. A close neighbor may even have a key and be able to give you permission to enter.
- **Homeowners' associations.** Subdivisions and gated communities usually have a homeowners' association. They have a list of homeowners and contact information.
- **The police.** In isolated locations and small towns, the police are a great source of information. They may actually recommend new sites to investigate; they are, after all, in the best position to experience the paranormal if they are called to a location and experience anomalous phenomena. Homeowners who are away will often

notify local law enforcement that they are out of town, so the police have their contact information or can direct you to the caretaker.

Some of these approaches will also work for commercial buildings. Ask neighboring businesses; they may share a landlord or know the owner. Ask the police; they are probably aware of who owns the building because they watch abandoned areas to keep an eye out for vandals. Other information sources include:

- **City directories.** Sometimes called reverse directories, these large books list who occupies premises. If you have the address, you can find who last occupied the premises. Most public libraries allow you to reference them.
- **Courthouses and city halls.** Public records are accessible here. Be prepared to pay a small fee in some cases. Property records, tax records, and probate records can yield the information you seek. The courthouse is the place to obtain property maps and do a title search. The maps are at the county assessor's office, and both the deeds and titles will be available through the county clerk's office. A title search, which shows the records of who owned the house over the years, will reveal the owner's name.
- **The Internet.** Online resources have grown in recent years. Some towns have their tax assessment records online, and knowing the address is all you need to find the owner.

The Internet can be a wonderful resource. Older homes and businesses may be listed in the National Register of Historical Places. Don't forget to check there if a building has historical significance.

Now What Happens?

Locating the owner is the first step. Getting her permission to enter is the next hurdle. If her property is really haunted, the owner may be defensive about it and may not want to discuss it. This is where a permission/confidentiality agreement and some gentle persuasion will help. Remind her that the information about the investigation is under her control, and if you find that something unusual is going on you may be able to clear the space for her.

What if the owner refuses to give her consent?
This happens far less often than you would imagine. Usually, when the benefits of the investigation are explained and the proper forms signed, the owner is glad to grant permission. If she won't, the investigation simply stalls.

Initially, the homeowner or landlord should accompany investigators to the site to open it and remain with them while a walk-through or initial research is done. This shows the proprietor the current state of the property and protects the investigators. If the owner hasn't been to the site in a while, she may be unaware of its true condition and any recent vandalism. Pictures taken at this initial walk-through will document the condition of the property and can prove invaluable if there is any later contention about group liability for any property damage.

Should the owner decline to go or is unable to accompany you, be sure to have her sign your consent/confidentiality form. This form must have the date, the physical address of the site, and a statement granting the group or researchers access to the premises. It should also include a reassurance from the group that the property will be left as it was found and that confidentiality will be maintained unless otherwise indicated. Add a check box to be ticked and initialed when the key is returned. The investigators and the building's owner should sign and date the form.

Medical Information and Preparedness

It is best to be prepared in the case of a medical emergency during an investigation. Every team leader wants to make sure that no one gets hurt on her watch. If someone does get hurt or falls ill, there must be a plan to deal with the situation quickly and effectively. Most groups ask that their staff keep information about their medications, medical conditions, doctors, and emergency contacts up to date and on file in a sealed envelope. These envelopes are taken on investigations in case a medical emergency arises and someone needs treatment.

Something to Consider

If you have certain medical conditions, carefully consider how stressful it might be to meet up with something unexpected during an overnight vigil in a cold, dark house. Being a paranormal investigator is not for the faint of heart, nor is it for you if you have:

- Heart problems
- High blood pressure
- Risk of stroke
- Diabetes
- Asthma
- Any chronic, debilitating illness

Investigators with existing medical conditions should be sure that they have adequate medication with them to complete the investigation and have informed the team leader of these conditions.

Being Medically Prepared

The longer you traipse around dark houses in the middle of the night, the more likely you are to end up with a boo-boo or two. Sometimes investigators in the field are twenty miles from the nearest town and they have only themselves and their fellow investigators to count on if an emergency arises. Emergencies can be caused by the psychological or physical stress of the investigation or by an accident that happens on the scene. Bring a first aid kit on every investigation. The first aid kit should contain these items:

- ❏ Band-Aids and bandages
- ❏ Aspirin and Tylenol
- ❏ Antiseptics
- ❏ Anti-itch cream
- ❏ Water

If a site investigation was done beforehand, investigators will know of any hazards in the environment, which can range from asbestos contamination to the possibility of snakebite—both unlikely. If someone on your team is bitten by something poisonous, bring its body to the emergency room if possible so it can be identified and the proper treatment administered.

ALERT!

Some groups keep epinephrine in the first aid kit. Anaphylactic shock can occur if an airway becomes obstructed due to bee stings or other shock reactions. Epinephrine keeps the airway from closing completely and can save someone's life until you can get him to an emergency room.

If at all possible, park as close to the site as you can. In case of emergency, you can get to a vehicle and to a hospital much faster.

Release Forms

Most groups now insist that members sign a medical consent form disclosing any treatment they are undergoing and listing any prescriptions they are taking and conditions that might cause problems in the course of an investigation. A separate form releases the organization from liability in the event the person is injured during the investigation.

SAMPLE RELEASE FORM
I, the undersigned, agree that in signing this document I release _____, its members, and their families of my own free will from any and all responsibility for any and all damage that may occur to me and personal property during the course of the investigation. I furthermore and of my own free will release _____, its members, and their families of any and all responsibility whatsoever for any physical or psychological harm that may at any time come to me as a result of attending and observing an investigation involving paranormal phenomena.

I acknowledge and understand that _____ will not in any way be held responsible for any medical or hospital costs associated with injuries or illnesses I may sustain in the course of the investigation.

In signing this release, I acknowledge that I waive liability and will hold _____ harmless for any injury arising from my participation.

I have read this agreement, understand it, and sign it voluntarily as my own free act and deed; no oral representations, statements, or inducements, apart from the foregoing written agreement, have been made.

I am at least eighteen (18) years of age and fully competent; and I execute this release for full, adequate, and complete consideration fully intending to be bound by same.

IN WITNESS WHEREOF, I _____ have hereunto set my hand on this ____ day of ____ in the year ____.

Signature: _____ Date: _____

Witness: _____ Date: _____

Organizations that do not ask observers and participants in an investigation to sign such forms are putting themselves at grave legal risk. If the parties involved are minors, their parents or guardians must sign the release form.

Getting Insurance and Covering Your Assets

Ghost hunting is risky business, and it doesn't hurt to have some insurance coverage. If you have a small group, it is probably best to have the individual members carry their own coverage. Make members insure their own individual equipment as well.

Full replacement cost insurance to cover the equipment should be discussed with your insurance agent. Your equipment should be covered whether it is taken on an investigation, left in the car, or stored at your home.

Other Kinds of Insurance

There are many ways to approach paranormal investigating. Most teams agree that they should do everything in their power to ensure that no one gets hurt and no accidents or mishaps occur to injure anyone during the investigation. This sort of care and prudence pays off. It builds trust, ensures things will run smoothly, and gives the team pride and a sense of professionalism.

The cost of replacing equipment isn't cheap. If the technology gets fried and suddenly stops working during an investigation, a little extra insurance coverage will seem like a very good idea indeed. You can purchase the insurance through an insurance agency; there is no need to disclose that it will be used on ghost hunts.

What can you do to ensure that your group remains safe on every investigation?

1. Obtain permission to investigate the site.
2. Leave if there seems to be a problem regarding your right to be there.
3. Follow proper investigative protocol.
4. Never investigate alone.
5. Bring along adequate equipment and supplies.
6. Bring a first aid kit.
7. Examine the site for hazards in the daylight prior to a night investigation.
8. Use walkie-talkies or other devices to keep team members in touch.
9. Make sure your transportation is reliable and maintain the vehicle(s) used by the team.
10. Have an agreed-upon signal to let members know that it is time to evacuate the premises in an emergency.
11. Bring plastic bags to cover equipment if there is bad weather during an outdoor investigation.

Remember, teammates do not put each other in jeopardy or play pranks that can lead to putting other teammates in danger. This is not to say that investigators can't have any fun during an investigation, but keep in mind that the site is important to someone. It may be someone's home or even place of burial. Try to act appropriately.

FACT

A team's greatest asset is its faith in a strong alliance with other team members. They must know without question that their teammates will always put the team's best interests and well-being before any other consideration, including gathering evidence.

If there are one or more sensitives in the group, pay close attention to them to ensure their safety. They are the most vulnerable to psychic and physical attack and entities are drawn to them more than other investigators. Should they start behaving oddly or seem to be exhausted, they should be taken away from the site before they become ill.

CHAPTER 18

Magical Record-Keeping

Ah, if only we could just wave our magic wands and make all the paperwork disappear. But no, as mere mortals and serious ghost hunters, we must keep very careful track of the information we uncover during investigations. Lone investigators and organizations alike share the same obligation to the client and the rest of the paranormal community—to keep good records and share nonconfidential data that will lead to a greater understanding of the phenomena observed for *all* researchers in the field. A high standard of professionalism preserves the reputation and the integrity of the group.

Case Files and the Case Manager

How will you organize and coordinate all the data and files you accumulate in the course of your investigations? First, it's helpful to know who's in charge of the group's record-keeping and data storage duties.

The Case Manager

As groups grow over time, it soon becomes apparent that the organization benefits greatly from having a person known as a case manager. The case manager's responsibilities include noting the intake of new cases and managing the data from ongoing investigations.

The case manager's job does not end there; she is in charge of filing and organizing the old cases so their data is accessible to both the organization and to the client. It may be a thankless job, but some people love it, because it gives them ready access to case files and the information that they provide. The case manager is also the person who does background research prior to the actual investigation. She digs out facts and background history and acts as the go-to person for the team in regard to basic information and setup. The case manager is the backbone of the team. When the right person is in the job the workflow goes very smoothly and the group functions at its optimal level.

FACT

A little organization at the beginning can go a long way toward quickly building a sterling reputation for reliability and professionalism, which are truly invaluable assets to a group of this kind. If you aren't sure you can keep your records organized, partner up with someone who can.

Intake and Client Screening

Since the case manager is the first point of contact when a potential client calls the group for help, she must quickly ascertain whether the person is desperate, frantic, in danger, or just curious about paranormal activity. She must be a good judge of human nature, too, as ghost hunting groups are targeted for more than their fair share of hoaxes.

The case manager should ask the following questions during a request-to-investigate interview:

1. What sort of phenomena are you experiencing? Are there moving shadows or are you glimpsing something out of the corner of your eye?
2. Do you ever experience unexplained cold spots?
3. Do you hear footsteps or other unexplained noises, such as tapping or voices saying your name?
4. Do your children ever report seeing someone who isn't there?
5. Do animals seem to follow something you can't see with their eyes or have a fearful reaction without any apparent reason?
6. Have you noticed any strange odors?
7. Do things disappear and then inexplicably reappear later?
8. Do you ever feel you are being watched?

If the client answers "yes" to more than three of the questions, the case manager should schedule an investigation for the near future. If there are children in the home or a sense of peril, the investigation should be scheduled immediately.

Request to Conduct Investigation

Groups use a form to apply to investigate a site. This form is perhaps the most commonly used instrument for gaining access to a site and protecting the group from future liability. Even solitary investigators or small groups should use a form. There is no way to legally conduct an investigation without it, and those who do so are setting themselves up for a lot of trouble.

Without this basic form, investigators can be arrested and charged with trespassing or perhaps breaking and entering. Neither does much for the perpetrator's reputation.

To ensure that this form is legally binding, have an attorney draw it up or purchase one from a website that guarantees the form's viability. This is a little like buying insurance. If the client later alleges that the group did not have permission to enter the premises or did damage to it, having the contract and dated photos of the site can save you from a lawsuit, or worse.

Permission Forms

It is a good idea to have an attorney draw up a simple form that keeps the rights and obligations of both parties clear.

When a client first approaches a paranormal group seeking help, the group evaluates the situation and decides if an investigation is warranted. Likewise, the client has to grant permission to the group or individual to conduct the investigation, and he must also decide whether he wants the group to release any information that may be discovered during the course of the investigation. If a client is reluctant to fill out paperwork, go over it with him and make sure he understands it. Answer any questions the client has. Make it clear that the investigation cannot proceed without it and that signing the paperwork will only take a few minutes.

How many kinds of permission forms are there? Organizations don't really have one unified version of each form that they use; each group makes up forms based on necessity, and forms are tailored to fit the individual needs of the organization. Individuals and very small groups can get by with basic permission and release forms, but at bare minimum they should have an application to conduct an investigation, which the client can fill out, and a form granting the group permission to conduct a field investigation.

Release Forms

The release form, like the permission forms, comes in several different varieties. The release form serves to ensure that the rights of both the investigating group and the client are protected. Releases help both sides of the investigation feel comfortable with each other and ensure that neither side is leaving itself open to damage. The investigators may have to agree to keep the client's information confidential, and both sides may have to agree not to hold the other liable in the case of injury or damage during the course of the investigation.

Make sure you have at least two different kinds of release forms:

1. **Permission to release confidential information.** This release gives the investigators permission to publish information that they gather concerning the case. If the client declines this form, then you must both

sign an alternate form that binds the investigators to protecting the client's confidentiality.

2. **Release from liability.** This form should protect both the client and the investigators.

FACT

A client's privacy *must* be respected if she chooses to remain anonymous, and team members should be discreet when making any sort of reference to the investigation. The client's identity, address, and phone number should never be given out without her express written permission.

Only when concerns of this nature have been cleared away can both sides proceed without fear of reprisal. Of course, basic trust between the parties is a prerequisite for such an arrangement. This is when a paranormal group finds that having a sterling reputation as professionals is a huge advantage. Always maintaining professional standards and procedures will quickly allow even new groups to develop a good reputation. This means having group members who are conscientious and considerate in their approach to clients, the property being investigated, and the integrity of the evidence gathered. The whole package has to be there or word will quickly spread in the community that a group is unreliable.

Interview Questionnaires

It is vital to interview potential clients and witnesses. They are the ones with the inside information and they will usually initiate contact with the investigators. It is the paranormal investigator's duty to properly assess the request.

- Is the client believable and not a hoaxster?
- Is the client mentally stable and not under treatment for a psychiatric disorder or substance abuse problems?
- Is the situation the client describes a dangerous one that needs immediate attention?

The answers to these questions are almost impossible to determine with just a phone call. Someone from the group must interview the client and ask the proper questions in person. With a questionnaire in hand, he can ask the client to fill out the answers.

ALERT!

Clients have been known to change their minds in the middle of an investigation and withdraw their permission to investigate. This is frustrating, but stay calm and try to remedy whatever concern the client has to save the situation and your investment of time and effort.

Although people may balk at answering personal questions, filling out a form can be a little less threatening. The interviewer can look the form over and ask follow-up questions. The form is an icebreaker, and it provides a permanent record of the initial meeting. Facts pertinent to the case can be readily available to the team as they conduct the investigation. This form should include the date and case number, the location, the name of the person being interviewed, and a description of the phenomena the client has observed.

Site Investigation Forms

Site assessment and investigation forms are a prerequisite for most investigations, whether they are residential or commercial. This form allows the investigators and team leaders to record their experiences on the site in a very organized way. They must include a place to record the following information:

- The investigator's name
- The names of all investigators at the site
- The date, time, and temperature
- The location address
- The equipment in use
- Any unusual events

The personal investigator's log is sometimes part of this form. It can also be a separate form, depending on how much information the team thinks its members should be recording during an investigation. In the personal log, the investigator has more space to write down impressions and personal experiences, which is not always the case in more bare-bones site investigative forms.

Assessment and Client Reports

Some sort of internal assessment and client recommendation form is needed to properly condense the other forms. In such a report, the team leader usually distills all the data from the various site investigative forms into one overarching report. The team leader will attempt to identify patterns or determine whether the data indicates a particular course of action. It is the bird's-eye view of the investigation, and it can often point the way to further study of the phenomena and give the team an idea how to proceed.

Team leaders can't be everywhere at once. Only when they read and digest the information from their team's verbal and written reports will they have a comprehensive picture of what actually happened during the investigation. They may have some idea of what is happening, but it's often impossible to judge the full impact until all the data has been reviewed.

Meticulous Records and Analysis

All members of a paranormal group are involved in record-keeping to one degree or another. During the probationary period of training, investigators learn about equipment and procedures, and they are also taught how to interpret and record equipment readings. Each individual investigator logs all the facts and occurrences that might conceivably be of any relevance. There may not be any obvious correlations between the bits of data and evidence, but sometimes it all fits together like a jigsaw puzzle to form a whole, coherent picture.

The Lead Investigator's Role

After an investigation has been completed, the lead investigator or team leader gathers the other investigators' notes and case logs for review. Some groups go so far as to have the logs printed on two- or even three-part forms in order to have a copy for the investigator, the team leader, and the organization's files.

The team leader should go over the written records carefully, looking for anything that may be significant. Information can be derived from cross-checking and comparing the records—for example, did different teams experience the same sort of phenomenon, such as a cold spot or seeing a shadowy figure, at the same location? Did something happen at the same time to all investigators at the site? If so, further investigation is necessary.

Haphazard Records

If the lead investigator's review of the written material still leaves gaps in his understanding of the event, he will follow up with any team members whose reports seem incomplete. If an investigator consistently forgets to fill in information that is relevant to the investigation, the team leader needs to emphasize the importance of keeping good, detailed records.

ALERT!

The most important assets an investigator can have are reliability and integrity. If a team member does not keep good records, she is letting other team members down and effectively sabotaging the investigation. Periodic reviews can help team members stay on track and alert them to areas where they can improve.

CD or DVD Digital Storage

The records, logs, and evidence for each investigation must be keyed and correlated to one another in a master organizational system. A lot of the evidence gathered during the course of the investigation is digital—audio, video, and photography. In most organizations, as soon as a new case opens, the case manager assigns it a case number and sets up a file folder for it. The individual investigators on a case can handle their stored digital media in one of several ways:

1. They remove the digital media cards and slip them into small baggies with the case number and their names, then hand them over to the team leader. The team leader submits them for evidence review.
2. Investigators take the storage medium out at home and upload it to their computer, where they label it by case number and make a copy of the files for the evidence review process.
3. Investigators review the files individually and hand over copies of any files that appear to contain unexplained activity.

Investigators still use regular film cameras, but the photos are usually scanned into a computer database for easy file storage, enhancement, and transfer. Physical photos and negatives can be labeled and stored in binders for easy access in the office.

Choosing a Method

There are pros and cons to each approach. Media storage can be lost or misplaced, and it isn't cheap to replace. It does, however, allow the team leader to keep control of the data. Team members may feel more comfortable with this option if the media cards belong to the group and they are not expected to turn over their own property.

In the second approach, the individual investigators are responsible for making sure the evidence eventually reaches the group. If they are not well-trained and conscientious investigators, evidence can be accidentally damaged or destroyed.

The third approach, in which the individual investigators decide which files to hand over, has the least merit but can be quite a time-saver for the evidence reviewers, removing hours of tedium from their job. The best candidates for this approach are investigators with years of working experience.

This approach works best when the team has completed many investigations together and implicitly trusts each member's judgment.

Organization of Files and Folders

Whatever approach is used for preserving and reviewing the digital files, the group should agree upon and follow a clear procedure. The files should be uploaded and put in a folder on the computer that is named according to case number. For example, the first investigation of 2009 could be named 09-001-Ellis. The first two digits are the year and the middle three denote the case number. The client's name finishes up the case number.

Subfolders should have the case number and the type of files to be found within them, such as 09-001-Ellis-Audio, 09-001-Ellis-Photos, 09-001-Ellis-Video. If more than one investigator did audio or EVP work, it may be necessary to create a subfolder within the audio subfolder with the case number, the subfolder name, and the name of the investigator, such as 09-001-Ellis-Audio-Melissa.

Keeping files this organized is easy once everyone understands the system. The case manager may have to go in and sort things out occasionally, but everyone should attempt consistency in naming and record-keeping.

Photo copyright Melissa Martin Ellis, 2007.

Scanned photos taken with regular film cameras can be more easily stored and shared with other investigators when they are converted to digital files.

E-QUESTION

How important is it to back up files?
It is vital. After the subfolders and files are created, they should be immediately backed up to CD, DVD, an external hard drive, or an online file storage service. CDs and DVDs can be stored with the rest of the case's hard files. Make two copies just to be safe.

New Member Interview and Assessment

As the popularity of investigating the paranormal grows, most groups are inundated with new member applications. At first, this may seem like a good thing, but you must screen and assess new members before you invite them to be a part of your team.

E-QUESTION

How do I tell an applicant that she hasn't made the team?
Try to let her down as easily as possible. Tell her that the requirements are difficult and that not everyone who applies is suitable to be part of a paranormal investigative team with all its pressures and stresses. She may not agree with your decision, but you must do what's best for your team.

Being a paranormal investigator is not for everyone. It requires a rare combination of traits: the drive to explore the unknown, an unquenchable curiosity, and a mature and responsible approach to the field. Choosing members wisely is as important as training them well, so designing a form to screen out thrill-seekers and the unstable or irresponsible is a very good idea. What questions you feel are appropriate to achieve those ends is up to each individual group, but each application should include questions about the prospective member's education and employment history and hypothetical situations that test the applicant's common sense.

CHAPTER 19

In the Public Domain

Information about paranormal investigations is everywhere. It is all over the Internet, on television, and in every bookstore. The paranormal is not just for Halloween anymore. The rich world of the paranormal and all its fascinating and diverse topics are in the public consciousness now perhaps more than at any other time in history. Your paranormal group can benefit from the exposure all this media attention brings.

Building an Online Presence

If you have a group of ghost hunters but you don't have a website, chances are the groups in your area who do have one are getting all the attention and referrals. It may not be strictly necessary when you're first starting out, but once you have become established and have been doing active investigations for about a year, it is time to start seriously thinking about your web presence. There are multiple reasons every ghost hunting group should have a website, including the following:

Photo copyright Melissa Martin Ellis, 2007.

Halloween, or Samhain as the Celts called it, is a time when it is believed the dead walk the earth. We still get satisfaction out of its ghoulish symbols.

- It attracts new clients.
- It attracts fellow paranormal enthusiasts who may want to find and join your group.
- It allows local media to find you if they want to do an interview on the paranormal.
- It gives members a place to interact and exchange information online.
- It can serve as an educational tool on paranormal topics for the community.
- You can offer classes and workshops.
- It allows clients to contact you via e-mail.

Check Out the Competition

So many groups are now on the web that yours may not be the first group in the area to go online. That's not bad news; there are plenty of ghosts to go around. A check of other groups' websites will help you in several ways. It will show you what they are doing, and you'll also have the opportunity to note what they aren't doing. Their site may be very basic and rudimentary or ultra-cheesy with the theme from *Ghostbusters* playing in the background. Grab a pencil and paper and make notes about the websites for any groups in your region. What is likeable about them? What are they lacking?

These sites have links to many ghost related website directories.

- *www.dmoz.org/society/paranormal/ghosts/personal_pages*
- *www.google.com/alpha/Top/Society/Paranormal/Ghosts/ Personal_Pages*

These two websites offer links to many other ghost-related sites and are a good way to check out a lot of sites in a short amount of time.

Even the most rudimentary website is better than no website at all. If you cannot afford a web designer, build your own site. Be sure to maintain and update the site frequently. Include your contact information and an assurance of confidentiality, and mention there will be no charge for your services. Testimonials can boost your credibility as well.

Gathering Resources

It is true that you are offering a free service to the public. In all likelihood, a website may seem like a total extravagance. But it's an absolute necessity. If you can't afford an elaborate site, start small and build it up over time. Even if your site only has your contact information and a little bit of text that states your policies, it is better than no web presence at all. If you are a nonprofit organization, the website may be tax deductible.

Your Ghost Hunting Website

Based on the research you've done online, get your team members together and identify your favorite sites. Start thinking about the features and the look of your website. Let your imaginations run wild.

Talk about the website's overall tone and message. Is it going to be somber or scary or comedic? Will it have a gallery, a forum, a blog? If you have a general idea of what you want for your site before you begin the hunt for a web designer, you will save time and money. If someone in the group is web and design savvy, he may be able to build a basic site for the group without going to a web pro.

Salem, Massachusetts, is one of the best places to capture paranormal images. Sometimes you can even capture a ghostly ecto-mist.

Photo copyright Melissa Martin Ellis, 2007.

Once you map out the basics, start getting into the details. Decide what domain name to reserve for the site, and discuss who is going to write the copy and maintain the site if you choose to run it yourself.

Before You Begin

Do a little background research to familiarize yourself with the basics before tackling the actual website projects. Check out books and videos about web development. It might be worth it to look into a course at your local continuing education center. Remember, if it all becomes too difficult, you can shop around for a web designer and dump the whole project on her. It will definitely cost more money, but the time you save might make it worth the cost.

Getting Up and Running

To realize your ideas and work toward a finished website, you must follow these steps:

1. Decide on content. Write the text and choose the graphics.
2. Reserve a domain name.
3. Find a web host.
4. Find a template that suits your design goals or a web designer who will follow your design.
5. Approve the finished template design and upload it to the web host.
6. Tweak the content.
7. Monitor the site for e-mails and client appeals for help.

ALERT!

Microsoft Word includes web templates, and basic sites can be built and uploaded once they have been put together. Of course, you need to obtain a domain name and a web host before you do anything. If you're clueless about any of this stuff, your best bet is to find a web designer to help get the site up and running.

Helpful Information

There are a lot of options when it comes to web hosts and website design. It is definitely a little intimidating to try to build your first website, but if you have the guts to be a ghost hunter, you probably have enough tenacity and gumption to build a website, too.

ALERT!

Websites with paranormal photography get a lot more hits than those that do not. Before putting photos up, be sure to remember that there may be privacy issues involved. Set up a system for noting which photos you can post on your website and which need to remain confidential. Always give photo credits and use captions, too.

The following sites have easy website building tools.

Google (*www.google.com/sites*)

This site has a single-click page creation utility called Google Page Creator. Creating a new page for your site takes a minute or two; it requires no knowledge of HTML markup language. There are different types of pages and templates.

Users can upload files and attachments up to 10MB in size. When you sign up for Google Apps, which is free, your account gets 10GB of storage for your website—quite enough to get the site up and rolling.

You can insert videos, presentations, and photo slide shows to enrich the content of the pages. There are no software downloads involved. The pages created are hosted on Google servers, and your URL will follow a conventional pattern: *http://yoursitename.googlepages.com*.

Yahoo (*http://geocities.yahoo.com*)

This option comes with some free features and low-cost upgrades for those who want a fancier site. The upgrades allow you to customize the design and other features. The setup fees range from $4.95 a month to $12, and from 500MB of storage space to unlimited storage. The site can handle Flash and other plug-ins and has twenty-four-hour customer service for the unlimited plan. View different template designs at *http://smallbusiness .yahoo.com/webhosting/sb/template.php.*

Microsoft (*smallbusiness.officelive.com*)

Microsoft offers a free web-hosting package, easy-to-use design tools, and site traffic reports. It says it offers everything you need to look professional on the web, and around-the-clock customer support is available.

Networking in the Community

Building an online presence is important, but building connections and cultivating a reputation in the region is just as integral to the success of the group—perhaps even more so.

It has become far more acceptable in recent years to talk about all things paranormal, but some folks will still look askance at anyone who has anything to do with the supernatural. This is why many clients don't want their names associated with it. How does a group overcome this bias?

The truth is that the bias against the belief in the supernatural world will never be overcome with a certain segment of the population. Some skeptics would not believe ghosts existed even if they saw the evidence with their own eyes. The paranormal investigator who goes head-to-head with this sort of skeptic is in for a wild and unpleasant ride.

FACT

Word of mouth is your best free publicity. If your clients like the service you've provided, they may be quite happy to spread the word that your organization is reliable and professional. This assumes they aren't concerned about maintaining confidentiality.

Preaching to the Choir

Statistics from a 2005 CBS News poll reveal that 48 percent of Americans believe in ghosts and that 22 percent believe they have encountered apparitions or have felt themselves to be in the presence of an apparition. These people don't need to be convinced of the validity of a paranormal organization's goals; they are already sympathetic.

The group of people who have had no paranormal experiences of their own or who are just plain neutral are the ones most paranormal groups hope to sway with their focus on the collection of hard evidence. They are the audience who is willing to be convinced if enough evidence is produced.

E-QUESTION

Why has there been such a shift toward belief in ghosts?
There's no doubt that shows like *Ghost Hunters*, *Most Haunted*, and *Paranormal State* have given the public something to think about and made it okay to say positive things about the world of spirits.

Building a Reputation

How does a ghost hunting organization build a good relationship with the local community? What are the factors that convince the public that the group is comprised of serious people who are conducting investigations with a measured scientific approach?

- Be an ongoing presence in the region by maintaining a physical location or office.
- Work over time to maintain a consistent public profile.
- Hold educational programs and workshops.
- Stick to professional protocols and standards.
- Have members of good character.
- Offer the organization's services to civic organizations and spread the word about the work.
- Conduct investigations in a professional manner and let word of mouth spread the news.

The last strategy is the one that may have the most impact. If the group has been around for a while and has conducted investigations with integrity, members of the community will hear about it and embrace it.

Ghost Photo Gallery

It isn't all hard work; sometimes ghost hunters can have a bit of fun and promote interest in their work at the same time. Put together a photo gallery and make it available both online and at your physical location. This can intrigue people and draw them to your organization, too. Nothing causes a reaction quite like a really good ghost photo.

The photos are great public relations tools. They attract clients, volunteers, and the media. If you are into the educational aspect of the business, the pictures you capture during actual investigations make wonderful additions to your presentation or workshop.

Planning a Web Gallery

When you are planning a website, consider the importance of having an online web gallery of ghost photography. Find a means of accepting digital files from photographers who would like to have their ghost photos analyzed. The sites that seem to get the greatest number of hits are those that have a very cool gallery interface that casual viewers can find and access. People want tangible proof of ghosts, and ghost photos are always a real draw.

The Ghostly Galleries

The site Ghost Study.com (*http://ghoststudy.com*) has a very slick website with good galleries. There is something for everyone, and the gallery of faked photos can help researchers distinguish real photos from photos that have been Photoshopped.

Another great site from host Stephen Wagner is About.com's ghost gallery at *www.paranormal.about.com/od/ghostphotos/ig/Best-Ghost-Photos*. This site has some really great shots that have become true classics. The first photo in the gallery is of the Brown Lady, a ghost said to haunt the oak staircase of Raynham Hall. In 1936, Captain Provand and Indre Shira, two photographers who were on assignment for *Country Life* magazine, captured the stunning image of a woman on the stairs. Another very chilling photo, shot in 1963, was taken by the pastor of a church in North Yorkshire, England. Called "the Specter of Newby Church," the photo shows a robed figure with a shrouded white face looking directly at the camera.

Ecto-mist or some aberration of the camera? Probably the latter; the shot was taken at twilight from a moving car and the low light conditions may have caused exposure problems.

Photo copyright Melissa Martin Ellis, 2004.

Other recommended sites include the following:

- The Connecticut Paranormal Research Society (*www.cprs.info*)
- The Rhode Island Paranormal Research Group (*www.triprg.com*)

Dos and Don'ts

If you are looking to be a respected member of the paranormal community, never post a photo that you have not investigated thoroughly. The possibility of being hoaxed always looms over paranormal investigators, so check out any photos that are submitted to be sure they are legitimate. If you do post one, simply identify it with the photographer's name and her account of what it represents.

When posting photos taken by team members, do remember to:

- Give proper photo credit.
- Enhance the photo only slightly, if you enhance it at all. Sharpening and contrast adjustments are fine when they are done in moderation.

- Indicate the circumstances under which the photo was taken.
- If appropriate according to the client's confidentiality wishes, include the date and location.

If a photo on the website just doesn't look that good upon reviewing it, either fix it or take it down permanently. It is very disappointing to web visitors to have to look through a mediocre gallery. It is better not to have any pictures rather than ones that aren't very good.

Helping Those in Trouble

Currently, paranormal investigators hold themselves to a rigorous standard. Their aim is to collect not only personal experiences, but also hard, scientific proof of the existence of ghosts.

But should this always be the primary objective of the group? What about the people who need a resolution to the problems that are haunting them? Aren't they entitled to some closure? The paranormal organization that is using the public merely to prove the existence of ghosts is not serving the community as well as it could be. Gathering evidence should never be done at the expense of people in distress. Sure, it is the way some groups approach the situation, but in the final analysis, the field should always be about finding a compassionate solution to an intolerable situation.

Different Case Types

There will be times when a group is called in to do an investigation simply to validate what is occurring. The client may be the proprietor of a commercial establishment that has a long history of paranormal doings; he may even have adopted the ghost as his mascot and feel that its presence gives a certain cachet to the premises. A paranormal team entering the site operates by certain standards, which should be explained to the client at the point of the initial meeting. Even if the client is okay with the ghost being there, does the ghost feel the same? In the case of residual hauntings, there is no actual interaction between the entity and the observers, so there is really no way to establish whether the entity wants to be released from the site. However, in the case of interactive hauntings, where the investigators have EVPs and there is a possibility of communication, every attempt should be made to do so. This will often mean bringing in sensitives to try to establish contact. If they are successful at doing so and learn that the spirit or spirits want to go into the light, they should feel an obligation to help them do so, whether the proprietor agrees or not.

Malevolent Hauntings

In the case of truly scary hauntings, the residents of a house are in dire need of help and the investigators should do everything in their power to bring relief to the victims of malevolent hauntings.

These cases aren't too frequent, but when they do occur they test everything the group has learned. These cases test the team in ways an ordinary ghost hunt never can. The investigation of a poltergeist or malevolent case requires a different skill set from the average haunting. It is both frightening and exhilarating for the team. To the client, however, it may be just plain terrifying.

People who are desperate to rid themselves of entities that are plaguing them are usually the most motivated clients. Keeping that in mind is an important aspect of the case, and helping them find relief should become the team's number one goal.

Lectures, Presentations, and Classes

With a few years of ghost hunting and paranormal investigating under your belt, you will be a walking encyclopedia of all things supernatural. You may decide that you wish to share that knowledge with the public and offer presentations, lectures, and classes.

Paranormal investigators may find themselves invited to be guest speakers at regional events. If their schedules permit, it is a very good way to increase exposure for the organization and talk about the fundamental approaches used by today's ghost hunters. Paranormal investigators who use technology and are getting verifiable results have captured the public's imagination. If a member of your team is invited to speak, do not let shyness or reticence cause him to miss the opportunity to do so; it dramatically increases the whole organization's profile. Try the team approach. If one person thinks he will get stage fright, two others can provide mutual support and backup.

Lecture Topics

A survey of ghost hunting organizations shows that most are asked to talk about their most exciting investigation, particularly if it was local. People do love to hear about haunted locations right in their own communities.

If your team has had a particularly active case that is not being kept confidential, bring along pictures, EVPs, and any other evidence you were able to gather, such as thermal images or video recordings. Put together a Power-Point presentation so the audience can see what you're talking about. Even if you must keep the client's identity confidential, you can change names and choose evidence that preserves the client's anonymity. People also love to hear about the whole scientific approach to the investigation and the logistics involved in deploying the teams and equipment.

Classes and Workshops

A lot of organizations find they can help defray their operating costs with supplemental events such as speaking engagements and paranormal classes and workshops. Although most investigators have extremely busy schedules, the revenue from these workshops can help buy new equipment and pay for travel expenses.

A good class or workshop should start with the fundamentals, from the first contact with the clients all the way through a step-by-step description of an investigation and the criteria used to gather hard evidence. One or two instructors can teach the sessions, which can range from entry-level to advanced classes. Sometimes, a particularly promising student is asked to join the organization.

A typical advanced class might be about EVPs, orbs, or infrared imaging. An advanced EVP class would cover the basic theory, how to apply it in the field, and what to do with the files to clean them up for evidence review. A course in digital photography for ghost hunters might discuss the basics of operating a digital camera, particularly under low-light shooting conditions, as well as using software programs such as Photoshop Elements to clean up the photos. Also vital would be a discussion of the proper resolution and size and format for the photos and how to archive them safely.

CHAPTER 20

Foretelling the Future

To say the pursuit of the paranormal has expanded in the last twenty years would be a gross understatement. There is an unparalleled interest in the supernatural, a trend that has been fueled by the crossover between science and the supernatural. When confronted with the unknown, we want to understand it, weigh it, measure it, and quantify it. It seems that science has only just begun to give us a glimpse of the possibilities and the tools to analyze the intersection between these two seemingly incompatible worlds.

20

Compiling and Comparing Data

Make no mistake; psychic researchers are not about gazing into crystal balls or reading the tarot anymore. They are all about data compilation and employing standardized procedures to gather that data. There is a network of loosely affiliated organizations around the world that gather evidence of an afterlife and correlate the data to identify patterns and quantifiable facts. If in the process they sometimes seem to be discarding evidence that at one time would have been saved and evaluated, it is only in the name of being scrupulous and thorough.

Organizations have the means to communicate quickly over the Internet. Groups can and do share evidence they have gathered during an investigation and receive input on the analysis of it. Digital files stream over servers and vast quantities of data are analyzed by many sets of eyes and ears, virtually simultaneously.

Celtic headstones mark graves over two hundred years old in Middletown, Rhode Island.

Photo copyright Melissa Martin Ellis, 2007.

Such collaborations are usually productive, but occasionally friction over analyses or methodology will drive a wedge between groups.

TAPS is a good example of such collaborations. On its website, it lists its affiliates, which are called "TAPS Family Members," in areas all over the United States. The website says the criteria for being a TAPS Family Member are quite stringent.

FACT

To be a member of the TAPS Family, an affiliation of paranormal researchers worldwide, you must have been in business for at least one year, have a website, have community references, and accept no payment for your services. Also, the group must be in an area where they need coverage.

New Avenues of Research

There are some exciting new developments in the field. Many are derived from new approaches, theories, and technology. The ghost box and the new theory of orbs are two examples.

Paranormal researcher Beth Fowler contributed an article to the Weekly Universe (*www.weeklyuniverse.com*) in which she introduced her theory of orbs. In brief, she theorizes that what are commonly called orbs actually are three different kinds of phenomena:

- Ghost lights, which can be seen with the naked eye
- Dust orbs, which are light reflecting off dust or other particles
- True orbs, which have consistency and seem to be in motion

Fowler's theory of orbs states that there are discernible differences between the three that researchers should consider before discounting all orbs. She offers two options—that if true orbs do exist, they are either balls of energy of unknown origin, or they are spirits.

Another new theory of orbs is the one presented by a former NASA scientist, Professor Klaus Heinemann, and Miceal Ledwith, a former professor of theology and former president of St. Patrick's College, Maynooth, in

Ireland. These two highly educated men have established to their own satisfaction, at least, that orbs should not be lightly dismissed. Heinemann was able to determine that digital cameras that had recorded orbs were not malfunctioning, and he became convinced that orbs were an actual paranormal phenomenon.

Instrumental Transcommunication

Some researchers in Europe claim they have achieved almost daily two-way communication with spiritual beings. These entities provide all sorts of advanced technical information through radio, television, VCRs, telephones, and computers. This is all part of a new and growing field called *instrumental transcommunications* (ITC). Research in this area has been ongoing since 1985, and researchers say some of the new approaches yield excellent results.

Throughout history, there have been many ways of communicating with the other side—Ouija board, mediums, automatic writing, etc. The technologies of the last century have given us EVPs, the Spiricom, and messages through televisions, radios, computers, and phones, which may all be lumped together in the category of instrumental transcommunication.

In Luxembourg in the 1980s, Maggy Harsch-Fischbach began experimenting with a tape recorder, trying to establish contact with entities. Within a week, she received her first voice contacts. Her husband, Jules Harsch, soon became involved with the experiments and they formed a group that met weekly. Soon they encountered an entity who claimed to be early EVP researcher Konstantin Raudive. With his help, the group efforts succeeded in establishing a very strong contact field with Raudive.

Soon deceased friends and relatives began contacting them, and Raudive appeared at nearly every session. Both the television and radios started to behave oddly, emitting strange noises and even tuning themselves. Sometimes group members would feel compelled to adjust the equipment with no vocalized coaching from their colleagues on the other side, and even more entities made contact.

A New Development

An entity calling itself "the technician" began communicating. A being who claimed never to have been human, he supervised all communications in cooperation with other higher beings. His knowledge of mathematics, electronics, physics, astronomy, history, and even, allegedly, the future seemed to be quite extensive. According to the technician, he functions as a guardian and guiding spirit and has helped the group become even more advanced in their research. The operation is named Timestream and its efforts are still ongoing.

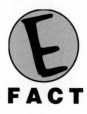

FACT

A large part of the Timestream experiment has shown that the experimenter's attitude, knowledge, and beliefs play a huge role in establishing a contact field with the other side. They are reportedly working to downplay this aspect so that communication can become more widespread and accepted.

The experimenters hope to eventually be able to bypass their own beliefs and thoughts to stabilize the receptivity to allow a wider segment of the population to receive the transmissions. It is believed they are getting close to their goal, which is to let everyone know that life continues after death.

New Technology and Tools

Geiger counters, electromagnetic field meters, motion detectors, audio recorders, barometric pressure monitors, and thermometers are all used when the hunt is on. Some of this technology has been around for decades and some is relatively new. The addition of radios, televisions, VCRs, computers, and telephones has expanded the paranormal researcher's horizons as well.

In the 1980s, George Meek, the inventor of the Spiricom, announced that "lengthy, two-way, normal voice communication with persons who have died have now taken place." Created by a mix of frequencies, the voice steals energy from the noise around it to produce language and audible speech.

The Ghost Pix website (*www.ghostpix.com/spiricom.htm*) has links to actual Spiricom recordings and a little background information on the Metascience Foundation and its founders, Meek and psychic Bill O'Neil. Dr. George Mueller, who passed away some six years before the Spiricom recordings, is not only heard on the tapes but is also credited with helping O'Neil and Meek in their research by "lending his expertise from the other side."

On Ghost Pix there is a downloadable two-hour recording of George Meek explaining the device as well as some long recordings of actual contacts he made through the Spiricom, including contacts with the long-deceased Dr. Mueller. There is a schematic and short excerpt from the longer files at *www.worlditc.org/k_06_spiricom.htm*.

E-QUESTION

Do spirits really have accents?
Yes, they do seem to have retained the accents they had in this world, and they even seem to speak the languages they spoke when they were alive. Their voices also retain qualities distinctive enough to be recognizable to those who knew them on the earthly plane.

Computers and Spirits

In the last twenty years, spirit messages have been received and recorded by all sorts of electronic media, but messages coming through computers are now gaining attention. There have been far fewer recorded instances of this sort of communication than through other devices. Perhaps some of the messages went unrecognized by their recipients or were seen as computer error. In a few instances, however, trained researchers have received other-worldly messages.

Three cases stand out:

- In 1980–81, EVP researcher Manfred Boden reported multiple cases of unexplained messages appearing on both his monitor and his printer. Strangely, the messages were rather negative, threatening, or menacing in nature.
- From 1984 through 1985, Kenneth Webster wrote a book entitled *The Vertical Plane.* In it he described receiving more than 250 messages on several different computers. They were allegedly from a spirit claiming to be Thomas Harden, a sixteenth-century Englishman, written in the vernacular of that time. The text chastised Webster for stealing what had apparently been Harden's home. Harden described Webster's computer as "a box with a multitude of lights sitting near my chimney." A records search later showed that someone by that name had actually lived in the house.
- In 1989, Holmes and Malkhoff, two independent EVP researchers, received an unusual computer printout. The text read, "Central to station Rivenich. We greet you all Fritz. Be patient to make a stone. [To?] Cry at the moment is simpler for us than to carry on a dialogue with Schweich. We cannot repeat everything. Even your ten commandments have only been written down once. Wilhelm Busch will come through again 7-22-89 at station Rivenich since the contacts are not transferable. God is Love and Love is God. Central greets you all from the third level 7-17-89 00:4."
- In 1992, EVP researcher Maggy Harsch-Fischbach reported that Friedrich Jürgenson, the deceased EVP researcher, had appeared briefly on her computer screen and sent messages concerning speculations from theologians on the other side.

Not only are these accounts pretty far out, but to whom would most people report such bizarre occurrences, even if they were so inclined? There is also a much greater likelihood of tampering, hoaxing, and hacking where computers are involved. Even if deliberate hoaxing is ruled out, the possibility still exists for accidental interference, particularly in networked computers.

Physicists tell us that at quantum levels, parallel universes may interpenetrate our own. Is it so far beyond the realm of possibility that computers may eventually connect us with these worlds?

ALERT!

Although Americans are fascinated with the possibility that ghosts are real, the rest of the world is getting in on the act, too. The enthusiasm for paranormal research is reflected in the popularity of such shows as *Ghost Hunters* and *Destination Truth*, both on the Sci Fi Channel.

New Ways of Analyzing Information

New audio software that scans EVPs for human voices and sophisticated meters, gauges, cameras, and recorders are all relatively cutting edge methods to help paranormal investigators analyze information. The new technologies continue to improve and expand our knowledge as we welcome a future in which much of the drudgery may be taken out of the evidence analysis phase of an investigation. New breakthroughs in two-way communication may at last be made viable for widespread use as ITC devices grow more sophisticated. We are at the beginning of a new cycle of paranormal exploration, in which the endlessly fertile minds of humans will devise new ways of parsing the data that has been so laboriously gathered.

Italian Interdisciplinary Laboratory

The Italian organization Il Laboratorio is a research group devoted to the study of paranormal phenomena. Not content with ordinary levels of investigative scrutiny, they take a very rigorous approach to the subject. They use the latest technologies and equipment to analyze the results of their experiments. They have been able to quantify the data they have analyzed so scrupulously that skeptics may be flabbergasted at their findings. They made a presentation at an EVP conference in 2006, which you can find at the American Association of Electronic Voice Phenomena web page (*www .aaevp.com/index.htm*). Click on "Articles" on the left side of the page, then look under "Researchers' Articles," and finally on "The Work at Il Laboratorio" by Paolo Presi.

Anomalous Results

In controlled experiments, scientists have come across many anomalies in EVPs. The acoustic measurements revealed the presence of significant structural anomalies deviating from normal human speech parameters, even when the sentence was spoken in a loud, clear voice.

A ringing sound, similar to that produced by a call bell, preceded the words. No one heard such a ring during the experiment. The measurements carried out on the second sentence confirmed the presence of important anomalies in the voice structure. The presence of the fundamental frequency without the consequent vibration of vocal cords is inexplicable. It must be said that, in normal human speech, only the vibration of vocal cords generates the fundamental frequency.

The researchers found anomalies associated with the vowel sounds and concluded that, quite simply, the sounds were not made by a human voice.

When paranormal investigators started using technology to explore the supernatural, skeptics termed it pseudoscience. Paranormal investigators who strictly follow the scientific method hope to debunk the debunkers with their methodology.

May I Ask Who's Calling?

The lab analyzed an EVP recorded during a telephone conversation. The voice of a young girl of sixteen who had been killed by a car was analyzed by software the FBI uses to identify images.

The acoustic map produced by the digital audio was subjected to a comparative analysis of the girl's living voice and a match was found. Even when the girl's audio file was buried in a sea of 950 other voices, the FBI Image Searching software identified it as a match.

Who Goes There?

Il Laboratorio also uses anthropometric face recognition software in its investigations. Features are mapped with the FaceIt software used by forensic detectives and airport security. It works by measuring the distances between certain facial reference points. The software has a recognition accuracy that reaches 98 percent and can even recognize people in disguise.

The lab used this software to analyze a photo of a young man, a musician named Massimo Castagnini, who died in a car accident. On the one-year anniversary of his death, his friends and band-mates decided to honor him by holding a concert party. One of his friends shot about seventy pictures of the event. When the film was processed, he noticed one picture was very unusual, with loud colors and wild luminous streaks.

The strangeness of the photo made Massimo's mother take a closer look and she and a few friends were greatly amazed to see what seemed to be a blurry, semitransparent face that bore an uncanny resemblance to Massimo. The figure appeared holding something that seemed to be a microphone in his hand. When comparing the analysis of the strange photo to an old photo of Massimo, the FaceIt software picked the young man's image out of a database of 2,048 faces.

FACT

The beauty of using computer software programs to conduct evidence analysis is that the risk of human error is taken out of the equation and the statistical likelihood of the event occurring by chance is plainly seen to be negligible.

Applying the Scientific Method

Perhaps the science of paranormal investigation can put an end to the misguided stereotypes of investigators as gullible and anti-scientific. At last, ghost hunters are gaining credibility and are being taken a bit more seriously. Yes, there are still many skeptics who claim what they are doing is pseudoscience, but as the evidence reaches some sort of tipping point, peoples' minds will open.

For the field to gain credibility and respectability, investigators know they must do two things. First, they must recognize when evidence could have a normal explanation. Second, they must follow the scientific method during investigations.

Following Scientific Protocols

An investigator employing the scientific method must remain both open-minded and skeptical. Phenomena must be questioned. To get to the root cause, the scientific investigator must ask questions based on the scientific method:

- Why is the event happening?
- Is there a natural, root cause?
- Is this incident connected to any other causative events?
- Is there other research or literature that has found connections between events you have observed?
- Have other researchers drawn the same conclusions?
- What is your hypothesis? Does it agree with your colleagues or is it new?
- How will you test your hypothesis?
- Can the hypothesis be tested under controlled conditions?
- What predictions were made based on the hypothesis?
- Were tests based on the hypothesis statistically significant?

After all these steps, if the predictions made on the hypothesis work out, it is time to publish your results in a reputable scientific journal. Other investigators will note the experimental protocols you used and they will try to reproduce your results. If your peers can repeat your experiments successfully, you may have come up with a new theory to explain the unexplained.

Breaking New Ground

In *PSIence: How New Discoveries in Quantum Physics and New Science May Explain the Existence of Paranormal Phenomena*, Marie D. Jones explores the connections between science and anomalous phenomena. She asserts that mainstream scientists, particularly physicists, are making many discoveries that may explain things we have always considered paranormal. There may be scientific explanations not only for poltergeists and ghosts, but other unusual sorts of phenomena such as UFOs and time travel. Ms. Jones explores the new discoveries in quantum physics and how they may actually explain some of the things we have always considered bizarre. Breakthrough discoveries are bringing them into the mainstream, as maverick scientists push the boundaries and paranormal investigators get more scientific in their approaches to the supernatural.

Wherever our investigations into the supernatural take us, we must wear our skepticism like armor. Even if we are inclined toward a belief in spirit communication, we must remember that we can't always know with whom—or what—we are communicating.

The End—or Is It?

Slowly but surely, the idea of employing the scientific method to explore the questions of life after death is gaining acceptance. A few brave souls in the scientific community are sanctioning more research into the paranormal. Ian Stevenson investigated claims of memories of past lives. In 1967, Chester Carlson, the inventor of the Xerox process, learned of Stevenson's research and offered to fund it. He bequeathed $1 million to the University of Virginia after his death so that Stevenson could continue his paranormal research. Stevenson resigned his position as chair of psychiatry and used the money from the endowment to establish the division of parapsychology. This allowed him to pursue paranormal research full-time and hire assistants to help. Stevenson said of his more conservative colleagues, "Not a few psychiatrists suspected that I had become unhinged." Nonetheless, Dr. Stevenson pressed forward.

He was a role model for the future, a man of science who was not afraid to ask tough questions. Dr. Stevenson died on February 8, 2007, at the age of eighty-eight in Charlottesville, Virginia. Who knows? We may not have heard the last of him. Mediums are already claiming they're getting messages from him—from beyond the grave.

Most Haunted Sites in America

The Alamo
San Antonio, Texas

Alcatraz
San Francisco, California

Bachelor's Grove
Midlothian, Illinois

Belcourt Castle
Newport, Rhode Island

Bell Witch Cave
Adams, Tennessee

Bobby Mackey's Music World
Wilder, Kentucky

Castle Hill Inn & Resort
Newport, Rhode Island

Gettysburg Battlefield
Southern Pennsylvania

Lemp Mansion
St. Louis, Missouri

Lincoln Theater
Decatur, Illinois

Moore Home / Axe Murder House
Villisca, Iowa

Myrtles Plantation
St. Francisville, Louisiana

Old Slave House
Junction, Illinois

Waverly Hills Sanatorium
Louisville, Kentucky

The White Horse Tavern
Newport, Rhode Island

Winchester Mansion
San Jose, California

Famous Ghosts

Jean Harlow: the famous "blonde bombshell" actress who died at the age of twenty-six

Harry Houdini: his ghost is said to haunt the Plaza Hotel in Las Vegas

Thomas Ince: one of the most respected directors of the silent film era

Andrew Jackson: the seventh president of the United States

Jesse James: outlaw and train robber

Thomas Jefferson: the third president of the United States

Robert E. Lee: Confederate general in the Civil War

John Lennon: musician; former member of the Beatles

Liberace: known for his piano playing skills, charisma, and diamonds

Abraham Lincoln: the sixteenth president of the United States

Marilyn Monroe: actress who died mysteriously in 1962

Elvis Presley: singer, musician, and actor; he has been seen by stagehands at the Las Vegas Hilton

George Reeves: the star of the 1950s television series *Superman*

Betsy Ross: credited with sewing the first American flag

Bugsy Siegel: a colorful Las Vegas underworld figure

Dylan Thomas: a Welsh poet and writer

Mark Twain: popular humorist, novelist, and writer

Rudolph Valentino: one of the greatest Hollywood romantic idols

John Wayne: actor; he has been seen on his old yacht, the *Wild Goose.*

Orson Welles: considered one of Hollywood's greatest directors

Glossary

akashic records
The concept of a vast psychic record of all thoughts and emotions, some human, some not, which is sometimes accessible to advanced souls.

amulet
A symbolic magical object imbued with energy, meant to protect its wearer from harm; usually a necklace, ring, or pendant.

angel
A nonhuman entity; a winged celestial being, usually benevolent and kind and possessed of powers and knowledge beyond human comprehension.

anomaly
An occurrence for which there is seemingly no normal explanation.

apparition
The projection or manifestation of a paranormal being.

astral plane
A dimensional plane at a higher vibration than the earthly plane, where entities both good and bad can be encountered during astral travel in the astral body.

aura
An energy field that surrounds the physical body and is a reflection of the astral body, which can be influenced by thought and emotion.

banishing
A ceremonial, magical ritual to cast out negative energy and influences; it can refer either to a spiritual cleansing of a person or property, or to the closing of a magical rite.

cleansing
A ritual in which negative energy and entities are banished through prayers that are spoken aloud and may be adapted to the user's needs.

clearing
Synonym for *cleansing*.

demonologist
A person, sometimes clergy, sometimes not, who studies and banishes demons.

digital audio recorder
Small recorders of good sound quality; the files can be transferred to a computer.

digital video recorder
A video camera the files from which can be transferred to a computer.

dowsing
A means of locating different substances and energies by the means of two rods, which

cross when the energy field that is being searched for is encountered.

ectoplasm
An ethereal substance that is supposedly exuded by the bodies of mediums and can form into objects and entities.

ectoplasmic mist
A substance that forms out of thin air and looks like a thick fog.

electronic voice phenomena (EVP)
An utterance not heard as it is being spoken but is audible later when the recording is played back.

electromagnetic field (EMF)
electrical charges, found in varying degrees in anything that uses electricity or generates a magnetic field.

elemental
A nature spirit that can be either good or evil.

entity
A classification for a disembodied being, which

may be a ghost, a spirit, an elemental, or a demon.

exorcism
A ritual performed to drive a devil or demon from the body or the house it is occupying.

ghost
A spirit who may or may not have been a living human being or animal, which can sometimes appear to be semitransparent.

haunting
The repeated appearance of ghosts, spirits, or poltergeists.

hex
A magical spell, cast to influence a person's life; usually used as a curse.

hypnosis
A state of altered consciousness, self-induced or created by an external agent. Franz Anton Mesmer first popularized this practice, which he called mesmerism.

instrumental transcommunication (ITC)
Two-way, real-time communication with

spiritual beings. The entities provide advanced technical information through radio, television, VCRs, telephones, and computers.

intelligent haunting
An entity that is aware of the presence of humans and may be interactive.

levitation
A rare phenomenon in which objects or persons are lifted or sometimes hurled through the air. Encountered occasionally in cases of poltergeist activity.

K2 meter
An EMF meter that measures magnetic and electrical fields and may be recalibrated for paranormal investigative use.

materialization
The brief physical appearance of an entity, seen as it is happening.

matrixing
The natural tendency for the human mind to try to interpret sensory data into recognizable patterns.

medium
A person with the ability to communicate with the dead, sometimes called a sensitive.

metaphysics
The school of philosophical thought that seeks to understand the meaning of existence and the human soul.

MiniDV
A small version of the camcorder that records and plays MiniDV tapes.

necromancy
The art and practice of communicating with the dead to obtain knowledge of the future or other hidden events.

poltergeist
The famous "noisy ghost." A rare form of haunting wherein random objects are moved and sounds and speech are produced by unseen entities, which seems to crave attention and recognition. Frequently a child or adolescent is at the center of the phenomena.

psychokinesis
A paranormal phenomenon in which objects are moved solely by the powers of the psychic's mind. See *telekinesis*.

reincarnation
The belief that a soul will move on to another body after death to work out its karmic debt.

residual haunting
A psychic recording of an event that is traumatic or violent. It is repeated over and over; the entity involved does not interact with onlookers.

saging
See *smudge sticks*.

séance
The attempt by a group to contact the spirit world. A medium is usually the channel for the energies to manifest through.

sigil
A magical charm that forms an energy barrier and protective shield. It can be visualized or drawn.

smudge sticks
A Native American tool made of sage used for purification, healing, and cleansing ceremonies. The smoke is thought to clear negative energies.

spirit
A ghost; an entity that once existed on the earthly plane but has passed on.

synchronicity
Uncanny coincidences that seem too convenient to be truly coincidental.

telekinesis
The psychic phenomenon where objects are moved solely by the powers of the mind.

vortex
A rip in the fabric of space-time that opens into the spirit world and lets entities from the other side in.

ward
A magical construct that guards a person or a place.

wraith
The semitransparent image of a person that appears shortly before or after his or her death; also sometimes used when talking about a ghost.

APPENDIX D

Bibliography

Faces of a Ghost Hunter, by Gloria Young (Lulu.com, 2004).

Ghost Hunters: The Victorians and the Hunt for Proof of Life after Death, by Deborah Blum (New York: Penguin: 2006).

Ghost Hunters: True Stories of Unexplained Phenomena from the Atlantic Paranormal Society, by Jason Hawes and Grant Wilson, with Michael Jan Friedman (New York: Simon and Schuster, 2007).

Ghosts Caught on Film, Photographs of the Paranormal, by Dr. Melvyn Willin (Devon, UK: Charles and David, 2007).

Ghost and Ghoul, by Thomas Charles Lethbridge (Garden City, NY: Doubleday, 1962).

The Haunted House Handbook, by D. Scott Rogo (New York: Grosset and Dunlap, 1978).

Hauntings and Poltergeists, by Loyd Auerbach (Oakland, CA: Ronin Publishing, 2004).

Hostage to the Devil: The Possession and Exorcism of Five Contemporary Americans, by Dr. Malachi Martin (New York: HarperOne, 1992).

The Lost World of the Kalahari, by Lauren van der Post (Fort Washingon, PA: Harvest Books, 1977).

Mysteries, by Colin Wilson (New York: Putnam, 1978).

The Occult, by Colin Wilson (London: Watkins, 2006).

The Orb Project, by Dr. Klaus Heinemann and Miceal Ledwith (New York: Atria Books/ Beyond Words, 2007).

Poltergeist, by Colin Wilson (St. Paul, MN: Llewellyn Publications, 1995).

PSIence: How New Discoveries in Quantum Physics and New Science May Explain the Existence of Paranormal Phenomena, by Marie D. Jones (Franklin Lakes, NJ: Career Press, 2006).

The Welcoming Silence: A Study of Psychical Phenomena and Survival of Death, by D. Scott Rogo (University Book, 1973).

Index

THE EVERYTHING SERIES!

BUSINESS & PERSONAL FINANCE

Everything® Accounting Book
Everything® Budgeting Book, 2nd Ed.
Everything® Business Planning Book
Everything® Coaching and Mentoring Book, 2nd Ed.
Everything® Fundraising Book
Everything® Get Out of Debt Book
Everything® Grant Writing Book, 2nd Ed.
Everything® Guide to Buying Foreclosures
Everything® Guide to Fundraising, $15.95
Everything® Guide to Mortgages
Everything® Guide to Personal Finance for Single Mothers
Everything® Home-Based Business Book, 2nd Ed.
Everything® Homebuying Book, 3rd Ed., $15.95
Everything® Homeselling Book, 2nd Ed.
Everything® Human Resource Management Book
Everything® Improve Your Credit Book
Everything® Investing Book, 2nd Ed.
Everything® Landlording Book
Everything® Leadership Book, 2nd Ed.
Everything® Managing People Book, 2nd Ed.
Everything® Negotiating Book
Everything® Online Auctions Book
Everything® Online Business Book
Everything® Personal Finance Book
Everything® Personal Finance in Your 20s & 30s Book, 2nd Ed.
Everything® Personal Finance in Your 40s & 50s Book, $15.95
Everything® Project Management Book, 2nd Ed.
Everything® Real Estate Investing Book
Everything® Retirement Planning Book
Everything® Robert's Rules Book, $7.95
Everything® Selling Book
Everything® Start Your Own Business Book, 2nd Ed.
Everything® Wills & Estate Planning Book

COOKING

Everything® Barbecue Cookbook
Everything® Bartender's Book, 2nd Ed., $9.95
Everything® Calorie Counting Cookbook
Everything® Cheese Book
Everything® Chinese Cookbook
Everything® Classic Recipes Book
Everything® Cocktail Parties & Drinks Book
Everything® College Cookbook
Everything® Cooking for Baby and Toddler Book
Everything® Diabetes Cookbook
Everything® Easy Gourmet Cookbook
Everything® Fondue Cookbook
Everything® Food Allergy Cookbook, $15.95
Everything® Fondue Party Book
Everything® Gluten-Free Cookbook
Everything® Glycemic Index Cookbook
Everything® Grilling Cookbook
Everything® Healthy Cooking for Parties Book, $15.95
Everything® Holiday Cookbook
Everything® Indian Cookbook
Everything® Lactose-Free Cookbook
Everything® Low-Cholesterol Cookbook

Everything® Low-Fat High-Flavor Cookbook, 2nd Ed., $15.95
Everything® Low-Salt Cookbook
Everything® Meals for a Month Cookbook
Everything® Meals on a Budget Cookbook
Everything® Mediterranean Cookbook
Everything® Mexican Cookbook
Everything® No Trans Fat Cookbook
Everything® One-Pot Cookbook, 2nd Ed., $15.95
Everything® Organic Cooking for Baby & Toddler Book, $15.95
Everything® Pizza Cookbook
Everything® Quick Meals Cookbook, 2nd Ed., $15.95
Everything® Slow Cooker Cookbook
Everything® Slow Cooking for a Crowd Cookbook
Everything® Soup Cookbook
Everything® Stir-Fry Cookbook
Everything® Sugar-Free Cookbook
Everything® Tapas and Small Plates Cookbook
Everything® Tex-Mex Cookbook
Everything® Thai Cookbook
Everything® Vegetarian Cookbook
Everything® Whole-Grain, High-Fiber Cookbook
Everything® Wild Game Cookbook
Everything® Wine Book, 2nd Ed.

GAMES

Everything® 15-Minute Sudoku Book, $9.95
Everything® 30-Minute Sudoku Book, $9.95
Everything® Bible Crosswords Book, $9.95
Everything® Blackjack Strategy Book
Everything® Brain Strain Book, $9.95
Everything® Bridge Book
Everything® Card Games Book
Everything® Card Tricks Book, $9.95
Everything® Casino Gambling Book, 2nd Ed.
Everything® Chess Basics Book
Everything® Christmas Crosswords Book, $9.95
Everything® Craps Strategy Book
Everything® Crossword and Puzzle Book
Everything® Crosswords and Puzzles for Quote Lovers Book, $9.95
Everything® Crossword Challenge Book
Everything® Crosswords for the Beach Book, $9.95
Everything® Cryptic Crosswords Book, $9.95
Everything® Cryptograms Book, $9.95
Everything® Easy Crosswords Book
Everything® Easy Kakuro Book, $9.95
Everything® Easy Large-Print Crosswords Book
Everything® Games Book, 2nd Ed.
Everything® Giant Book of Crosswords
Everything® Giant Sudoku Book, $9.95
Everything® Giant Word Search Book
Everything® Kakuro Challenge Book, $9.95
Everything® Large-Print Crossword Challenge Book
Everything® Large-Print Crosswords Book
Everything® Large-Print Travel Crosswords Book
Everything® Lateral Thinking Puzzles Book, $9.95
Everything® Literary Crosswords Book, $9.95
Everything® Mazes Book
Everything® Memory Booster Puzzles Book, $9.95

Everything® Movie Crosswords Book, $9.95
Everything® Music Crosswords Book, $9.95
Everything® Online Poker Book
Everything® Pencil Puzzles Book, $9.95
Everything® Poker Strategy Book
Everything® Pool & Billiards Book
Everything® Puzzles for Commuters Book, $9.95
Everything® Puzzles for Dog Lovers Book, $9.95
Everything® Sports Crosswords Book, $9.95
Everything® Test Your IQ Book, $9.95
Everything® Texas Hold 'Em Book, $9.95
Everything® Travel Crosswords Book, $9.95
Everything® Travel Mazes Book, $9.95
Everything® Travel Word Search Book, $9.95
Everything® TV Crosswords Book, $9.95
Everything® Word Games Challenge Book
Everything® Word Scramble Book
Everything® Word Search Book

HEALTH

Everything® Alzheimer's Book
Everything® Diabetes Book
Everything® First Aid Book, $9.95
Everything® Green Living Book
Everything® Health Guide to Addiction and Recovery
Everything® Health Guide to Adult Bipolar Disorder
Everything® Health Guide to Arthritis
Everything® Health Guide to Controlling Anxiety
Everything® Health Guide to Depression
Everything® Health Guide to Diabetes, 2nd Ed.
Everything® Health Guide to Fibromyalgia
Everything® Health Guide to Menopause, 2nd Ed.
Everything® Health Guide to Migraines
Everything® Health Guide to Multiple Sclerosis
Everything® Health Guide to OCD
Everything® Health Guide to PMS
Everything® Health Guide to Postpartum Care
Everything® Health Guide to Thyroid Disease
Everything® Hypnosis Book
Everything® Low Cholesterol Book
Everything® Menopause Book
Everything® Nutrition Book
Everything® Reflexology Book
Everything® Stress Management Book
Everything® Superfoods Book, $15.95

HISTORY

Everything® American Government Book
Everything® American History Book, 2nd Ed.
Everything® American Revolution Book, $15.95
Everything® Civil War Book
Everything® Freemasons Book
Everything® Irish History & Heritage Book
Everything® World War II Book, 2nd Ed.

HOBBIES

Everything® Candlemaking Book
Everything® Cartooning Book
Everything® Coin Collecting Book
Everything® Digital Photography Book, 2nd Ed.

Everything® Drawing Book
Everything® Family Tree Book, 2nd Ed.
Everything® Guide to Online Genealogy, $15.95
Everything® Knitting Book
Everything® Knots Book
Everything® Photography Book
Everything® Quilting Book
Everything® Sewing Book
Everything® Soapmaking Book, 2nd Ed.
Everything® Woodworking Book

HOME IMPROVEMENT

Everything® Feng Shui Book
Everything® Feng Shui Decluttering Book, $9.95
Everything® Fix-It Book
Everything® Green Living Book
Everything® Home Decorating Book
Everything® Home Storage Solutions Book
Everything® Homebuilding Book
Everything® Organize Your Home Book, 2nd Ed.

KIDS' BOOKS

All titles are $7.95

Everything® Fairy Tales Book, $14.95
Everything® Kids' Animal Puzzle & Activity Book
Everything® Kids' Astronomy Book
Everything® Kids' Baseball Book, 5th Ed.
Everything® Kids' Bible Trivia Book
Everything® Kids' Bugs Book
Everything® Kids' Cars and Trucks Puzzle and Activity Book
Everything® Kids' Christmas Puzzle & Activity Book
Everything® Kids' Connect the Dots
            Puzzle and Activity Book
Everything® Kids' Cookbook, 2nd Ed.
Everything® Kids' Crazy Puzzles Book
Everything® Kids' Dinosaurs Book
Everything® Kids' Dragons Puzzle and Activity Book
Everything® Kids' Environment Book $7.95
Everything® Kids' Fairies Puzzle and Activity Book
Everything® Kids' First Spanish Puzzle and Activity Book
Everything® Kids' Football Book
Everything® Kids' Geography Book
Everything® Kids' Gross Cookbook
Everything® Kids' Gross Hidden Pictures Book
Everything® Kids' Gross Jokes Book
Everything® Kids' Gross Mazes Book
Everything® Kids' Gross Puzzle & Activity Book
Everything® Kids' Halloween Puzzle & Activity Book
Everything® Kids' Hanukkah Puzzle and Activity Book
Everything® Kids' Hidden Pictures Book
Everything® Kids' Horses Book
Everything® Kids' Joke Book
Everything® Kids' Knock Knock Book
Everything® Kids' Learning French Book
Everything® Kids' Learning Spanish Book
Everything® Kids' Magical Science Experiments Book
Everything® Kids' Math Puzzles Book
Everything® Kids' Mazes Book
Everything® Kids' Money Book, 2nd Ed.
**Everything® Kids' Mummies, Pharaoh's, and Pyramids
            Puzzle and Activity Book**
Everything® Kids' Nature Book
Everything® Kids' Pirates Puzzle and Activity Book
Everything® Kids' Presidents Book
Everything® Kids' Princess Puzzle and Activity Book
Everything® Kids' Puzzle Book

Everything® Kids' Racecars Puzzle and Activity Book
Everything® Kids' Riddles & Brain Teasers Book
Everything® Kids' Science Experiments Book
Everything® Kids' Sharks Book
Everything® Kids' Soccer Book
Everything® Kids' Spelling Book
Everything® Kids' Spies Puzzle and Activity Book
Everything® Kids' States Book
Everything® Kids' Travel Activity Book
Everything® Kids' Word Search Puzzle and Activity Book

LANGUAGE

Everything® Conversational Japanese Book with CD, $19.95
Everything® French Grammar Book
Everything® French Phrase Book, $9.95
Everything® French Verb Book, $9.95
Everything® German Phrase Book, $9.95
Everything® German Practice Book with CD, $19.95
Everything® Inglés Book
Everything® Intermediate Spanish Book with CD, $19.95
Everything® Italian Phrase Book, $9.95
Everything® Italian Practice Book with CD, $19.95
Everything® Learning Brazilian Portuguese Book with CD, $19.95
Everything® Learning French Book with CD, 2nd Ed., $19.95
Everything® Learning German Book
Everything® Learning Italian Book
Everything® Learning Latin Book
Everything® Learning Russian Book with CD, $19.95
Everything® Learning Spanish Book
Everything® Learning Spanish Book with CD, 2nd Ed., $19.95
Everything® Russian Practice Book with CD, $19.95
Everything® Sign Language Book, $15.95
Everything® Spanish Grammar Book
Everything® Spanish Phrase Book, $9.95
Everything® Spanish Practice Book with CD, $19.95
Everything® Spanish Verb Book, $9.95
Everything® Speaking Mandarin Chinese Book with CD, $19.95

MUSIC

Everything® Bass Guitar Book with CD, $19.95
Everything® Drums Book with CD, $19.95
Everything® Guitar Book with CD, 2nd Ed., $19.95
Everything® Guitar Chords Book with CD, $19.95
Everything® Guitar Scales Book with CD, $19.95
Everything® Harmonica Book with CD, $15.95
Everything® Home Recording Book
Everything® Music Theory Book with CD, $19.95
Everything® Reading Music Book with CD, $19.95
Everything® Rock & Blues Guitar Book with CD, $19.95
Everything® Rock & Blues Piano Book with CD, $19.95
Everything® Rock Drums Book with CD, $19.95
Everything® Singing Book with CD, $19.95
Everything® Songwriting Book

NEW AGE

Everything® Astrology Book, 2nd Ed.
Everything® Birthday Personology Book
Everything® Celtic Wisdom Book, $15.95
Everything® Dreams Book, 2nd Ed.
Everything® Law of Attraction Book, $15.95
Everything® Love Signs Book, $9.95
Everything® Love Spells Book, $9.95
Everything® Palmistry Book
Everything® Psychic Book
Everything® Reiki Book

Everything® Sex Signs Book, $9.95
Everything® Spells & Charms Book, 2nd Ed.
Everything® Tarot Book, 2nd Ed.
Everything® Toltec Wisdom Book
Everything® Wicca & Witchcraft Book, 2nd Ed.

PARENTING

Everything® Baby Names Book, 2nd Ed.
Everything® Baby Shower Book, 2nd Ed.
Everything® Baby Sign Language Book with DVD
Everything® Baby's First Year Book
Everything® Birthing Book
Everything® Breastfeeding Book
Everything® Father-to-Be Book
Everything® Father's First Year Book
Everything® Get Ready for Baby Book, 2nd Ed.
Everything® Get Your Baby to Sleep Book, $9.95
Everything® Getting Pregnant Book
Everything® Guide to Pregnancy Over 35
Everything® Guide to Raising a One-Year-Old
Everything® Guide to Raising a Two-Year-Old
Everything® Guide to Raising Adolescent Boys
Everything® Guide to Raising Adolescent Girls
Everything® Mother's First Year Book
Everything® Parent's Guide to Childhood Illnesses
Everything® Parent's Guide to Children and Divorce
Everything® Parent's Guide to Children with ADD/ADHD
Everything® Parent's Guide to Children with Asperger's
            Syndrome
Everything® Parent's Guide to Children with Anxiety
Everything® Parent's Guide to Children with Asthma
Everything® Parent's Guide to Children with Autism
Everything® Parent's Guide to Children with Bipolar Disorder
Everything® Parent's Guide to Children with Depression
Everything® Parent's Guide to Children with Dyslexia
Everything® Parent's Guide to Children with Juvenile Diabetes
Everything® Parent's Guide to Children with OCD
Everything® Parent's Guide to Positive Discipline
Everything® Parent's Guide to Raising Boys
Everything® Parent's Guide to Raising Girls
Everything® Parent's Guide to Raising Siblings
**Everything® Parent's Guide to Raising Your
            Adopted Child**
Everything® Parent's Guide to Sensory Integration Disorder
Everything® Parent's Guide to Tantrums
Everything® Parent's Guide to the Strong-Willed Child
Everything® Parenting a Teenager Book
Everything® Potty Training Book, $9.95
Everything® Pregnancy Book, 3rd Ed.
Everything® Pregnancy Fitness Book
Everything® Pregnancy Nutrition Book
Everything® Pregnancy Organizer, 2nd Ed., $16.95
Everything® Toddler Activities Book
Everything® Toddler Book
Everything® Tween Book
Everything® Twins, Triplets, and More Book

PETS

Everything® Aquarium Book
Everything® Boxer Book
Everything® Cat Book, 2nd Ed.
Everything® Chihuahua Book
Everything® Cooking for Dogs Book
Everything® Dachshund Book
Everything® Dog Book, 2nd Ed.
Everything® Dog Grooming Book

Everything® Dog Obedience Book
Everything® Dog Owner's Organizer, $16.95
Everything® Dog Training and Tricks Book
Everything® German Shepherd Book
Everything® Golden Retriever Book
Everything® Horse Book, 2nd Ed., $15.95
Everything® Horse Care Book
Everything® Horseback Riding Book
Everything® Labrador Retriever Book
Everything® Poodle Book
Everything® Pug Book
Everything® Puppy Book
Everything® Small Dogs Book
Everything® Tropical Fish Book
Everything® Yorkshire Terrier Book

REFERENCE

Everything® American Presidents Book
Everything® Blogging Book
Everything® Build Your Vocabulary Book, $9.95
Everything® Car Care Book
Everything® Classical Mythology Book
Everything® Da Vinci Book
Everything® Einstein Book
Everything® Enneagram Book
Everything® Etiquette Book, 2nd Ed.
Everything® Family Christmas Book, $15.95
Everything® Guide to C. S. Lewis & Narnia
Everything® Guide to Divorce, 2nd Ed., $15.95
Everything® Guide to Edgar Allan Poe
Everything® Guide to Understanding Philosophy
Everything® Inventions and Patents Book
Everything® Jacqueline Kennedy Onassis Book
Everything® John F. Kennedy Book
Everything® Mafia Book
Everything® Martin Luther King Jr. Book
Everything® Pirates Book
Everything® Private Investigation Book
Everything® Psychology Book
Everything® Public Speaking Book, $9.95
Everything® Shakespeare Book, 2nd Ed.

RELIGION

Everything® Angels Book
Everything® Bible Book
Everything® Bible Study Book with CD, $19.95
Everything® Buddhism Book
Everything® Catholicism Book
Everything® Christianity Book
Everything® Gnostic Gospels Book
Everything® Hinduism Book, $15.95
Everything® History of the Bible Book
Everything® Jesus Book
Everything® Jewish History & Heritage Book
Everything® Judaism Book
Everything® Kabbalah Book
Everything® Koran Book
Everything® Mary Book
Everything® Mary Magdalene Book
Everything® Prayer Book

Everything® Saints Book, 2nd Ed.
Everything® Torah Book
Everything® Understanding Islam Book
Everything® Women of the Bible Book
Everything® World's Religions Book

SCHOOL & CAREERS

Everything® Career Tests Book
Everything® College Major Test Book
Everything® College Survival Book, 2nd Ed.
Everything® Cover Letter Book, 2nd Ed.
Everything® Filmmaking Book
Everything® Get-a-Job Book, 2nd Ed.
Everything® Guide to Being a Paralegal
Everything® Guide to Being a Personal Trainer
Everything® Guide to Being a Real Estate Agent
Everything® Guide to Being a Sales Rep
Everything® Guide to Being an Event Planner
Everything® Guide to Careers in Health Care
Everything® Guide to Careers in Law Enforcement
Everything® Guide to Government Jobs
Everything® Guide to Starting and Running a Catering
  Business
Everything® Guide to Starting and Running a Restaurant
**Everything® Guide to Starting and Running
  a Retail Store**
Everything® Job Interview Book, 2nd Ed.
Everything® New Nurse Book
Everything® New Teacher Book
Everything® Paying for College Book
Everything® Practice Interview Book
Everything® Resume Book, 3rd Ed.
Everything® Study Book

SELF-HELP

Everything® Body Language Book
Everything® Dating Book, 2nd Ed.
Everything® Great Sex Book
**Everything® Guide to Caring for Aging Parents,
  $15.95**
Everything® Self-Esteem Book
Everything® Self-Hypnosis Book, $9.95
Everything® Tantric Sex Book

SPORTS & FITNESS

Everything® Easy Fitness Book
Everything® Fishing Book
Everything® Guide to Weight Training, $15.95
Everything® Krav Maga for Fitness Book
Everything® Running Book, 2nd Ed.
Everything® Triathlon Training Book, $15.95

TRAVEL

Everything® Family Guide to Coastal Florida
Everything® Family Guide to Cruise Vacations
Everything® Family Guide to Hawaii
Everything® Family Guide to Las Vegas, 2nd Ed.
Everything® Family Guide to Mexico
Everything® Family Guide to New England, 2nd Ed.

Everything® Family Guide to New York City, 3rd Ed.
**Everything® Family Guide to Northern California
  and Lake Tahoe**
Everything® Family Guide to RV Travel & Campgrounds
Everything® Family Guide to the Caribbean
Everything® Family Guide to the Disneyland® Resort, California
  Adventure®, Universal Studios®, and the Anaheim
  Area, 2nd Ed.
Everything® Family Guide to the Walt Disney World Resort®,
  Universal Studios®, and Greater Orlando, 5th Ed.
Everything® Family Guide to Timeshares
Everything® Family Guide to Washington D.C., 2nd Ed.

WEDDINGS

Everything® Bachelorette Party Book, $9.95
Everything® Bridesmaid Book, $9.95
Everything® Destination Wedding Book
Everything® Father of the Bride Book, $9.95
Everything® Green Wedding Book, $15.95
Everything® Groom Book, $9.95
Everything® Jewish Wedding Book, 2nd Ed., $15.95
Everything® Mother of the Bride Book, $9.95
Everything® Outdoor Wedding Book
Everything® Wedding Book, 3rd Ed.
Everything® Wedding Checklist, $9.95
Everything® Wedding Etiquette Book, $9.95
Everything® Wedding Organizer, 2nd Ed., $16.95
Everything® Wedding Shower Book, $9.95
Everything® Wedding Vows Book, 3rd Ed., $9.95
Everything® Wedding Workout Book
Everything® Weddings on a Budget Book, 2nd Ed., $9.95

WRITING

Everything® Creative Writing Book
Everything® Get Published Book, 2nd Ed.
Everything® Grammar and Style Book, 2nd Ed.
Everything® Guide to Magazine Writing
Everything® Guide to Writing a Book Proposal
Everything® Guide to Writing a Novel
Everything® Guide to Writing Children's Books
Everything® Guide to Writing Copy
Everything® Guide to Writing Graphic Novels
Everything® Guide to Writing Research Papers
Everything® Guide to Writing a Romance Novel, $15.95
Everything® Improve Your Writing Book, 2nd Ed.
Everything® Writing Poetry Book